PERSONAL ENCOUNTERS

STORIES, IDEAS, LESSONS
FROM JEWISH LIFE

Jack Shechter

D1715682

Printed in the United States of America

ISBN 978-1-66785-564-6

Published by Oaks Press
Thousand Oaks, California

Dedicated to my late father
Louis Shechter
Whose example has stimulated me through the
years to write about people and everyday life…
and to write legibly when handwriting was
once the way.

ABOUT THE PEOPLE
ENCOUNTERED IN THIS BOOK

I need to note that in all cases in this book the encounters through the years were personal. The one exception was Franz Rosenzweig who passed away before I was born. Yet my encounter with this great man was quite personal.

Contents

Introduction... i

PART ONE

1 Synagogue Personalities...1

Howard Rosenberg: A Frugal Synagogue President...... 3

Allan Grinberg and His Rabbi: "Better to Hold Back
      Than Having to Push"..5

Hazzan Mordecai Heiser: On Pulpit Procedure and
      Decorum...7

Herman Feldman and "A la Carte Judaism"................ 9

Samuel Perrin: On Calling a Rabbi by His First Name....10

Sarah and Ted Abrams: Quintessential Conservative
      Jews and Simchat Torah...................................... 12

Allan Neil, Caterer: *Marit Ayin* (The Appearance of
      Things)... 14

Suicide: Two Incidents... 16

Toby: Before and After Her Husband Passed Away...... 18

Laben Melnick: On Asking Forgiveness Before Yom
      Tov... 19

Jacob Spitz: Veteran Educator and His Young Rabbi...... 21

Walter Reis: On an Inner Connection with a Rabbi...... 23

John Harris: On the Most Memorable Eulogy in My
      Rabbinate.. 24

Sam Deaktor: A Person is Judged by the Kind of
      Arguments He Gets Into.....................................26

2 The Unusual... 29

Ishmael Sowa: Paganism and Living Religion.............. 31

Rene Rodriguez...and the Passion for Learning............34

A Cultured Swiss Lady and Chaim Potok's Novel,
    The Chosen.. 37

Jack Ostrow: "Chairman of the Board"....................... 39

Dennis Prager: Master Teacher...................................... 41

Joseph Telushkin: How to Keep a Whole School
    Laughing for Eight Consecutive Hours................... 43

Rabbi Alex—An *Atarah*: His Father's, His, Now Mine.... 46

Rabbi Chaim's Compassionate Concern for a
    Congregant in Pursuit of His "Beshert"................. 47

Martha: A Woman's Odyssey.......................................48

A Woman in a Jacuzzi: On Listening...........................50

Three Frugal Philanthropists....................................... 52

3 Colleagues...55

Jack Riemer: Savior of Preachers.................................57

Israel Silverman: Teacher Even for the Few................. 60

Five Seminary Faculty Wives...................................... 62

Zev Nelson and Boston's Soloman Schechter Day
    School...64

Isaiah Zeldin and Los Angeles' Stephen Wise Day School.. 66

Harold Schulweis and His Master Class.....................68

Max Vorspan: Visionary Partner.................................70

Solomon Freehof: Jewish Responsa Authority..............71

Herman Halperin: A Wise Rabbi Emeritus-To-Be.........73

4   Charismatics... 75

Louis Finkelstein: Chancellor.................................... 77

Yitzkhak Hutner: Imperious "Rosh Yeshiva"................79

A Young Hasidic "Rebbe" at the Head of the Table........ 81

Marshall Meyer: Two Kings, One Crown.....................82

Zalman Schachter Shalomi: Religious Creativity........... 83

Shlomo Carlebach: Troubadour Traditionalist............... 86

Edward Koch: Mayor..88

The Vishnitzer Rebbe: On Being in One's Presence.......... 90

Mr. Groner: Modeling Prayer.....................................92

Beryl Baumgarten: A Hasid at the Seminary................. 93

The Quintessential Charismatic: The Lubavitcher Rebbe.. 94

5   The Especially Well-Known.............................. 103

Leon Uris: Exodus... 105

Chaim Potok: Novelist..107

Admiral Hyman Rickover: "The Faith of the Fallen
    Jews"...110

Wolf Blitzer: Television Journalist............................. 113

Hans Kung: Catholic Renegade................................ 114

Harvey Cox: Christian Theologian and His Journey to
    Judaism..116

Yosef Yerushalmi: Student, Scholar, Charismatic.......... 118

Isaac Bashevis Singer: Novelist, Vegetarian................123

Alexander Schindler: Reform Leader and Competitor....125

Gideon Hausner: Adolph Eichmann's Prosecutor......... 127

Mort Sahl: A Comedian's Take on American Life..........128

Martin Luther King.. 130

Harold Kushner: "America's Rabbi"....................….…132

Yigael Yadin: Soldier, Statesman, Archaeologist....……...134

Cardinal Roger Mahoney and Elie Wiesel………..…..........136

6   The Holocaust…………………..……………….. 137

Elie Wiesel: Voice of the .Shoah…………………….........139

Richard Rubenstein: Theologian.………………….......140

Wiesel and Rubenstein Meet for Dinner……………..…142

David Weiss-Halivni: Talmud Scholar…………..…......143

Shmuel Posner: Haunted Picture Framer………..…….. 146

Simon Wiesenthal: Stamps and Abraham Joshua
      Heschel.……………………………………..………148

Emil Fackenheim: Encounter with Christian
      Theologians.………………………………….. 149

A "Frum" Family on Yom Hashoah/Holocaust
      Remembrance Day……………………………… 150

7   Israel…………………………………………….. 153

An Arab Guide on the Temple Mount……………… 155

A Muslim Guard at the Dome of the Rock: A Sacred
      Locale.………………………………………….…158

Roaming the Kotel Area.………………………..…... 159

Encounter with a Shepherd.…………………..………......161

A Young Man Studying in a Yeshiva: How to Cut
      Bread………………………………………… 163

Our Christian/Arab/Israeli Driver.................................... 165

A Taxi Driver's Dvar Torah..167

Shimon Peres and His "Companion".......................... 169

An Elder in a Greek Orthodox Monastery: No Hands in
    the Pockets..171

8   **Jews in a Non-Jewish World**........................... 173

Alan Dershowitz on "Chutzpah"............................. 175

Rob Eshman: Editor of "The Tribe"........................... 177

Robert Gordis: "Yiddishe Kup" and Distinctiveness...... 178

Henry and Edith Everett: Proud Jewish Philanthropists... 180

People in the U.S. Army..183

A Non-Jewish Elderhostel Coordinator for Northern
    California...187

A Rabbinic Blessing on New Orleans' Antique Row......188

PART TWO

9   **Early Influentials**...191

Rav Frankel: A Fifth-Grade Hebrew Teacher............... 193

B.J. Cooper: An Eighth-Grade General Studies Teacher.. 195

Sam Lee and Harry Cohen: A Work Ethic.................. 198

Sadie Goldstein and How People Used to be Called to
    the Phone...200

My Father: Louis Shechter from Sborov, Poland, to
    America...202

Bea Bleifeld: An Affirming Aunt............................. 206

Sidor Belarsky: Jewish Folk Singer.............................208

Alter Landesman: Pointing the Way………….………..210

Shlomo Shulzinger, Bilha Shudowski and Two
    Seminary Professors: Learning via"Terror"…………212

10 Zaydeh: A Consequential Grandfather…………217

An Immigrant in Manchester, New Hampshire………..… 219

Our "Shul"/Synagogue…………………………….…..221

Caring for Family I: The Children.…................................. 223

Caring for Family II: A Nephew and His Family
    Brought to America from Milan, Italy………………. 224

Chickens for Shabbos………………………………… 225

Lernen…Learning…Study……………………………226

On Coming to the Synagogue Early………………………228

The Mikveh………………………………..……….......... 230

Tzitzis Inspection: The Small Talis………………...……... 231

My Bar Mitzvah Speech: Why the Subject of Tefillin?......232

The Shabbos Table………………………………….......... 234

Kiddush Cup and Besomim (Spice) Box……………..........236

Zaydeh Toward the End………………………………....237

11 Herschel Schacter: A Special Uncle……………….. 241

The Rabbi of Buchenwald……………………..……….. 243

My Entry into Yeshiva University……………..…..........244

My Son Reuven at Yeshiva University……………......... 245

My Entry Into the Jewish Theological Seminary…………246

12 Mentors..249

Abraham Joshua Heschel: Herald of Jewish Spirituality... 251

Mordecai Kaplan: A Mentor for Community............254

Wolfe Kelman: Leader of Rabbis.........................257

Simon Greenberg: Model Rabbi...........................261

Israel Levinthal: Master Preacher and Synagogue
    Leader...264

Nahum Sarna: A Prized Teacher...........................271

Jewish Study in the Modern Age: Franz Rosenzweig
    (The Single Non-Personal Encounter in This Book)..........273

13 Non-Jewish Guides.............................277

H. Eberhard von Waldow...................................279

Markus Barth...281

Paul Lapp..283

Rolf Knierim...285

14 Empowering Others...........................287

Michael Melnick: A Bar Mitzvah Blessing...............289

Shelly Blumenfeld: Artist.................................290

Baruch Goldstein: The Saga...............................293

Neil Weinberg and the Introduction to Judaism/
    Conversion Program.....................................296

Ari Vernon: A Student and His Teachers..................300

An Email from Herbert Rosenblum.........................303

After Fifty-Five Years A Woman Says "Thank You"......304

A "Shidduch"...309

15 Experiences Vis-Á-Vis Young People.........................311

Lori Young: A Young Woman Leaves Home for an
Iowa Farm..313

Jason Narot...Formerly "Narotsky"...........................316

Vincey Caparizzo, Jr. and Judah's Yarmulka................317

A Young Man's Eyes Riveted on Mine...................... 319

Asher Meir: *Yasher Koakh* ("Well Done") and How to
Shake Hands.. 321

A Single Woman at the Door.............................323

Strolling Along the Third Street Mall in Santa Monica,
California.. 324

Mendel Morris: On Nascent and Realized Piety...........326

Paul Daniels and "Jewish Radar"........................... 328

Marty Smilowitz: Boyhood Friend.......................... 329

Shelley: From "Shaytel" (Wig) to Prancing in the Mall...330

16 Friends...331

Gilbert Rosenthal: Natural Rapport...........................333

Mervin Gray: A Bond with Rabbis........................... 335

Louis Shub: Unconditional Friendship.......................337

Elijah Schochet: Bound in Spirit..............................339

Allan Blaine: A Winsome Persona..............................340

Leah: Lifelong Friend...A Poem............................. 342

Acknowledgements... 347

About the Author..349

INTRODUCTION

About this Book

It is strange how vividly early memories come back to one. And the older one gets, the more does the mind insist on recalling the past. When we are young, we live in the future, in dreams and hopes of what is to be. When we begin to feel the approach of old age, the process is reversed. Instead of living in the future, we instinctively relive the past.

Nature (for the religionist, God) has fashioned human beings with many different sensibilities, with special inclinations manifest in various areas of life. Thus, some have special propensity for history, some for politics, sports, psychology, for human relations, for literature, for religion. We could of course, go on and on.

My special inclination for years has been with biography and autobiography, for the lives and times of individual people. I have been seized with the desire to study and conjure with the successes and failures, the virtues and foibles of the single person.

During my lengthy sojourn on this planet, when young and later as rabbi and university educator, I've obviously had many interactions with family members, as well as numerous encounters with interesting and often complicated people in special ways. I do believe that a lesson, a story, a useful idea can be gleaned from these encounters; these might help readers derive some insight into the multi-dimensional and fascinating character of the human condition.

Hence this book.

The Two Parts

Both parts of this volume have as their points of departure individual personalities. However, they are intended to exhibit different perspectives. Part One points to issues beyond the personal, focusing on what might be designated "collective" or "communal," which is to say that, in general, the vignettes tell stories, depict ideas and project lessons of a general nature. Part Two, on the other hand, is more directly personal, in that the pieces seek to say something about individuals who influenced me or those who I might have influenced, and what might be described as the "fallout" of these experiences.

The above are generalizations. The parts, no doubt, in many respects, overlap.

My Father, Louis Shechter: On Writing

שֵׂכֶל הָאִישׁ הוּא תַּחַת חוּטוֹ שֶׁל עֵט

A person's sensibility is beneath the point of his pen.

—Moses Ibn Ezra

The following is an excerpt from a letter my father wrote to my sister Evelyn. Note its detailed descriptive character:

> *I am sitting in my room in Brighton Beach writing this letter. It is hot in Brooklyn—and I like it very much here, going swimming every day, taking things easy in the evening, promenading on the boardwalk, watching the fireworks which takes place every Tuesday night.*
>
> *Last night, we were on the boardwalk—what a crowd, and a* tumel. *Thousands of people were packed on the boardwalk, not a seat to be found. Mother spotted a single seat and sat to watch the ocean, the sailboats, the swimmers that were still in the water—the young girls and boys who were having fun on the beach, lighting fires, etc., and, of course, the fireworks. It was a spectacle that was rare to find outside of New York...*

I am writing like I would be a visitor from California—but it is a fact that New Yorkers don't know New York. It takes an outsider to appreciate what New York has to offer. As there was no seat for me, I took a walk on the boardwalk to Coney Island. I walked slowly, watching the melting pot of humanity—old and young, some gay, some depressed, some galloping, some hardly walking, some faces white as snow, some faces brown, black, red and what not, languages galore—Jewish, Italian dominating and yet all peaceful, friendly towards one another.

While walking back, I was thinking—reading the newspapers, you will find most of it—HATRED, WAR—preparations for war, cold war, hot war, and what not. What a comparison to the crowd on the boardwalk, and the crowds in all the capitols of the world. They ought to spend a night on the boardwalk in Brighton Beach and take a lesson...

And now note the following excerpt from an essay I wrote when I was twelve years old.

I had responded to an assignment of a short essay about a subject of our choice and chose to write about a scene in my Brooklyn, New York, neighborhood. It was a bustling, block-long market area on Prospect Place, a short distance from where I lived. Observe an excerpt of its detailed descriptive character:

Pushcarts lined both sides of the street; they were loaded with all manner of fruits and vegetables, pots and pans, flatware, paper goods, fish and meats, hardware items—and more. Bearded men with skull caps and those without beards and skull caps manned the pushcarts, along with animated women, mostly middle-aged. The bargaining over price was loud and intense. The women customers, clothed in colorful printed dresses, sturdy shoes, with their "pockabooks" (i.e., purses) closely pressed to their bodies, roamed from pushcart to pushcart, haggling over their purchases. It was a busy, colorful, tumultuous scene—typical of a day in Brooklyn, New York, in the 1940s...

When one of my classmates read the essay, he was puzzled. What was the point of the essay? He asked. All it is, is a description of something we all know about. I did not know what to say to him then or even to myself—until years later when I came upon the above letter written by my father. The phrase that caught my attention was: *I am writing like I would be a visitor from California...It takes an outsider to appreciate what New York has to offer.* You see, my father was an immigrant from Poland; he came to America from an entirely different physical and social milieu, and so he looked on the scene about him from the point of view of an outsider looking in, and this is what made for his detailing of what for him was an essentially alien, now familiar, picture.

I came to understand a mindset similar to that of my father that prompted me to describe that Prospect Place pushcart scene in such objective, even lyrical detail. You see, I came to Brooklyn, New York at age eight from Englewood, New Jersey, where I was born. Englewood was another world of open space, verdant parks, immaculate main streets, where women shopped in clean, neat stores manned by well-spoken clerks and managers. *Like my father, I was an "outsider" looking in at an alien, now familiar, scene.*

This is my theory about the matter. Obviously I have no way of proving it, although such theories have been put forth by literary experts. The various sketches in this book might confirm that I inherited a writing style and mindset similar to that of my father. I really don't know, given the mystery of genetics; yet I would like to think that something of my father's writing ways have been at work within me.

PART ONE

– Chapter One –

SYNAGOGUE PERSONALITIES

My work in the rabbinate has been filled with a host of experiences with people characterized by:

> Sadness, heartbreak, irony, undercover emotion, bold ego, courage, unwarranted self-confidence, ambition, outsized talent, exaggerated humility—and much more that mark the human condition.

The panoply of vignettes is this section portray some of these human phenomena. They also limn something of the nature of the contemporary rabbinate, of lessons learned early on, lessens I should have learned earlier, lessons, alas, I've not yet learned. In the latter case, since it is now rather late for me, perhaps the readers of these vignettes might glean something of value for themselves.

HOWARD ROSENBERG:
A FRUGAL SYNAGOGUE PRESIDENT

Beth Israel Temple Center in the small Ohio town of Warren, was my first pulpit following departure from the chaplaincy at Fort Chaffee, Arkansas. I was twenty-eight years old; Leah and I had a two-year-old son and a second son just born. My salary was $8,500 a year.

I worked long and hard and do believe effectively for the congregation. I revamped the Religious School, instituted a well-received adult education program, introduced a variety of cultural program initiatives, reinvigorated the religious services, formed a well-attended junior congregation, and personally taught the confirmation class. It was, in my opinion, good work for a young vigorous rabbi on behalf of a small congregation in a small town.

Toward the end of my second year with Beth Israel, negotiations for a new contract took place. I asked for a raise of $1,000 citing my family needs and "accomplishments." Howard Rosenberg was the synagogue president and chief negotiator. He was firm: the congregation could afford only $500. The job as director of the United Synagogue Region in Boston became available at the very juncture of the contract negotiations. Rosenberg prevailed and let me go. My request, he said, was excessive. We moved to Boston.

Two months later, Pam Newman, one of my Beth Israel confirmation students, died in an auto accident. I hurried to Warren to be with the family. At the shiva home following the funeral, Howard Rosenberg approached me. With a visibly chagrined look on his face, he recalled our contract negotiations and said to me, "Letting you leave us for $500 was one of the biggest mistakes I've ever made."

Even if half of my claimed accomplishments were true, and even if I had only one son, Rosenberg's concern for his synagogue was indeed short-sighted. He recognized that, but as destiny would have it, his view allowed me to enter the Jewish communal arena, which meshed with my natural inclinations. I owe Howard Rosenberg my thanks.

The Greek poet, Lucillius, tells of a man who preferred death because the funeral expenses were cheaper than calling in a doctor.

ALLAN GRINBERG AND HIS RABBI:
"BETTER TO HOLD BACK THAN HAVING TO PUSH"

I came to my congregation in Pittsburgh, B'nai Israel, with an ambitious plan for the synagogue's revitalization. The animating idea of the program was that of "Synagogue-Center," that is to say, an institution with an array of programs and activities that would appeal to the "whole person" — from pre-school age to the golden years. This included religious and cultural activities, formal and informal education, social, athletic, social action events and the like...this all for all ages and groups within the orbit of the synagogue. It was proposed and accepted by the Board of Directors and carried with it a very heavy financial commitment.

Allan Grinberg was president of the congregation at the time. He had a strong frugal streak in him and sought throughout the process to temper my youthful drive and determination. He grudgingly acknowledged the positive budding results, being swept along by the irresistible tide of enthusiasm on the part of the synagogue's leaders and constituency.

I had invited Dr. Simon Greenberg, the vice chancellor of the Jewish Theological Seminary, to lecture at our Adult Institute. In a conversation with Dr. Greenberg, Allan complained about the rabbi imposing so much on the congregation. Dr. Greenberg responded, "If you were plowing with an animal in your field, wouldn't it better to have hold to it back rather than to have to push it?"

———————————

Lazybones, go to the ant;	לֵךְ־אֶל־נְמָלָה עָצֵל
Study its ways and learn.	רְאֵה דְרָכֶיהָ וַחֲכָם׃
Without leaders, officers or rulers,	אֲשֶׁר אֵין־לָהּ קָצִין שֹׁטֵר וּמֹשֵׁל
It lays up its stores during the summer,	תָּכִין בַּקַּיִץ לַחְמָהּ
Gathers in its food at the harvest.	אָגְרָה בַקָּצִיר מַאֲכָלָהּ׃

How long will you lie there, lazybones;   עַד־מָתַי עָצֵל תִּשְׁכָּב

When will you wake from your sleep?   מָתַי תָּקוּם מִשְּׁנָתֶךָ׃

A bit more sleep, a bit more slumber,   מְעַט שֵׁנוֹת מְעַט תְּנוּמוֹת

A bit more hugging yourself in bed   מְעַט חִבֻּק יָדַיִם לִשְׁכָּב׃

And poverty will come calling upon you.   וּבָא־כִמְהַלֵּךְ רֵאשֶׁךָ

—Proverbs 6:6f

HAZZAN MORDECAI HEISER:
ON PULPIT PROCEDURE AND DECORUM

When I came to B'nai Israel in Pittsburgh, I joined the staff along with the congregation's Cantor Heiser. He was in his fifties and I was in my thirties. He had a fine tenor voice, was a skilled musician and had trained a talented multi-voice choir which poured forth beautiful liturgical music. He had been with the congregation for over twenty-five years. A product of Germany, he was trained in the old-time tradition of *hazzanut*, his repertoire consisting of the likes of the nineteenth century's liturgical music composers Lewandowski, Janowsky et al.

Hazzan Heiser also harbored characteristic Germanic ways: structure, discipline, formality and a total commitment to dignity and decorum on and off the *bimah*. When I came to the congregation, it was clear that I was a product of the American milieu and a different generation. However, I was enamored by the impressiveness of the synagogue sanctuary and with the hazzan's ways. And so, three things, among others, emerged from our working relationship:

First was the way we entered the pulpit at the start of services. I was at a distance on one side of the pulpit at its entry, the hazzan on the other side. He prevailed on me to watch his signal as the choir began singing the *Ma Tovu*; when I saw the signal we emerged onto the pulpit in slow cadenced form in concert with the music. We marched in precisely the same way until we reached our chairs at the very same time, stood there until the music ended, and then sat down on our respective chairs in tandem with each other.

Second was the way we waved the etrog and lulav on the pulpit during the Sukkot Festival. Our waves needed to correspond precisely with the pace of the Hallel chanting of the choir. And they had to be waved in concert with the waves of the hazzan. He trained me to do this correctly and did so with the help of a graphic chart. This is the way the procedure worked:

A wave to the north with one musical *hodu,* pause; a wave to the west with a *hodu,* pause; a wave to the south with a *hodu,* pause; a wave to the east with a *hodu,* pause; a wave toward the heaven with the music, pause; a wave downward to earth and the musical conclusion. After a few services, I got the procedure right and thus remained in Hazzan Heiser's good graces.

Third the physical position of the hazzan vis-à-vis the congregation while chanting the service was to face the congregation. It seemed logical to me that this chanting be addressed to God and not the congregants and so the hazzan ought to turn around from his podium and face the Holy Ark as he pleaded to and praised the "Holy One, Blessed be He." I shared this view with the hazzan; he would have nothing of it.

Now, I was with the congregation for ten years and for seven of those years continued to urge my view on the hazzan, to no avail. Then suddenly, he "came around" or rather he "turned around" and faced the Ark during his chanting. This lasted for the final three years of my tenure—one of my rabbinate's major accomplishments.

I was in the process of coaching my ten-year-old grandson, Eric, in the proper way to point and shake the lulav when pronouncing the blessing…

- *To the north: point directly and shake*
- *To the west: point directly and shake*
- *To the south: point directly and shake*
- *To the east: point directly and shake*
- *Heavenward: point directly upward and shake*
- *Downward: shake*

The reason, I told him, is that God is everywhere in the world. To this Eric asked: "Is God in the diagonal?"

HERMAN FELDMAN AND "A LA CARTE JUDAISM"

Contemporary Judaism has been characterized by the term "a la carte Judaism," which is to say that Jews now pick and choose what religious observance, idea or principle they wish to embrace or eschew at any given time. The erstwhile disciplined structure of observance and thought wherein a whole system is embraced as a required way of life is, for the vast majority of the non-Orthodox, a thing of the past.

This condition once came home to be me in vivid form as a rabbi in Pittsburgh. Herman Feldman, a veteran and strong supporter of our congregation, was a faithful member of our morning minyan; he rarely missed a Shabbat morning service; he was at my side during all festival observances. I had come to rely on him psychologically as a congregant who would be there even when most others were not. His consistent presence, joyful demeanor and embracing character were major assets to our religious activities.

It was Simchat Torah evening. I had announced with some fanfare a renewed way of its celebration: honoring our leaders; carrying the Torah in procession; more lively music and dance; drink and refreshments—and the rest.

Herman was nowhere to be found. When I later asked him where he was on Simchat Torah and that we truly missed him, he replied unapologetically, "I was at the opera."

In restaurants, a la carte is the practice of ordering individual dishes from a menu, as opposed to table d'hote where a set menu is offered. It is an early century loan from French meaning "according to the menu" (Merriam-Webster Dictionary).

The individual dishes to be ordered may include side dishes, or the side dishes may be offered separately in which case they are also considered a la carte.

—Wikipedia, The Free Encyclopedia

SAMUEL PERRIN:
ON CALLING A RABBI BY HIS FIRST NAME

For five years I served as director of the New England Region of the United Synagogue of America, the national association of Conservative synagogues, headquartered in Boston, Massachusetts. Dr. Samuel Perrin of Pittsburgh was one of the prominent national leaders of the association.

Though only thirty-five years old at the time, I became a candidate for the rabbinic position of B'nai Israel in Pittsburgh, an eight-hundred-member congregation of which Sam Perrin was a past president and who continued on as one of its influential leaders. Sam knew of my work with the United Synagogue, and, despite my age and minimal pulpit experience, strongly endorsed me for the job. This was a major factor in my being selected for the post.

Sam felt close to me during the initial years with the congregation, justly feeling that he had a stake in my work. He supported and encouraged me. However, there was a problem: he had insisted on calling me by my first name—*Jack* eschewing the title, *Rabbi*. I resisted and, as tactfully as I could, asked him to address me as *Rabbi*. Sam felt rebuffed, hurt and our relationship was strained ever since that conversation took place.

Now, while it is true that at the time (the late '60s and early '70s), addressing a rabbi by his first name was not common, I have always regretted my stance toward Sam Perrin, not only because it alienated a friend and important ally, but because I think I was a bit too eager to protect the dignity of the rabbinic position—and no doubt, of my own personally. In addition, I hadn't taken into consideration the positive intent of the other; Sam Perrin was a smart man and respected professional; he was a passionate Jew and committed leader of his synagogue. He wanted to be a friendly supporter.

I've long since learned a valuable lesson from that incident; it was about the necessary limits to the admittedly important status of the rabbinic position and to embrace the sincere motives of the Samuel Perrins of synagogue life.

O, how times have changed!

Rabbi Yitkhak Hutner was head of the mesivta (high school) which I attended. Dr. Ariel Mayse of Stanford University wrote the following about Rav Hutner's teaching about pedagogy and traditional religious education; it was published in the periodical Religion, *2019:*

> One of the key themes of Hutner's teachings is his emphasis on the paramount importance of discipleship. The relationship between the student and master, at once distant and intimate, was central to his educational project. Hutner understood the enigmatic, allusive power of charismatic leadership. Honor due to teachers was also an important theme in his teaching; his students' recollections make clear that in his own life Hutner very much stood on ceremony.

SARAH AND TED ABRAMS:
QUINTESSENTIAL CONSERVATIVE JEWS
AND SIMCHAT TORAH

When I use the term *Conservative* here, I mean it in a dual sense. In terms of a denominational designation, i.e., the Conservative Movement as distinct from the Reform and Orthodox movements; and in terms of outlook on religious practices, i.e., conservative as distinct from liberal or progressive.

Sarah and Ted were Conservative Jews in both these senses. Sarah's mother was one of the great ladies of the congregation when it was founded prior to 1920 and in its magnificent synagogue structure erected in the mid-1920s. Sarah was reared in the ways of the classical Conservative Movement during its heyday. She and her husband, Ted, embraced its thought and practice with passion and tenacity. They attended religious services with unfailing regularity. When they arrived for services, one was struck by Sarah's careful grooming, elegant dress and confident stride. Ted was at her side with his erect posture, starched shirt with tie that perfectly complemented his immaculate suit along with handkerchief tucked neatly in suit jacket. A dignified couple indeed.

Sarah and Ted expected and reveled in the beauty and dignity of B'nai Israel's religious services which were characterized by orchestrated order, decorum, beautiful classical liturgical music; this all in a huge and majestic sanctuary.

And then a problem. On Simchat Torah I called on our congregants to come onto the *bimah* and dance and sing as the Torahs, clutched tightly by their carriers, circled the *bimah*. I then led a string of congregants down the center aisle in song. As a new, young rabbi, unschooled in the dignified and decorous ways of classical Conservative religious services, such behavior, even in celebration of Simchat Torah, was quite unsettling to Sarah and Ted.

At a subsequent meeting of the board of directors, Ted

described the rabbi's actions on Simchat Torah and protested, arguing that such behavior was undignified, raucous and inappropriate given B'nai Israel's traditions; it was a serious violation of its norms. A vigorous discussion about the matter ensued. I was not present at that meeting. No action was taken except that I was to be informed about the proceedings.

As a result, the following year I moved the Simchat Torah celebration to the Social Hall. We hired a *klezmer* band to enliven the music and dancing, a daring innovation at the time, even more unusual for our classical Conservative congregation. I danced and sang with the huge number of congregants present as we wended our way around our social hall. I stayed in my flowing black robe for the celebration. We punctuated each *hakafah* (circling with the Torahs) with refreshments and the required whiskey, and for the rest of my stay at B'nai Israel, we had a Simchat Torah celebration, which Sarah and Ted never attended.

Rabbi Benjamin Lichter was the rabbi of Congregation B'nai Israel in Pittsburgh since its founding in 1920. He served the congregation for some four decades in accordance with its classical Conservative norms which he personally embraced and embodied. He was a lifelong bachelor.

I sent the above vignette to my colleague, Rabbi Jack Riemer, who was born and bred in Pittsburgh. He responded with this note:

Dear Jack: Sarah and Ted were right. I cannot imagine Rabbi Lichter dancing with the Torah on Simchat Torah. He wore a frock coat and striped pants, with a fresh flower in his lapel every day.

ALLAN NEIL, CATERER: *MARIT AYIN*: (THE APPEARANCE OF THINGS)

On Catering

B'nai Israel congregation in Pittsburgh had a large, strikingly appointed Social Hall. Many congregational, community and personal events took place in it. We had a large well-equipped kitchen manned by a full-time caterer, Allan Neil, who delivered excellent kosher meals, both meat and dairy. It was one of the synagogue's major units—financially, socially, religiously and otherwise.

At the meat meals Mr. Neil provided each table with imitation butter, margarine, which was *pareve* i.e., non-dairy and hence perfectly legal kashrut wise. I had another take on that matter. As the rabbi of the synagogue, I "decreed" that margarine was not to be used at meat meals because it gave the appearance of real dairy butter and thus could be mistaken for the real thing.

I cited the rabbinic concept of מַרְאִית עַיִן (literally: *what the eye sees*), which means the appearance of things. People might not make the distinction between the technically legitimate margarine and dairy butter and hence could be misled by conflating the two, leading to vitiating the distinction between the kashrut principle of the separation of meat from dairy.

As a young rabbi not yet forty years old, I was convinced that this was a compelling argument. I insisted my *decree* be adhered to. Mr. Neil strongly objected. This was not good for business he urged; it's legally okay; the people insist on it; we'll lose *customers*; we need the income; the synagogue lay leaders want it; Rabbi, you can't contravene all that; you're a young rabbi still naïve about the practical ways of the synagogue world.

I stood by my position for exactly four catering occasions, whereupon I relented. The only thing I accomplished was labeling the margarine: "non-dairy." So much for the rabbinic concept of *marit ayin* insofar as a food "business" was concerned.

On Shabbat

I was still preoccupied with the notion of עַיִן מַרְאִית in Pittsburgh days. I was in the habit of strolling through my East Liberty neighborhood on Shabbat afternoons. During these walks I would gaze at the windows laden with the attractive goods displayed at the retail stores on Main Street. At times I would walk into the alcove of the stores to get a better look at the merchandise. I never went into the stores; it was unthinkable to purchase anything on Shabbat.

Lo and behold, עַיִן מַרְאִית, *what the eye sees*, entered the picture. Some in the community saw me gazing at these store windows and spread the rumor that the rabbi was shopping on Main Street on Shabbat! I had given the appearance of doing so. And so thereafter, since I didn't think it appropriate to pin a label on my suit lapel stating "only looking" during these afternoon strolls, I stopped taking them. The rabbinic concept of *marit ayin* would seem to remain valid at least insofar as a non-food matter was concerned.

Marit Ayin in Talmudic Times

Six things, though not prohibited actions, are unbecoming for a Torah scholar:

- *He may not go out perfumed into the marketplace*

- *He may not go out of the house alone at night*

- *He may not go out wearing patched shoes*

- *He may not converse with a woman in the marketplace*

- *He may not participate in a meal with the ignorant*

- *He may not be the last to enter the study hall*

- *And some say that he may not walk with an upright posture.*

—Berakhot 43b

SUICIDE: TWO INCIDENTS

אֵין בְּשַׂר הַמֵּת מַרְגִּישׁ בְּאִזְמֵל

The body of the deceased does not feel the knife.

I have hesitated to set the following thoughts to paper for deep sadness pervades their details. However, human life comprises not only joy, happiness, contentment, and the overcoming of difficulty, but also tragedy. This is the existential reality of the human condition. It is probably the reason, for instance, that Shakespeare's tragic plays are much more gripping and popular than his comedies. In the spirit of acceptance of this reality, the rabbis had something to say about this condition when they ordained that:

כְּשֵׁם שֶׁמְבָרֵךְ עַל הַטּוֹבָה, כַּךְ מְבָרֵךְ עַל הָרָעָה

Just as one has to bless God for the good, one has to bless Him for the bad.

—Talmud, Berakhot 48b

Two Incidents…

The woman was an active member of my congregation in Pittsburgh. She evinced emphatically cheerful demeanor, greeting me always with warmth and ever complimentary fashion. She called my wife, Leah, every Friday afternoon without fail to wish our family a "good Shabbat." Her husband, Harry, was a hardworking and benign man, and her two sons handsome and good students in high school, though a bit lethargic in our religious school.

One morning she was found in the basement of her house. She had hanged herself. Obviously, the trauma in the community was pervasive and my role as the rabbi conducting the funeral, internment and shiva was among the most difficult I've ever experienced. Sometime later at a morning minyan, I struck up a conversation with a young relative of this woman. He had been saying kaddish for one of his parents. He knew the family well, and so I asked him how he could explain what happened. He responded that he knew the real woman. She lived a life of inner chaos; she inexplicably had a deep fear of her benign husband; she was ambivalent about the nature of her sons. He understood quite well, he said, why that woman took her own life. He left it at that.

Another member of B'nai Israel in Pittsburgh was an active member of our men's club. A short, rather stout man, he was a salesman of hardware items, very outgoing in demeanor, full of nervous tension, acerbic when discussing synagogue politics, an eager usher at our religious services, and along with his wife and children a decided presence in our midst.

The man once told me that his father had taken his life by walking into the ocean and never returning, and that he was contemplating doing the same. I lectured him about the fact that Jewish religious tradition was emphatically opposed to such an act. He listened with a skeptical look on his face. Later, in Los Angeles, word got to me that the man walked into the ocean as did his father and floated back to shore with a calm demeanor on his lifeless face.

Scripture says: "For your lifeblood too, I will require a reckoning" (Genesis 9:5). Rabbi Eleazar taught that this means "I will require a reckoning from you for your own lifeblood."

— *Tractate Bava Kamma 91b*

Suicide is considered to be a grave sin both because it is a denial that human life is a divine gift and because it constitutes defiance of God's will for the individual to live the lifespan allotted to him. As it is put in Ethics of the Fathers (4.21): "Despite yourself you were fashioned, and despite yourself you were born, and despite yourself you live, and despite yourself you die, and despite yourself you will hereafter have an account and reckoning before the Holy One, blessed be He.

— *Louis Jacobs, The Jewish Religion*

TOBY:
BEFORE AND AFTER HER HUSBAND PASSED AWAY

Toby was a congregant of mine at B'nai Israel in Pittsburgh. Her husband was Saul. For many years Toby was confined to a wheelchair due to a paralysis diagnosed by her physicians. She depended wholly on the care, concern and loyalty of her husband, whose compassion for her was legendary in the community. Toby's condition was relatively secure; she had a confident demeanor; she reveled in the loyalty she commanded from her husband.

Suddenly, Saul died. Within a few days, Toby got up from her wheelchair and walked with sure steps. When I saw her confident stride, I was astonished—but understood.

Loyalty implies a faithfulness that is steadfast in the face of any temptation to renounce, desert or betray.

—Merriam-Webster Dictionary

LABEN MELNICK:
ON ASKING FORGIVENESS BEFORE YOM TOV

At my Pittsburgh congregation, I was ever eager to maintain a decorous service and atmosphere; this included limiting the already rather lengthy traditional Conservative service. Part of the effort was my determination to keep the number of *aliyot* at the standard seven even when some could not get a coveted *aliya* with its accompanying *mi-she-bayrach* (prayers for the sick or happy occasion), or when a prominent congregant was involved.

Dr. Laben Melnick, an especially sensitive spirit, was president of the congregation when one such rumble occurred. An important congregant demanded an aliya we could not offer. Whereupon Dr. Melnick, who sat on the *bimah* rose from his chair and approached me and rather emphatically insisted that I allow the *aliya*. I stood my ground; he then repeated his demand, this time not realizing the microphone was on and had caught his unusually disrespectful tone. I prevailed and that was the end of it.

Twenty-five years later in Los Angeles, where I had moved to work at The University of Judaism, I received a call from Laben Melnick. It was two weeks before Yom Kippur. He told me rather sheepishly that he regretted having spoken to me disrespectfully during that long-ago incident concerning the refused aliya. At the direction of his Pittsburgh rabbi, he was calling to ask for *mechila* (forgiveness) for only the sins committed against fellow men can be forgiven by the aggrieved. Also, his rabbi cited for him the passage in the Midrash (*Lamentations Rabbah 3*) that "the gates of repentance are always open." He was especially regretful, he emphasized, because the whole congregation had heard his disrespectful tone.

My response: "Of course, Laben, I forgive you."

"Rabbi, please put it in writing; this is very important to me," Laben pleaded.

"I will, Laben," but I did not get to write him the forgiveness note immediately.

A week later, I got another call from Laben. "Rabbi, please, I beg you to send me the written *mechila*." The urgent, pleading sound of his voice prompted me to immediately pen and dispatch the note.

A wise teacher once said to his followers: "We can learn something not only from what God has created, but also from what man has created."

"What can we learn from a train?" a follower asked. The teacher responded: "From being one minute late, a person can lose much."

"And from a microphone?" "That what we say here is heard there."

JACOB SPITZ:
VETERAN EDUCATOR AND HIS YOUNG RABBI

When I came to B'nai Israel as its rabbi, I was thirty-five years old—young for a congregation of 800 families. The synagogue was housed in a magnificent building which contained fifteen classrooms for its religious school. Jacob Spitz, a seasoned and veteran educator for two decades, was director of the school. He was fifty-five years old.

Now, the structure of the synagogue staff was such that the rabbi was in overall charge of the religious school, responsible for its basic philosophy and general well-being. I had some knowledge and experience about Jewish educational theory and practice, but those did not begin to match those of Jacob Spitz, our educational director.

Mr. Spitz was a mild, somewhat passive person and I was that young, self-confident, hard-driving rabbi in charge of things. We met each week for a formal meeting and regularly on ad hoc basis during a given week. This was the scenario:

I'm sitting behind my broad, neatly organized desk in a ma-hogany wood-paneled office; the floor is covered with luxurious wall-to-wall carpeting; my college and Seminary diplomas are prominently displayed; plush green drapes grace the windows; my extensive Judaica library covers a wall from floor to ceiling.

Mr. Spitz walks into the place in his usual humble, deferential manner. I talk curriculum, teachers' tasks, school projects, etc. etc., and Mr. Spitz just sits there and listens, nods and agrees with everything I say. "What should we do?" I would ask, to which he answers, "We should do what you've suggested." "What do you think?" I ask. He answers, "I agree with you, Rabbi." And so go our exchanges, punctuated here and there with a quiet, bland comment, suggestion, report from Mr. Spitz, and always with a deeply respectful and deferential demeanor.

Invariably, when our meeting is concluded and Mr. Spitz exits the room with his standard, "Thank you, Rabbi," I feel that this thirty-five-, thirty-six-, thirty-seven-, thirty-eight-year-old rabbi has arrived at sagehood.

I learned a good deal from the likes of Mr. Spitz:

- *Listen more and talk less.*

- *Value older experience as much as the new.*

- *Do not assume that quiet deference makes for lack of substance.*

- *Engage co-workers who are not afraid to challenge, to argue.*

- *Never assume that just because one is a rabbi he/she possesses all wisdom.*

- *Rabbi: never allow a Mr. Spitz to trap you into believing how great you are!*

WALTER REIS:
ON AN INNER CONNECTION WITH A RABBI

During my rabbinic work in Pittsburgh, I toiled mightily to fashion a program for the youth of the congregation. One of the ventures that met with success was the USY (United Synagogue Youth) organization which at one time engaged well over a hundred teenagers in religious, experiential Jewish learning, athletic and social activities. Indeed, the program thrived.

After a weekend outing as three busloads of the USYers were heading home, tragedy struck. During a stop for refreshments, three of the girls went for a stroll along the country road when a car speeding along struck all three girls. Only one of them survived. When we all heard what happened, the pain and anguish I experienced was indescribable.

The girls had been taken to the hospital. I went to the place where the returned buses were parked. As I stood there alone, I pounded away at the sides of one of the buses in anger and grief, subconsciously blaming myself for what happened. It was a very difficult time, indeed.

Years later, after having left Pittsburgh for Los Angeles, I received a call from Dr. Walter Reis, a psychiatrist, a man of religious sensitivity, a member of the congregation. He had long since forged an invisible bond with me, as congregants often do with their rabbis.

Dr. Reis just wanted to talk to me to *hear my voice*, he said. We talked. Then he told me that he knew all about how, standing alone near those buses that had carried the three USY girls many years ago, I pounded away at one of them in great grief. I was startled by what Dr. Reis said because I always thought that encounter with the bus was a solitary one, a private moment of grief.

The psychological Jew.

JOHN HARRIS:
ON THE MOST MEMORABLE EULOGY
IN MY RABBINATE

John Harris and his wife, Anne, lived in an apartment on the grounds of B'nai Israel's synagogue in Pittsburgh. John was the building's full-time superintendent; he took care of every facet of the synagogue's physical needs. He and I became good friends; we saw each other every day; we planned things cooperatively; we joked and exchanged stories and generally got along very well. Once when I jokingly chided John for having forgotten to wear his skullcap, he responded: "Rabbi, ah's Reform."

Alas, John suddenly suffered a heart attack and passed away; he was in his late forties. How sad, how tragic it was; we were all chagrined; Anne was now a widow; I lost a friend.

Anne insisted that I have the chief role at John's funeral, which was held in a black church in the Homewood section of Pittsburgh. I painstakingly prepared the eulogy, which told John's story with our synagogue as well as his early life in the South. It spoke of his warmth, love of life, his bond with Anne, his sense of humor, his focused work ethic, his dreams for a life of continually elusive prosperity—and more.

As I stood on the pulpit of that church facing a sea of black faces speaking with a passion I rarely displayed at the much more subdued Jewish funerals, I was greeted with spontaneous enthusiasm. Every time I said something positive or noteworthy about John, the assemblage burst forth with "yeah," "sure," "good," "yes, Rabbi," "you got it right," and more. Since I said so many good things about John, that eulogy lasted longer than any other I ever delivered. Never in my career was I more exhilarated when delivering a eulogy, for, you see, Jewish funerals are far more quiet, subdued, sad and restrained.

Following the church service and internment, family and friends came to John's apartment to console Anne and to reminisce. I came as well. As I entered the apartment, I was greeted with a warmth and enthusiasm I've rarely experienced in my days. "You sent John away in style, Rabbi...,"you're a good man of God, Rabbi." I felt as if I were some sort of Hollywood celebrity walking the red carpet. Believe me, dear reader, this kind of greeting was never repeated during my life's sojourn.

I had moved to Los Angeles. Anne, who was allowed to stay in the apartment on the synagogue grounds following John's demise, passed away. She had been ill and had left word that she wanted me to deliver the eulogy at her funeral. I demurred, indicating to the caller that the current rabbi of B'nai Israel ought to do so.

SAM DEAKTOR:
A PERSON IS JUDGED BY THE KIND
OF ARGUMENTS HE GETS INTO

Sam Deaktor was an immigrant to America who did very well, indeed, in his adopted country. He came to own a number of "Giant Eagle" supermarkets, making him a man of considerable means. He was a prominent member of the B'nai Israel congregation in Pittsburgh, of the Jewish community-at-large and a generous donor to both. A truly ironic puzzle about Sam: he would consistently win in lotteries, collect a goodly sum and proudly walk about—the last person in the community who needed the winnings! Of course, he did not lack for personal problems. When I asked him one day, "How is everything, Sam?" he replied, "Rabbi, everything covers a lot of territory."

Sam was the pillar of the daily minyan (morning worship service) of our synagogue. For the some twenty-five persons who attended the service regularly, he provided a full-scale breakfast along with the whiskey most minyanaires enjoyed — myself excluded. ("What kind of a rabbi are you?" he once exclaimed when I declined the liquor).

Sam was proud of his philanthropy and wasn't shy about reminding all who would listen about it. One morning he got into a heated argument with Herman Feldman another of our minyan's regulars and also an elder of the congregation.

Herman claimed that his charitable giving easily matched and even exceeded Sam's. "How do you know what I give?" Sam protested. "I easily give more than you do." They kept arguing, whereupon they agreed to show the records and let their rabbi (me) decide the matter. "Gentlemen," I said, "listen to me:"

I quoted the rabbinic passage in *Pirke Avrot* (Ethics of the Fathers 5:20):

כָּל מַחֲלֹקֶת שֶׁהִיא לְשֵׁם שָׁמַיִם סוֹפָה לְהִתְקַיֵּם

Every controversy that is for God's sake will be of lasting worth in the end.

This verse indicated that Sam and Herman's argument was about a high and holy and mighty important purpose—helping people and causes in need, a true mitzvah. And that theirs was, therefore, a good and constructive argument. They both calmed down, never stopped giving and rarely argued about the matter again at our *minyan*.

And so, from our daily minyan I relearned something important about the Jewish mindset. People argue—they always did and always will. The Jewish idea is to argue about the important things.

Note: Dear reader, on my word of honor, this is a true story!

– Chapter Two –

THE UNUSUAL

unusual *adjective* **1** *an unusual characteristic*, uncommon, out of the ordinary, atypical, abnormal, rare, singular, odd, strange, curious, surprising, unexpected, different, unconventional, uncustomary, unorthodox, irregular; **2** *an unusual talent*, extraordinary, exceptional, singular, rare, remarkable, outstanding.

—Oxford American Dictionary

ISHMAEL SOWA:
PAGANISM AND LIVING RELIGION

Ishmael Sowa was a native of Ghana, a small nation on the southwest coast of Africa. He had been ordained a Presbyterian minister and was in America studying for a master's degree in biblical literature at the Pittsburgh Theological Seminary. He had already translated sections of the New Testament into his native African tongue and, upon returning home, planned to translate portions of the Old Testament.

My wife, Leah, a classmate of Ishmael at the Pittsburgh Seminary, had arranged a dinner at our home in order to introduce Ishmael to me, for relaxed conversation and perhaps to learn from each other something about our respective religious ideas and practices. We were the first Jews Ishmael had ever met and Ishmael was the first native African we had ever met. After telling him about some of the Jewish religious ways, I asked Ishmael to delineate for Leah and me the nature of native African religion and his reactions to it as a Christian. A warm, friendly and articulate man, he proceeded to do so.

Many Africans today are "pagans," Ishmael began. They literally worship rivers, stones, trees, bones. They offer animal sacrifices to these objects, accompanied by elaborate rituals and incantations. Instead of the Jewish-Christian-Muslim "Thou shalt: and "Thou shalt not," they have "taboos" that regulate and control family life and social relationships. These taboos, unlike the regulations of monotheists, partake of magic and superstition in that a specific prohibition against touching, saying or doing something problematic is rooted in fear of immediate harm from a supernatural force. The Africans' belief in life after death is so strong that, like the ancient Egyptians, they bury food, water and eating utensils with their dead so that the deceased will continue to have nourishment during their life in the great beyond.

The River God

Ishmael told us that on the day before his departure for America, his father took him to the river to pray to the river god for a safe journey. I later learned that what Ishmael was referring to was a widespread practice, when for example, the Masai of East Africa cross a stream, they throw a handful of grass into the water as an offering to the stream's "spirit." The grass, the source of life for their cattle, plays an important role in their tribe's superstition and ritual.

Among the Baganda of Central Africa and the Ghanians in southern Africa, before a traveler forded any river, he would ask the spirit of the river to afford him a safe crossing and, as an inducement, throw a few coffee beans as an offering into the river. At certain spots at the rivers Nakiza and Sezibwa in Uganda was a heap of grass and sticks on either bank, and every person who crossed the river threw some grass or sticks on the one heap before crossing, and on the other heap after crossing: this was his offering to the spirit of the river for a safe passage through the water.

From time to time, more costly offerings were made at these heaps; the worshipper would bring beer, or an animal, or a fowl or some bark-cloth, tie the offering to a heap, and leave it there after praying to the spirit. The worship at each of these rivers was conducted by a priest.

The nature of this phenomenon was explained by Mircea Eliade in his *Patterns in Comparative Religion*, p. 203-204:

> These spirits live and govern in the depths of the waters. Like the very elements in the waters, the divinities are at odds with each other and capricious; they do good and evil with equal carelessness, and like the sea, they generally do evil. More than any other gods they live outside time and history. Their life is perhaps less divine than that of the other gods, but it is more closely connected with the element they represent—the waters.

It was these practices, Ishmael said, that prompted him and so many other Africans of his educated group, to adopt the religion of the western world.

The above encounter with Ishmael Sowa took place some thirty-five years ago. Following Ishmael's stay in Pittsburgh, he returned to Ghana and proceeded to his work of translating the Hebrew Scriptures into his African language. I heard nothing about him since—until the year 2011—over three decades later.

Leah and I were at the Newark Airport beginning our trek back from New Jersey where we had spent the Sukkot holiday with our son Judah and his family. Because of her knee problem, Leah required a wheelchair at the airport to get her from place to place. A young Ghanaian woman worker at the airport met us and wheeled Leah. I struck up a conversation with the young lady, who was quite informed and articulate about life and religion in her native Ghana. She had graduated from college in Ghana and was working at her present job to finance study in America to qualify for American accreditation.

I told her about Ishmael Sowa and our encounter with him in Pittsburgh. She proceeded to wax lyrical at the mention of the name Ishmael Sowa. He is famous all over the African continent, she exclaimed. *He is an old man now; he lives in Accra, the Ghanaian capital; he has translated portions of the New and Old Testaments into numerous native Ghanaian tongues;* he is a great man whose work has helped to transform the pagan religion of much of Africa. *She explained—much as Ishmael Sowa did for Leah and me thirty five years ago—something of the nature of African religious practice and how Christianity has replaced it; this because of the work of Ishmael Sowa and others in Ghana.*

The young Ghanaian woman was very impressed that we had known Ishmael Sowa personally.

RENE RODRIGUEZ...AND THE PASSION FOR LEARNING

I was enroute from the parking lot to Office Depot, an office supply store, to replenish some of my home supplies. A swarthy, dark-eyed man approached me thinking I looked like someone he knew. Though not the case, he insisted on talking to me.

We entered the store together. I don't know why, but he asked me if I was Jewish. Yes, I was, and that unleashed a torrent of talk. His name was Rene Rodriguez. He was a native of Puerto Rico and came to the United States at age eight. His father had left home and his mother died from neck cancer. He was brought to Manhattan in New York by an aunt to live with her, his grandmother and the aunt's two daughters. They all lived in a cold, sparsely furnished, two-bedroom apartment. It was a hard life living as they did from hand to mouth.

Things looked up for Rene in elementary school primarily because of his Jewish teachers. One such teacher, Mr. Goldstein, gave him an extra sandwich during lunch periods when he saw the lad didn't have enough to eat.

Another teacher, Mrs. Cohen, encouraged and urged him to study hard, to master reading and writing, to be different from the other Puerto Rican kids who were more indolent than he was and were looked down upon by the other students. Mrs. Cohen often stayed with him after school hours to help him with his homework. Periodically, too, she invited him to her home on weekends for study.

These experiences stayed with him all his life. How grateful he was to the Jewish people for that.

But there was more. When he was in junior high school, his science teacher, Mr. Schwartz, saw that he wore tattered shirts and sweaters during the freezing winter. With tears in his eyes, Rene said his teacher bought him his first warm coat, the thought of which keeps him warm to this day.

Persistence

With palpable passion, Rene said that because of these Jewish teachers who affirmed him, who cared for his needs, who consistently urged him to get a good education so that he would one day be a successful "somebody," he persisted in that direction. He continued his studies and graduated high school which few of the other Puerto Rican kids did. He went on to a technical school to study mechanics. He then joined the U.S. Air Force and studied for a pilot's license, which he got. When he came out of the air force, he studied in college on a scholarship and got a degree in aeronautic technology.

Now Rene has been in his own business selling, repairing and supplying copiers, printers and fax machines using the skills he acquired during his studies. That's how I met him at Office Depot; he was on one of his stops throughout Southern California doing business, doing quite well, he said, and able to take good care of his family.

When he finished his narrative, I told him how impressed I was, and that as a Jew and a rabbi I understood this great emphasis of the Jewish people on education. When I mentioned "rabbi," he enthused: how eternally grateful he was to the Jewish people, "who made me who I am today."

The Conversation Was Not Yet Over

Rene told me about a local Jewish-owned electronic store which had been vandalized. He was enraged and spoke in protest at a town meeting. He was then asked to appear on a local television program during which he told of Jewish benevolence, emphasis on learning and all the rest, and that such behavior at a Jewish store—any such store—was intolerable. Whereupon a group of skinheads sought him out and smashed the windows of his car and his house, as well as calling him and threatening him on the phone. To which Rene said to me, "There's no way these guys intimidated me. I am from Puerto Rico!"

Finally, the encounter was over. Rene Rodriguez gave me his

business card. I gave him my card. We embraced. He proceeded to his business with the Office Depot manager. I went out of the store musing about Jewish compassion and the passion for learning, and the difference it can make in a person's life.

The beneficial effect of learning is analogous to infection: it enters and spreads.

—*L. Stein,* Journey Into the Self

A CULTURED SWISS LADY AND
CHAIM POTOK'S NOVEL, *THE CHOSEN*

Some years ago, I was visiting Dr. Markus Barth in Basel, Switzerland. Son of the renowned Protestant theologian Karl Barth, the younger Barth had been Professor of Biblical Literature at the Pittsburgh Theological Seminary where he served as one of my doctoral studies advisors. I served a synagogue in Pittsburgh at the time.

At his home, he introduced me to his sister. She was a woman with erect posture and well-defined facial features, dressed in stylish Swiss fashion, was well-spoken and with good command of English. She greeted me smoking a pipe! The woman impressed me as highly cultured and well aware of her father's worldwide fame.

Being in the presence of a rabbi, she proceeded in animated fashion to tell me that she had read Chaim Potok's novel, *The Chosen*. She related how deeply she had been taken by the book, and the insight she had gotten into the distinctive Hasidic mindset as it clashed with the way of living and thinking of the modern Jewish Orthodox.

Here was a Protestant woman herself living religiously and psychologically far removed from the Jewish experience. Yet from a depiction of a particular way of life, at a particular time and place, with its own flavor and nuance, as limned in Potok's novel, this woman got genuine insight into a vibrant slice of Jewish life. And it wasn't Judaism in general that moved her, but a particular setting that spoke to her mind and heart. It was from that bounded framework that she was able to resonate to the universal issues of friendship and generational conflict.

James Joyce's great novel, Ulysses, *is a successful attempt at the complete recapture insofar as it is possible in fiction of the life of a particular time and place. The scene is Dublin, Ireland, its streets, homes, shops, newspaper offices, pubs, cemeteries, hospitals, brothels, schools. The novel is a series of remarkable Homeric parallels, the incidents, characters, and scenes of a Dublin day corresponding to those of the Odyssean myth. Joyce attempts to reproduce not only the sights, sounds and smells of Dublin, but also the memories, emotions and desires of its people in the drab modern world.*

Ulysses *is a widely discussed novel and one of the most influential in 20th century literature. Why? Because from Joyce's depiction of Dublin in particular we get insight into the nature and condition of urban life in general in locales throughout the world. And more: even as William Blake saw the universe in a grain of sand, so did Joyce see the universe in Dublin, Ireland on June 16, 1904, a day distinguished by its utter normality. Almost every variety of human experience is crammed into the happenings of a single day. Seen through the eyes of a single Jew, Leopold Bloom, the run-down city that is Dublin is a figure of hope and hopelessness, morality and dogged survival.*

The point: from the particular we gain insight into the general. From the rich soil of one's own specific milieu and experience, from one's unique life and ways, we get understanding of others outside one's own setting.

—*From* Journey of a Rabbi *(Vol 1, p. 345)*

JACK OSTROW: "CHAIRMAN OF THE BOARD"

There are some extraordinary people in the world of Jewish in-stitution-building. For many years Jack Ostrow was chairman of the board of directors of the University of Judaism in Los Ange-les, California (at which institution I served as dean of continu-ing education for two decades).

Jack was *the* pillar of financial support and lay guidance of the university throughout his three-decade tenure. He was born in the Brownsville section of Brooklyn, New York, and grew up in a home of poverty. (This is the same neighborhood, inci-dentally, where I grew up and thus I was quite familiar with such situations.) Jack once told me that as a youth, in order to sleep at night, he had to place three wooden boards across two stands, arrange for a thin mattress and flat pillows and in cold weather sleep under the heavy coats used for the outdoors. His parents were Yiddish speaking immigrants committed to "secu-lar" Jewish life and who had not yet adjusted to life in the new world of America.

But Jack was smart and enterprising; he learned to work at odd jobs, earned some money, managed it carefully and slowly emerged as a budding fiscal entrepreneur. He subsequently moved to Los Angeles and became manager of the finances of prominent Hollywood personalities, including the likes of the famous actor, Burt Lancaster. Jack's own fortune grew into the millions.

As a non-business pre-occupation, Jack became committed to Jewish life, joined a Conservative synagogue in Beverly Hills, and was involved in the growth and development of the Univer-sity of Judaism as chairman of its board of directors. The "UJ," as we all called it, was the educational institution founded in 1947 by Dr. Mordecai Kaplan and Rabbi Simon Greenberg of the Jewish Theological Seminary, which institution was, at the time, the West Coast branch of the seminary, the center of the Con-servative Movement in America.

In the early years, Jack was practically alone in support of the young institution, though, as time went on, he was able to involve others of means and otherwise supportive of the cause to help in the finances and its needs. Jack's own commitment and passion for the institution was, indeed, quite remarkable, as per but one characteristic example:

Dr. Max Vorspan, vice president of the UJ, had initially involved Jack in the internal affairs of the institution. That was when he (Ostrow) initially joined in the school's activities in the arts realm. Max once visited me in my office with a check in hand. He told me that the UJ that particular year ran into a $500,000 deficit which had to be closed if the institution was to carry on its work. Max then showed the check he had in hand…

It was made out to the "University of Judaism" for $500,000 and was signed "Jack Ostrow." This was the first and last sight of such a check my eyes ever beheld.

"Great oaks from little acorns grow."

DENNIS PRAGER: MASTER TEACHER

During my tenure as Dean of Continuing Education at the University of Judaism, I had determined as a basic strategy to seek out and engage especially articulate and informed teachers with special ability to relate to and communicate with adults who learn in ways quite different from children. (In this field of education, we called the method with adults *andragogy* versus *pedagogy*.)

Dennis Prager was one such instructor. Once, I introduced him to Louis Jacobs' *Principles of the Jewish Faith*, which contained a systematic interpretation of Maimonides' "Thirteen Articles of Faith." This book served as the basis for one of his courses concerning the principle theological affirmations of Judaism. On another occasion, we agreed that he would expound on each unit of the Pentateuch over an extended period of time until the *Pentatetuch* was completed. These offerings and a number of others were presented to many hundreds of searching adults for some fifteen years.

Prager was, indeed, the kind of thinking person and able communicator who eagerly embraced such substantive intellectual fare. He had been Director of the Brandeis Institute in Simi Valley, was a well-known talk show personality specializing in serious intellectual and popular contemporary issues, and an author of several books on Judaism of lucid and accessible content. He had an imposing physical presence and resonant voice and his reasoned explication of Judaic concepts was consistently compelling.

A "Eureka" Moment

Once, walking the classroom hall at the University to gather feedback about our study offerings, I encountered a young woman standing alone in tears; it was during a recess of a Prager class. I asked her why the tears, to which she responded that as a result of Prager's analyses, she now believed she could find her way back to a Judaism that was meaningful to her, something heretofore lacking. She continued that here was a breakthrough for her in how to think about ways to mesh the traditional Jewish way and the modern way comfortably. It appeared that the learning experience with Prager was for this a "eureka" moment of discovery.

In light of this "eureka" encounter, an instructive aside: in choosing instructors for the University's continuing education program, I had always emphasized the importance of our instructors having advanced academic degrees or established Judaic scholarship. My superiors at the University insisted that we maintain this criterion.

I did—with an exception: Dennis Prager, in fact, did not have the above credentials. However, it was quite clear to me that he possessed unusual general and Judaic intelligence and a surpassing capacity to transmit often complex theological ideas and religious practices in lucid and compelling fashion. During the first five years of his teaching at the University, I regularly heard rumbles from my superiors about Prager's "credentials" and I succeeded in either ignoring or resisting the rumbles—and Dennis Prager remained on the University of Judaism's Continuing Education teaching staff during these five years and throughout the following ten years.

Academic chairs are many, but wise and inspiring teachers are few.

—*Albert Einstein,*
The World As I See It, *p. 243*

JOSEPH TELUSHKIN:
HOW TO KEEP A WHOLE SCHOOL LAUGHING
FOR EIGHT CONSECUTIVE HOURS

For many years I arranged a Sunday Institute program at the University of Judaism. One such venture was with Rabbi Joseph Telushkin about Jewish humor. Some one hundred people attended in a large classroom off the university's majestic balcony.

The laughter was incessant. Every hour or so, I would visit the room to observe and witness hilarity. It was so persistent that I decided to open the classroom doors to enable others to listen. Soon they stood near the doors and joined the laughter. The hilarity continued even during the recesses and lunch time for what else was there to talk about?

Gradually, as the day progressed, dozens more of curious, from throughout the building gathered near the large classroom widely opened into the balcony. And they joined in ever hearty laughter. It seemed like the whole school was laughing.

This all went on for eight straight hours. I do not exaggerate.

THE PROGRAM

See the following for details published in the winter 1993 edition of the continuing education catalogue depicting the various learning offerings.

Jewish Humor:
What the Best Jewish Jokes Say About the Jews

with
With an incisive, deeply informed, highly entertaining scholar and teacher

Rabbi Joseph Telushkin

Author of *Jewish Humor, Jewish Literacy, The Nine Questions People Ask About Judaism, Why the Jews: The Reason for Anti-Semitism* and three mystery novels

Sunday, February 7, 1993 • 9:30am-5:30pm

Sigmund Freud once wrote of Jewish jokes: "I do not know whether there are many other instances of a people making fun to such a degree of its own character." Why this should be so is the subject of this Institute on Jewish Humor, an erudite, opinionated, and hilarious examination of comedy as the mirror of a culture. This program is woven around more than 100 of the best Jewish jokes—some classic, some newly minted.

Through humor, Rabbi Telushkin identifies the keystones of Jewish character: family love and torments, relations with God, the push of anti-Semitic oppression and the pull of assimilation; *chutzpah* and its flip side, self-denigration; the love of learning, the passion for arguing, the commitment to justice—and others.

Among the specific issues the Institute will address are:

- How Jews cope with persecution and discrimination
- How Jews view money and financial success
- What Jews think about sex
- How Jews see rabbis and other religious leaders
- What Jews think about violence (there is one kind they like)
- How Jews think about assimilation and intermarriage
- How Jews see Jews of other denominations and ethnic backgrounds

Tuition: $75 per person

Includes lunch, materials, and registration fees

"The long-standing Jews in prominence in American comedy—over the last forty years—is shown by the phenomenon that 80 percent of the country's leading comics have been Jews." This estimate was made by Steve Allen, a non-Jewish comedian and historian of American comedy (Funny People, p. 20).

"American comedy," Allen believes, *"is a sort of Jewish collage industry"* (p. 11). A listing of twenty of the most prominent American-Jewish comedians indicates the disproportionate success of Jews in this area: Woody Allen, Jack Benny, Milton Berle, Fanny Brice, Mel Brooks, Lenny Bruce, George Burns, Sid Caesar, Billy Crystal, Rodney Dangerfield, Danny Kaye, Sam Levenson, Jerry Lewis, Groucho Marx, Jackie Mason, Zero Mostel, Joan Rivers, Mort Sahl, Phil Silvers, Henny Youngman.

RABBI ALEX—AN *ATARAH*:
HIS FATHER'S, HIS, NOW MINE

Rabbi Alex was a colleague in Los Angeles. He had served a congregation in Northridge before joining the staff of the neighboring University of Judaism as a vice president (I was dean of continuing education). Both his father and uncle were Conservative rabbis; later his son followed suit as a rabbi. Alex was intelligent, articulate and resourceful; he also harbored personal struggles. We got along well professionally and personally—despite his more liberal religious tendencies which were at variance with my own more traditional ones.

Once Alex approached me with an *atarah* (a silver adornment worn around the neck area of a talit) in a plastic bag. He removed it and handed it to me and said it had belonged to his father. Why give it to me, I asked, and not keep it for yourself? I know you will use it and often, he replied. Why don't you give it to your son? I asked. His answer: I want you to have it. I persisted in protest. He would not budge in his determination that I have the *atarah*. I relented and accepted it.

Alex subsequently left the University of Judaism and took a large pulpit in San Francisco. After a few years he left San Francisco and occupied a pulpit in a small town—Warren, Ohio (where, by coincidence, I began my pulpit career after leaving the Army as a chaplain). He served in Warren for a very brief period. Shortly after he died, unfortunately at a young age.

I attached the *atarah* to my talit and have been wearing it ever since Alex gave it to me.

Alex's atarah *is a sterling silver assemblage of small squares sewn onto the neck area of a tallit. The name* atarah *means crown or wreath. Its etymology is from the Hebrew noun* עטרה *the verb of which is* עטר *which means "to surround."*

RABBI CHAIM'S COMPASSIONATE CONCERN FOR A CONGREGANT IN PURSUIT OF HIS "BESHERT"

Once during a stay in a staunchly Orthodox neighborhood during Passover, I visited a synagogue populated by "newly Orthodox" congregants. There and then, I then relearned one of the important tasks of a spiritual leader…

During one of the rabbi's *droshes* (homilies), he described an urgent entreaty on the part of one of his loyal congregants. The man was seeking a *kallah* (a bride) and had a set of qualifications he was requiring and asked his rabbi to help him in his search. The stipulations included the following:

- He was seeking a woman who never watched television.

- He wanted a wife who never read the newspaper.

- He needed a woman who never used a computer.

- He was seeking a wife who never listened to a radio.

- He wanted a woman who never would touch or be touched by a man before marriage.

"Please, Rabbi, help me find my *beshert*, the woman destined to be my mate for life," the man pleaded.

The rabbi, a compassionate and embracing spiritual leader, told the man that he was presenting him with a difficult task. However, because of his congregant's earnestness and loyalty to *Yiddishkeit* (the Jewish way of life) and to the *shul* (synagogue), he would do everything in his power to find the man the wife he so fervently sought.

When the service was over, I approached the rabbi wishing him a "good Shabbos" — and "good luck."

MARTHA: A WOMAN'S ODYSSEY

The following is an entry in the diary I kept during a month-long stay in Mexico City as a student rabbi while yet at the Jewish Theological Seminary. The stay was for the High Holy Day—Sukkot period with a small enclave of Conservative leaning Jews in the country.

One night after a busy day, I came back to the rooming house where I was staying, where Martha, the cook/housekeeper, was watching television. I asked if it would be possible to have some tea; she immediately obliged. She also took off my blue jacket and removed some paint spots on it. (They had painted the kitchen and pantry that day.) After the tea, we sat down to watch television which featured a boxing match, of all things. It was a grueling and bloody thing. After the fight, the announcer introduced an ex-boxing champion who asked for money for a group of unfortunates as a result of a flood in Thailand. The crowd proceeded to throw money into the ring.

Apparently prompted by the scene on the screen and by a question I asked her about her situation, Martha proceeded to tell me her story.

She was born to a well-to-do family in Switzerland and married a man whom she described as "a gentleman from head to toe." He was ambitious and a bit restless and they traveled together throughout Europe, the United States and South America for almost three years. Feeling the need to settle down, her husband asked her where she would like to live. Martha said, "I will go to Mexico," because life was easy there, the climate was good and opportunities for an ambitious businessman were many. He agreed. And so they moved to Mexico City. Her husband opened a ribbon factory and they prospered.

They lived in a huge house in Homas, an exclusive residential section of the city, in a home Martha described as larger and more beautiful than the one she was now working in. They had no children but many friends, dined out, attended parties, took vacations and frequent trips to interesting sites. They had a really good life.

The Downfall

And then seventeen years ago, Martha's husband died at age fifty-two (she was forty-one.) He left her 365,000 pesos, which was about $35,000—a lot of money in those days. But Martha trusted everybody (she still does, she said). She kept lending money for various business ventures—50,000 pesos here, 30,000 pesos there—and never got repaid. And seven years ago she sold her big house and planned to live on the money received.

She never had to work, and didn't until finally she lost absolutely every peso she had. Now she had to go to work: Martha became a lowly, unkempt, obedient housemaid. She said she now lives purely on memories, yet she doesn't mind her condition too much. She does cry, but goes on living. She wouldn't mind it so much if Bertha (her boss) were a kinder person. Bertha always finds fault with her and doesn't trust anybody.

Martha continued. She'd been out of this house three evenings in the last year and television was the only form of entertainment she had. It was a drab, dull, housemaid's life.

Even as Martha finished telling me her story, I sensed it came from the lips of a person with an innate dignity. She had a proud bearing that was intermingled with the realization of her lowly status in life. She was a poignant phenomenon.

———————————

I used to rule the world
Seas would rise when I gave the word
Now, in the morning I sleep alone
And sweep the streets I used to own.
      —*Coldplay (a British band), "Viva la Vida"*

A WOMAN IN A JACUZZI: ON LISTENING

I was relaxing in the warmth of the Jacuzzi in the gym when a woman in her early sixties entered. She began an endless monologue: twenty years ago when her husband served in the military in Japan, she was in a ski accident that injured her leg and the Jacuzzi helps ease her discomfort. She had three sons and wanted a daughter, so she had one and then another. Her sons work here and there, are basically okay but do cause her problems. All this spoken in extended and minute detail during which I murmured but a word or two.

Finally, the woman asked me what I was about. I told her I taught at a university; she immediately proceeded to expatiate about her brother who has worked for many years as an expert electrician at a nearby college. When I was able to get in a word edgewise, saying that my field was "religion," the floodgates opened.

She had gone to Israel with her Baylon church Catholic priest on a pilgrimage and had seen the sacred sites, Capernaum, Jerusalem, Bethlehem, Hebron, etc. It was a full and exhausting trip, very informative, and with the extended description and the minute details of the trip, I could see how that was so. I did not get in a word edgewise, even though I had just completed a book about the land of Israel.

She then launched into her work as a Sunday school teacher at her church. She had been a sixth-grade teacher in public school. With a barrage of specifics, she regaled me with the imaginative way she teaches her Sunday school charges about the holy land, the *Stations of the Cross* in Jerusalem, how she takes them from the *Book of Genesis* through Scripture to the advent of Jesus and all the rest. "It's only one and one-half hours in Sunday school," she said, "but I do stoke their imagination." She asked me not a word about my thoughts on the subject.

Finally, after what seemed to me an endless monologue, I emerged dripping wet from the Jacuzzi, full of information about the woman's life and experiences, draped myself in a towel and began exiting the pool area, whereupon the woman said to me, "I'd like to learn about religion and the Holy Land from you." Without a word in response, I proceeded toward the locker room. As I did so, I heard her striking up a "conversation" with someone else who had entered the Jacuzzi.

Two people were in conversation. The first was speaking some 90 percent of the time while the second was listening…and listening. As they were parting, the first person said to the second, "You are a good conversationalist." I suspect that the woman of our gym encounter thought I was a good "conversationalist.

The story is told about a clergyman who is standing at the door of his sanctuary greeting a long procession of people. He clasps each person's hand and says, "Wonderful!" to everything the person says. One of the people going trough the line says, "My grandfather was killed yesterday," to which the greeter responds, "Wonderful."

Yes, many of us, not just clergy, don't hear the other. We ask, "How are you?" and then keep walking and talking. Maybe we don't listen because we fear getting involved in other people's problems, or maybe we simply prefer the sonorous sound of our own voice or the overarching importance of our own concerns.

THREE FRUGAL PHILANTHROPISTS

I've known three gentlemen who were persons of considerable financial resources and major contributors to their synagogues and to the University of Judaism.

Sam S. established the library at his synagogue in Phoenix, Arizona with a magnificent gift of $200,000. He also endowed the Elderhostel program at the University of Judaism with a $400,000 gift. Every week he would call me at the university from Phoenix to inquire about our Elderhostel budget to make sure that we didn't fritter away his money on "non-essentials."

Leonard S. came from a family of wealthy supporters of their synagogue in Los Angeles' San Fernando Valley, where, among other gifts, they had the synagogue's chapel named for them. Subsequently he and his wife, via a huge financial contribution, had the University of Judaism's chapel named for their deceased son. This gentleman had sold his plumbing supply business to an English company for $90 million. He told me matter-of-factly that whenever he was confronted by a parking meter, he would circle the block for a place to park his car to avoid having to pay the meter's money requirement.

Philip W. endowed a number of programs at his West Los Angeles synagogue as well as a major lectureship at the University of Judaism to the tune of $250,000. For all of the programs at the university the gentleman attended, he insisted on receiving the senior discount for study course tuition and tickets for lectures and concerts.

"In Defense of Scrooge, Whose Thrift Blessed the World"

In the 1840s, Charles Dickens, author of "A Christmas Carol," didn't see how businessmen like his hero, Ebenezer Scrooge, were already lifting mankind from poverty.

Who benefited from the accumulated wealth of Scrooge and Marley? First Britain and then all mankind. Since Scrooge and Marley never consumed the wealth they created, its use was a gift to all. It funded the factories and railroads, the tools and jobs that fed and clothed millions of British subjects and then billions around the world. Their unspent wealth was of no use to them, but it was of sublime use to humanity.

Even as Dickens's Ghost of Christmas Present pulled back his robe to reveal the children who embodied Ignorance and Want, the wealth accumulated by Scrooge was already beginning the long drive that would do more to end ignorance and want than all the governments and charities that ever existed. Scrooge's wealth accumulation would have benefited far more people than anything he gave to charity after his reclamation, and many times more than government would have helped had they taken his wealth and spent it.

—Wall Street Journal, *December 24, 2020*

– Chapter Three –

COLLEAGUES

My career has been blessed with encounters with outstanding rabbinic leaders. Characteristic of what follows has been experiences with older colleagues who I have always admired, learned from, and been enriched by their example, teaching and presence. Some had foibles.

JACK RIEMER: SAVIOR OF PREACHERS

Rabbinic Tasks

Consider this: the rabbis of old used to preach twice a year, at *Shabbat Hagadol* before Passover and at *Shabbat Shuva* between Rosh Hashana and Yom Kippur. The rabbi of today preaches each and every Shabbat and each and every festival throughout the year, in addition, of course, at the unusually demanding High Holy Days.

Consider also: in addition to preaching, the modern rabbi serves as teacher off the pulpit, as programmer and administrator for his congregation, as counselor, as visitor of the sick, as representative to the larger community, as husband/wife or father/mother—and more.

How, in heaven's name, is such a person to become an effective sermonizer? Where is the time to prepare, to study, just to think, to interact with colleagues in order to produce sermons of substantive content and religious and personal inspiration? This all is a constant problem and struggle for the rabbi of today. I can testify personally to this, having served a demanding congregation in Pittsburgh for a decade.

Riemer to the Rescue

There is a prolific rabbi in America who has for many years come to the rescue. He is Jack Riemer, in my opinion America's premier homiletician for a good half-century. During this period, Rabbi Riemer has authored engaging, relevant, biblical and rabbinic-based sermonica that has been circulated throughout the rabbinic world. Each piece is based on the weekly Shabbat or holiday biblical portion; most have a compelling and memorable message; each is almost always useful for colleagues faced with the inexorable demands of his/her preaching schedule.

For obvious reasons the literally hundreds of rabbis who use Rabbi Riemer's materials are reticent about the source of their sermonizing because, after all, the rabbi needs to be original and have his own voice. And so, countless sermons during the past half-century have had their origin in the creative mind and prolific pen of Jack Riemer "incognito." He has been a savior in this regard for the rabbis of America.

Over the years in my role as continuing education programmer at the University of Judaism, I had arranged seminars for rabbis at which leading preachers presented their sermonica to colleagues in preparation for the looming High Holy Days. For many such occasions I invited Rabbi Riemer to present his materials. Whenever he appeared on the program, numerous colleagues at the seminars took home, and used his resources. And significantly I would receive requests for the materials from colleagues throughout the country. I reprint below one such typical importunity:

> Dear Jack:
>
> I would deeply appreciate your sending me a set of the sermon material that Jack Riemer will present on Wednesday to our colleagues.
>
> Would you be good enough to *rush it* to me (since time is so short) to my *home address*?
>
> I trust that I will be able to reciprocate this favor in a tangible way in the future.

A Rabbinic Resource Department: Proposed, Rejected

I once sought to have Rabbi Riemer engaged full time at the University of Judaism to head up a special "Rabbinic Resource Department." Its purpose was to produce a monthly packet for the rabbi containing full sermons, a comment on the Haftorah, a prayer and a synagogue bulletin article, all integrated around a single theme. This would be distributed to those subscribing to the venture. Such an undertaking is common among the various Protestant denominations, including Presbyterian, Lutheran and Methodist. I thought that institutionalizing Rabbi Riemer's

homiletical genius would be a further boost to the very preoccupied rabbis in America.

Jack was willing. The university leadership was not. Sad.

---

*Let the speaker be called what he will...so long as he expounds
the word of God from the Bible and Agada, extracts pure gold
from old and new fields, teaches the present generation its true
work and reaches all hearts by skillful speech. Then the divine
spirit will return to thy temples, O daughter of Zion, and will
become manifest in deeds flowing from words of enthusiast.*

—Zunz, *Gottesdienstliche Vorträge*, 1832, p. 481

ISRAEL SILVERMAN:
TEACHER EVEN FOR THE FEW

Israel was a good personal friend during our Boston years together. He served his Brookline congregation, Temple Beth Zion,
while I was director of the New England Region of the United
Synagogue. I "held his hand" during the illness of his first wife,
Toby, and, alas, after her passing. He knew of my affection and
regard for him when later he asked me to be a signing witness to
his and Gloria's *ketubah* at their marriage.

I once visited Israel during a Shabbat afternoon in his synagogue. He was in the midst of lecturing during the *seuda
shleesheet* (the "third meal"), the period between the *mincha* and
maariv services. I counted seven people listening to him. He was
speaking with enthusiasm and emphasis on biblical and rabbinic
sources as he referred to his copious notes; it was clear that he
had prepared meticulously for that learning session. He held
forth as if seventy listeners were before him.

In Israel's mindset, the sacred texts of which he was master
deserved to be understood and embraced by whoever cared to
listen. Numbers were quite irrelevant.

---

*The overwhelming importance of the individual person, who is
to be spoken to as if one is addressing a "whole world" (i.e., a
massive number of people), is encapsulated in the following
Talmudic passage (Sanhedrin 4:5):*

לפיכך נברא אדם יחידי ללמדך. שכל המאבד נפש אחת
מעלה עליו הכתוב כאילו איבד עולם מלא.
וכל המקיים נפש אחת מעלה עליו הכתוב כאילו קיים עולם מלא.

ומפני שלום הבריות.   שלא יאמר אדם
לחבירו אבא גדול מאביך.   ולהגיד גדולתו של הקדוש ברוך הוא.
שאדם   טובע כמה מטבעות בחותם אחד וכולן דומין זה לזה.
ומלך מלכי המלכים הקדוש ברוך הוא טבע כל אדם

בחותמו של אדם הראשון ואין אחד מהן דומה לחבירו.
לפיכך כל אחד ואחד חייב לומד בשבילי נברא העולם

It was for this reason that man was first created as one person [Adam], to teach you that anyone who destroys a single life is considered by Scripture to have destroyed an entire world; and anyone who saves a single life is as if he saved an entire world.

And also to promote peace among the creations, that no man would say to his friend, "My ancestors are greater than yours." And also, to express the greatness of The Holy One [blessed be He]: For a man strikes many coins from the same die, and all the coins are alike. But the King, the King of Kings, The Holy One [blessed be He] strikes every man from the die of the First Man, and yet no man is quite like his friend Therefore, every person must say, "For my sake the world was created."

FIVE SEMINARY FACULTY WIVES

I was a rabbi in Pittsburgh. During a visit to New York and the Jewish Theological Seminary, I was invited to a gathering of seminary faculty and wives at the home of Rabbi David and Zipporah Weiss-Halivni. They wanted to hear directly about my various initiatives in Pittsburgh, and I was eager to hear their take on some of the Jewish-religious issues of the day.

The five faculty wives present were the following:

- A Ph.D. in library science
- A prominent landscape artist
- An editor of children's books
- A Ph.D. in psychology
- A Ph.D. in biology.

I asked the group what they thought about women serving in the rabbinate, being counted to a *minyan* along with the men, receiving *aliyot* at services.

All five women were adamantly opposed, citing the traditional ban on these matters. When I pointed out that they, along with many women doctors and lawyers and college professors are active in the "outside" world, meet and work with professional men and women all the time, they responded with one voice: the religious public domain is different. When I asked why it was different, their response was: it just is—that this domain has a different set of criteria for such matters.

These truly accomplished professional women have not integrated their general and religious public domains—a puzzling dichotomy between the secular and religious ways of thinking and acting. This is a phenomenon that I believe could use some research and analysis.

Two decades ago the Conservative Movement admitted women into the rabbinate. It was a controversial period of debate, heated disagreement, and reluctant acceptance by many of the more traditional minded colleagues. My friend Rabbi Allan Blaine was among the traditionalists.

Two decades later, the Conservative Movement was seriously considering admitting gays into the rabbinate. Again, much heated discussion, debate and disagreement. A decision had not as yet been made.

At the fiftieth anniversary occasion of Allan's and my ordination that took place in Boston at the annual convention of the Rabbinical Assembly, I asked Allan what he thought about the gay rabbi issue, to which he exclaimed:

"Are you kidding? I haven't gotten over the women rabbi decision yet!"

ZEV NELSON AND BOSTON'S
SOLOMON SCHECHTER DAY SCHOOL

One Monday morning in September 1961, I, as director of the
United Synagogue in New England, along with Harry Lakin,
president of the New England Region of the United Synagogue,
and Rabbi Jerome Bass, a local Conservative rabbi, especially
supportive of the cause, entered a classroom in Brookline's Congregation Kehillat Israel's educational wing. We were there to
witness the start of a new Jewish educational venture—a Solomon Schechter Day School. Six youngsters and two teachers
were in that classroom. Thus began a major venture sponsored
by the New England Region of the United Synagogue and Rabbinical Assembly.

The six youngsters were enrolled in first grade. The following
year, four additional children joined these six for a second grade,
and twenty children entered the school's first grade. We were
elated by this modest beginning and especially pleased with the
substantive Judaic and general studies the youngsters experienced. We were convinced of the need for such an intensive Judaic education for our children, and the day school in the Conservative Movement was becoming another effective means of
realizing that end.

The story of the struggle and hardship we faced in order to
keep the school alive could fill many a page. Indeed, were it not
for the passionate commitment and indefatigable effort of one
man—Rabbi Zev Nelson of Temple Emeth of Chestnut Hill with
whom I had extensive contact on this and other synagogue matters—it is doubtful the school would have survived during this
incubation period. In face of much indifference on the one hand,
and palpable resistance on the other, Rabbi Nelson's endlessly
outstretched hand for fiscal and moral support was a true phenomenon of dedication to a sacred cause.

The problems we faced in the years that followed remained
formidable—scarcity of funds, rabbinic resistance because of

"competition" with Boston's quality afternoon Hebrew schools, concerns about "parochialism," etc. But, under the determined leadership of Rabbi Nelson, we were committed to the day school cause and therefore determined as he was to see the school thrive.

In one of my reports to our constituents, I said this:

One day we will look with pride at this institution and be thankful we had the courage and conviction to grapple with and overcome the immense obstacles inherent in such a pioneering venture.

Indeed, the Solomon Schechter Day School of Boston has enrolled thousands of youngsters through the past fifty years and has become a signature Jewish educational venture in New England.

ISAIAH ZELDIN AND LOS ANGELES'
STEPHEN WISE DAY SCHOOL

Day schools in the Reform movement are rarities. Isaiah Zeldin's vision and extraordinary commitment in founding fifty years ago the Stephen S. Wise Day School as an integral part of his prominent Los Angeles temple was and is the exception.

The elementary school along with the Milken middle and high schools constitute one of the largest and most effective Jewish educational institutions in the country. Over the past decades it has trained thousands of young people who have imbibed the values and have practiced much of the living patterns of the faith and peoplehood of Israel. This has been accomplished by combining the best of traditional Jewish religion and culture with that of the larger secular world the contemporary Jew inhabits.

Rabbi Zeldin is the reason for this phenomenon. He was a staunch Zionist following in the footsteps of the prominent Rabbi Stephen Wise, along with possession of a zealous commitment to intensive Jewish education. This, along with unusual charisma, learning and public presence and a strong capacity for translating vision into practice, made his school a phenomenon in the Jewish world of the twentieth and twenty-first centuries. He knew how to raise the needed funds and how to inspire and motivate his lay leaders.

I write this as a firsthand observer having served as dean of continuing education at the University of Judaism which was immediately adjacent to the day school on a mountain bluff of Bel Air. For over two decades I watched "Shy" (as we called him) Zeldin's work and regularly interacted personally with him about the school's progress. I saw the school slowly grow, admired its founder and driving force.

Incidentally, my wife, Leah, served the institution as assistant principal for Judaica for some eighteen years and, among other things, she pioneered the integration of Jewish and general studies into a seamless curriculum which was, in no small measure, a factor in the school's substantive educational content.

———————————————

Vision looks inward and becomes duty. Vision looks outward and becomes aspiration. Vision looks upward and becomes faith. Vision spawns reality.

—Stephen S. Wise, Sermons and Addresses, 72

HAROLD SCHULWEIS AND HIS MASTER CLASS

Along with so many others, I had always considered myself among Rabbi Harold Schulweis' many admirers. His theological insights and passionate patterns of action are the stuff of legend in the Los Angeles community as well as throughout the country. As the rabbi of Valley Beth Shalom in Encino, California, his prolific pen, creative synagogue programming and magnificent preaching and lecturing have influenced both fellow colleagues and especially the Jewish laity in significant measure. Indeed, his contribution to the Jewish cause during his lengthy career has enriched the Jewish world.

As dean at the University of Judaism, I pressed Harold Schulweis into the cause of Jewish life outside his own synagogue. Thus, for example, I sent him on lecture tours throughout the west coast Jewish community; I arranged for him year after year to occupy the university public lecture program attended by thousands and he was one of our classroom teachers.

Here I want to example an aspect of his teaching, his master class: an unusual capacity to transmit substantive ideological learning material to laypersons. A quotation from a university continuing education catalog...

> *Rabbi Harold Shulweis* of Valley Beth Shalom in Encino, California, one of America's leading Jewish thinkers, presents a "Master Class in Jewish Theology: Four Modern Jewish Philosophers in Search of Spirituality." He and his students will embark on this search through an examination of:
>
> - *The Religious Existentialism of Martin Buber*: Seeing the human individualism in each Jew
>
> - *The Prophetic Vision of Abraham Joshua Heschel*: The need for spiritual balance
>
> - *The Halachic Faith of Joseph Soloveitchik*: Law as spiritual liberation

- *The Religious Naturalism of Mordecai Kaplan*: Judaism through a humanistic and programmatic lens.

This master class was geared to lay persons with particular interest in what could be considered arcane subject matter for such an audience.

A special added feature to the program was four pre-class dinners with Dr. Shulweis for those enrolled in the course. These took place in the UJ dining center, where students and teacher joined for dialogue about the coming class subject matter.

The result: well over one hundred students attended both the dinners and class sessions. The students resonated to the experience's substance and its master teacher with a passion I rarely observed in my over two decades as the university's adult education dean.

Israel said to Moses: Our teacher, Moses, lo, you say to us "The Torah is not in heaven, nor is it beyond the sea" (Deuteronomy 30:12-13). Then where is it? He answered: It is in a very near place, in your mouth and in your heart, that you may do it; it is not far from you, it is near to you...

The rabbi said: Solomon said seven things about the sluggard, but what Moses said was greater than all of them. How so? People say to the sluggard (in Moses' name):

Your teacher is in the city,

Go and learn Torah from him.

—Deuteronomy Rabbah,
Chapter Eight, Section Six

MAX VORSPAN: VISIONARY PARTNER

Max Vorspan was a key figure in the growth and development of the University of Judaism in Los Angeles. His natural focus was on the "Jewish civilization" aspects of Judaism, and he resonated to the role of the arts in Jewish life—to theater, music, painting, sculpture, dance—as ways to enrich the Jewish experience in America.

Blessed with a creative and highly imaginative mind, Max was full of new ideas and constantly projected visions of what the university should do and become. He also had a signature sense of humor which was rooted in the "offbeat" aspects of life. He was often impractical and unrealistic, traits that sprung from his ever restless and imaginative mind. Yet because of his winning ways and masterful speaking he engendered powerful loyalties for the university along with munificent financial support. Max was a special person, indeed.

For two decades we worked together at the university, he as a senior vice president and me as dean of continuing education. We had a natural bond based on a mutual concern for the arts and the need for creativity in programming for the institution. We met and constantly exchanged ideas and plans. At the end of many working days, Max would come into my office to relax; I'd take out a bottle of wine from my desk drawer, pour two glasses, and we would talk.

For a way to characterize our working relationship, the following image comes to mind: Max would project the sparks of vision into the atmosphere and I would harness the sparks and translate them into programmatic reality. It was a good combination of skills that made for a fruitful relationship. This probably accounts for Max's unfailing support of my work in the face of the consistent *Sturm und Drang* of university life.

The place where two men meet to seek the highest is fruitful ground.

—Felix Adler

SOLOMON FREEHOF:
JEWISH RESPONSA AUTHORITY
A Visit in His Basement Book Binding Facility

Dr. Solomon Freehof was a leader of Reform Judaism in America and throughout the world. He came to Pittsburgh's Rodef Shalom as its rabbi after serving as professor of homiletics at the Hebrew Union College in Cincinnati. In these positions he gained a reputation as an insightful scholar and writer as well as that of a brilliant orator.

Throughout his career Solomon Freehof's principal scholarly interest had been the development of Jewish law, as seen in the vast legal literature of the Responsa. He had linked Reform Judaism to the Responsa literature through his volumes, *Reform Jewish Practice,* which provide modern solutions which he believed were natural extensions of the scholarly literature of the past. His volumes of Reform Responsa reflect the problems and mood of contemporary America. In addition to these works, Dr. Freehof has published a number of books which have introduced the responsa literature to the general reader.

During Dr. Freehof's later years, I served Congregation B'nai Israel as rabbi in Pittsburgh, a neighbor of Freehof's Rodef Shalom. This unusual man was deeply proud of his vast collection of responsa literature which he had collected over the years. Many of the written responsa were originally in tattered form, thin pamphlets, the seams loose, the pages yellowed with age, the covers' lettering hardly visible.

Freehof had a plan: he fixed up the basement in his home as a book binding facility equipped with strong thread, white paint with paintbrush and all manner of supplies. With these he restored each of his responsa publications with new black covers, new stitching and clear lettering identifying the items' author and content. The neatly arranged revamped collection of rabbinic responsa literature, huge in number, sat on the basement's shelves. It was a library sight to see.

The caring scholar wanted me to see what we had done. And so, as an embracing gesture of a young rabbinic colleague who he surmised would appreciate his creative labors, he invited me one day to his home basement to view his huge collection of responsa. As I surveyed the vast assemblage of pamphlets and books, large and small, I was astonished at the love and care Dr. Freehof invested in the sacred word.

The Responsa literature extends for a period of over a thousand years down to the present day. The majority of the questions to which the authors addressed themselves concerned Jewish law in all its ramifications. New situations and circumstances, different in many ways from those which obtained in former ages, posed problems of conduct for which no direct guidance could have been expected in the classical sources. Yet it was believed that Judaism, if properly investigated, had an answer to every question, was capable of showing which way was right and which wrong in matters of ritual, social and family life, reaction to the Gentile community and communal endeavours.

The central theme of the Responsa literature is the discovery of the right way for a Jew to behave; what it is that God would have him do. With their mastery of the sources, especially the Talmud (the major fount of wisdom for those who engaged in this task), the famous Respondents were able to give advice on all the practical problems that were the concern of their questioners; most of their replies came to enjoy authority in subsequent Jewish law.

Although most of the emphasis in the Responsa is undoubtedly on practice, there are to be found in nearly all the great Responsa collections discussions of a theological nature; naturally so since new conditions pose problems for belief as well as for practice. From time to time, questions were asked regarding fundamental principles of the Jewish faith, the answers being arrived at by more or less the same methods that were used to propound the law in a particular case.

—Louis Jacobs, preface to his *Theology in the Responsa*

HERMAN HALPERIN:
A WISE RABBI EMERITUS-TO-BE

The world of the rabbinic search—the process by which a congregation seeks to locate the best spiritual leader for its members, is a complicated one indeed.

A typical synopsis of the qualifications of a potential rabbinic candidate, based on the written resume, portrays a person of pronounced quality; he or she is a good sermonizer, an outstanding educator, a skilled organizer, a compassionate pastor, an effective participant in the large Jewish community, and a devoted family man/woman. The virtues of the person go on and on, buttressed by a set of warm and laudatory letters of recommendation from various prominent persons with whom the candidate has been associated over the years. Nary a word about the candidate's shortcomings, large or small.

Often recommendations are solicited via phone in addition to writing. I once received such a call from Herman Halperin, a wise, long experienced colleague who was rabbi emeritus of a synagogue in search in Pittsburgh. He was assisting in the process of selecting a successor. His was a prominent Conservative congregation and this was, of course, no small matter.

Herman asked me, a neighboring rabbi, about Rabbi X who was a candidate for the position, and a very good friend of mine. I proceeded to extoll my friend's manifold virtues, depicting a person with the plethora of qualities listed above. Whereupon the veteran and seasoned rabbi emeritus-to-be asked: "Tell me, Jack, what are his weaknesses?"

Rarely in my life have I been so taken aback. I thought fast: the candidate's weaknesses were that he worked too hard; he was too conscientious. This was the best I could do. I knew, of course, that my comment contained yet more virtues disguised as weaknesses, and that my recommendation was not a fully candid one, as my wise rabbi emeritus-to-be colleague subsequently told me.

Over the years, I've tried various scenarios which might disentangle the push and pull of this condition: be honest yet helpful, etc. I really haven't yet figured this one out.

I have heard that there are more than three hundred times in the Babylonian Talmud where a discussion ends with the Hebrew word "תֵּיקוּ," "let it stand," i.e. the issue remains unsolved, the question unanswered, the solution not found. Tradition has interpreted the word teiku *as follows using the Hebrew lettering:*

תִשְׁבִּי = *the prophet Elijah (in the Messianic age)*

יְתָרֵץ = *will answer*

קוּשִׁיוֹת = *questions*

אַבָּיוֹת = *problems*

The prophet Elijah will in the Messianic Age answer all (unanswered/unsolved) questions and problems.

– CHAPTER FOUR –
CHARISMATICS

Merriman-Webster's Collegiate Dictionary (Tenth Edition), page 192, defines charisma this way:

> *A personal magic of leadership arousing special popular loyalty or enthusiasm for a public figure. A special magnetic charm or appeal.*

The persons depicted in the following section have been outstanding leaders in their respective fields. To some, the elements of charisma defined by Webster are theirs quite naturally; to others not quite naturally. Hence, in the case of the latter, in order to assure and secure their leadership roles, the elements which make for charisma have had to be "orchestrated," including distance, aloofness from followers and other measures. In the case of the former, such orchestration has supplemented with the leader's natural charismatic endowments.

Such are the complexities of prominent leaders, invested as they have been with the burdens, responsibilities and privileges of leadership which require "popular loyalty or enthusiasm" as the dictionary has it.

What follows is a set of vignettes seeking to illustrate this phenomenon.

LOUIS FINKELSTEIN: CHANCELLOR

During the course of a lecture appearance at my Pittsburgh synagogue by Dr. Louis Finkelstein, the chancellor of The Jewish Theological Seminary, I brought my Christian seminary professor, Dr. Eberhard von Waldow, to Dr. Finkelstein's hotel room for an informal meeting.

Dr. Finkelstein was a major rabbinic scholar, author of the two-volume The Pharisees, a biography of Rabbi Akiba, a commentary on Avot D'Rab Natan (a collection of rabbinic lore), producer of a critical edition of the midrash Sifra, and other seminal works. He had also authored an important article about the origin of the synagogue in the distant past. Professor von Waldow who was particularly interested in the synagogue article told me how eager he was to meet its author. And so it was arranged.

Now Dr. Finkelstein was not only a scholar of distinction and a leader of a major seminary, but also an imposing persona. He was relatively tall, had chiseled features, a pointed, neatly trimmed beard and a penetrating gaze when he spoke to you. He wore a black skull cap surrounding straggling strands of hair, and spoke with a soft voice, strangely halting, yet with authority. Altogether he was a man of decided charisma.

When Dr. von Waldow and I came into his hotel room, Dr. Finkelstein greeted us with restrained cordiality. Von Waldow immediately assumed a reverential and respectful demeanor. He asked about the synagogue article, whereupon Dr. Finkelstein launched into a detailed, scholarly and insightful discussion. Clearly a sage was holding forth. As I watched the scene, Dr. von Waldow, a serious scholar in his own right, sat silently, attentively listening and assumed the stance of a disciple in the presence of a master.

Later, when we reminisced about the encounter, Dr. von Waldow said, "I thought I was in the presence of Jesus Christ."

Abraham Ibn Ezra in the introduction to his commentary on the Pentateuch writes this:

The thoughts of God are so deep, who can know the mysterious way in which He moves? By Him alone all are actions weighed. It is possible that God brought it about that Moses would be raised in the royal palace so that his soul would be able to attain to a high degree through education and study there provided.

Ibn Ezra points here to God's plan for the future leader of the people having to have a regal presence and aristocratic demeanor which would endow him with the special characteristics suitable for a leader.

—Louis Jacobs, *The Jewish Religion: A Companion*

YITZKHAK HUTNER: IMPERIOUS "ROSH YESHIVA"

My high school years were spent at the Mesivta Rabbi Chaim Berlin in the Brownville section of Brooklyn, New York. Rabbi Yitzkhak Hunter, a man of arresting demeanor and imperious manner, was the Rosh Yeshiva, the principal and revered founder and leader of the school. I once knocked on the Rosh's office door to ask him about something; when he opened it and stood there glaring at me with his piercing eyes, I felt like running in the opposite direction.

The following was the scene in the *Bais Midrash* (study hall) of the Mesivta. The students would be studying Talmud loudly and with animation, when suddenly a voice is heard announcing, "The Rosh Yeshiva is entering!" Immediately a hush pervaded the hall; the students stood up and formed two straight aisles facing each other, whereupon Rabbi Hutner, chest out and head high, entered the hall and marched confidently to his seat while the Red Sea-like formation with its "both walls" remained in place. The Rosh Yeshiva took his seat. The formation then dissolved and the students went back to their Talmud a bit quieter and restrained now that their rabbi was in their presence.

As I've thought about that scene, which I recall quite vividly despite the many intervening years, three questions have come to mind:

First, could this have been a carefully orchestrated scenario designed to emphasize Rav Hutner's charisma?

Second, on the other hand, could the scene have been a spontaneous illustration of the profound respect for Torah learning and religious piety which Rav Hutner represented?

Third, or was it both of the above—spontaneity orchestrated?

Years later after penning the above vignette, I came across a fascinating analysis of the Rav Hutner's teachings about pedagogy and religious education. It was written by Dr. Ariel Evan Mayse of Stanford University and published in the periodical, "Religion," in 2019. Mayse writes:

> *One of the key themes of Hutner's teachings is his emphasis on the* paramount importance of discipleship. *The relationship between the student and master, at once* distant and intimate, *was central to his educational project. Hutner understood the* enigmatic, allusive power of charismatic leadership. Honor due to teachers *was also an important theme in his teaching; his students' recollections make clear that in his own life* Hutner very much stood on ceremony.

Hutner portrays the ideal teacher as a soulful educator, a fusion of the Lithuanian *rosh yeshiva* and *Hasidic* rebbe *offering far more than religious instruction or conveying ideas. Hutner argued that* students should be fundamentally transformed *by their encounter with the educator's religious personality and the essence of his being.*

(Note: emphasis added)

A YOUNG HASIDIC "REBBE"
AT THE HEAD OF THE TABLE

Once, during a visit in Israel, I searched out a small Hasidic enclave located in the Meah Shearim district of Jerusalem. Though moderate in size, it housed a well-known "dynasty" whose rebbe had just passed away, leaving his son as his successor. The son was a young man—no more than 25 years old, yet with dress, long beard and side-curls clearly appropriate for the role of Hasidic rebbe.

It was *Shalosh Seudos* time (the third meal on Shabbos afternoon). The rebbe's followers were eating modest fare and singing moving *z'mirot* (table songs). The young rebbe was sitting at the head table. He began to talk. I know Yiddish well, but could not make out a word he uttered.

His hands and arms began gyrating in unusual ways. His body twisted in circular fashion. He cut some apples in small pieces and flung them into the outstretched hands of his followers. Then with the Hasidism riveted on him, he rolled his eyes in such a way that we could only see the whites of his eyeballs; and then he quietly began a *nigun* (a wordless melody) in which the assembly gradually joined in trance-like fashion.

Could this have been a carefully orchestrated scenario designed to emphasize this rebbe's charisma? (See previous entry: Rav Hutner: Imperious Rosh Yeshiva)

MARSHALL MEYER: TWO KINGS, ONE CROWN

A Conservative spiritual leader, Marshall Meyer, achieved fame as a recognized human rights activist while living in Argentina for some two decades. He founded what emerged as a major influential Conservative synagogue as well as a rabbinical school in Buenos Aires that has trained numerous Spanish-speaking rabbis who practice throughout South America.

Danger and controversy stalking him because of his political activities in Argentina, upon returning to the United States, he became rabbi of Congregation B'nai Jeshurun in New York City. There he revived the Congregation which had been on the brink of demise, making it one of the largest and most creative institutions on the American scene. A tall, handsome person with a strong voice and eloquent speaking skills, Marshall was clearly a striking charismatic figure as the undisputed helm of the institutions he fashioned and the causes he advocated.

There was a one-year hiatus between Argentina and New York, and that was Marshall's appointment as vice president of the University of Judaism in Los Angeles. I was designated to greet him at the airport and arrange for him and his wife Naomi to be housed and settled. Within a few months of his arrival at the UJ at a gathering in his elegant home attended by the lay leaders at the university, Marshall projected his own vision of what his new institution could and should be—this without consultation with the sitting President of the institution, Dr. David Lieber. A short time later, at a retreat at Camp Ramah in Ojai Dr. Lieber informed Marshall that it was time for him to leave the university. He then departed for New York.

Rashi comments on the verse in Genesis 1:6 about God's creation of the sun and moon. "Both were created of equal size; but the moon who felt diminished because it complained that it was merely equal in size with the sun, and thus it was said:

אי אפשר לשני מלכים שישתמשו בכתר אחד

It is impossible for two kings to wear one crown.

ZALMAN SCHACHTER SHALOMI:
RELIGIOUS CREATIVITY

One day some years ago during a summer at Camp Ramah in Connecticut, I suddenly beheld an unusual sight: there he was, a rather tall man dressed in a long black caftan, bearded, with side curls and a *shtreimel*, a round fur headpiece atop his luminous face. It was Rabbi Zalman Schachter, the scholar-in-residence for the summer at our Conservative summer camp.

• It was Friday, late afternoon, at the camp's Shabbat worship service which Reb Zalman conducted. He swayed from side to side, forward and back, his arms reaching upward, his resonant voice chanting the liturgy, and his *niggunim* (wordless melodies), engulfing the entire camp population. The usually orderly, dignified and carefully orchestrated assemblage seemed stunned and puzzled—and appeared to be deeply affected.

• The next day's Shabbat morning service repeated the Friday evening experience with an added touch: instead of the young congregation standing still and erect for the *amida* (silent prayer), Reb Zalman invited those who wished to go off into the shaded tree area surrounding the worship setting and stand there as long as they wished in prayer—silent or otherwise.

• The Havdalah service Reb Zalman conducted was equally unusual. This experience was ordinarily quite moving at Ramah, only this time the singing and swaying had less passion as Zalman's sonorous voice carried all of us away with him.

An unusual feature was added to the ceremony: an empty Coke bottle was used to hold the Havdalah candle. Some smirked at this so-called innovation. Zalman later explained that this kind of ritual artifact was a way to connect an old religious ceremony with an object of contemporary familiarity so as to creatively integrate the traditional with the modern. Some were persuaded by his explanation, some were not.

• At times, we might chant the prayers in English, Zalman

suggested. This helps give the worshipper a sense of really talking with God because he is speaking directly with words he himself grasps. Rabbi Nahman of Bratzlav had urged his Hasidim to sometimes chant their prayers in the Yiddish vernacular, their native language. Most of us pray through a "glass darkly," and so it appears legitimate to use the understood vernacular periodically.

• He taught that ritual can be harnessed to teach social values and awareness of others. Blessings, for example, can be used, not only as a way to foster gratitude to God, but also to fellow man. Thus; when we bless the food we are about to eat, we might include the farmer, or the baker, or the truck driver, who were involved in the process of getting our food to the table.

• If recitation of the entire *amida* is felt to be too much, either because of length or constant repetition, pick just one passage that you identify with and focus on it alone. Example: the one about *malshinm,* slanderers who you wished would stop using their hurtful words.

• During one of Zalman's lectures to the staff, he suggested a new ritual dealing with personal spiritual development. Why not adapt the biblical seven-year cycle of nature to our own lives? Every seven years after our bar or bat mitzvah, he suggested, we conduct a ceremony of re-initiation with which we renew our pledge to God to study, practice and affirm the faith of Israel. In this way we'd keep in touch with our own personal spiritual development.

At one point during a weekday service, Zalman made an arresting suggestion. He quoted Reb Nahman of Bratzlav, who said that if you want to know God, you need only to listen to the beat of your heart. One need never be lonely for Him or out of touch with Him who fashioned your heart. You can always touch your pulse and say, "Oh, there you are!"

The Purpose of All of This?

It is to integrate the traditional with the contemporary in order to revive and revivify Jewish practice and idea for our time, to make them relevant and compelling for the modern Jew. "It's no good," Zalman urged, "educating youngsters to be Jewish for 1815! We have to give up nostalgia. We have to reinterpret our tradition for our new and ever-changing society." Yet more: there are abiding spiritual experiences in ever-changing forms of expression.

Creativity leaves us when we are imprisoned by precedent. It is in daring—to be outrageous, to play with the least probable possibilities, the ones more weird and spiritual--where we may find answers.

These possible forms dance before the mind's eye and from that vision emerges an unexpected form with its creative proposal and therefore its new way to understand and to map reality.

—Zalman Schachter

SHLOMO CARLEBACH:
TROUBADOUR TRADITIONALIST

On the book jacket of one of Rabbi Shlomo Carlebach's records, we read the following:

> *Shlomo Carlebach is at once a trend and a tradition, a remarkable musical experience: remarkable in that he is able to reflect the cherished radiance of Hasidism, of Jewish spirituality with simplicity and ease, remarkable in that he can kindle a new fire in many a young estranged and hungry heart.*

As is the case with so many others, my personal contacts with Shlomo Carlebach over the years have been memorable. I recall a half-century-old memory when a young singer with beard and cocked hat sat at the piano of the Jewish Theological Seminary alcove playing some of his favorite compositions. A few random students paused to listen to what appeared, at the time, a strange sight. Shlomo was at an early stage seeking some attention for his nascent career.

And then, Leah and I were shipped off to far-away Arkansas to assume my job as a U.S. military chaplain. I recall vividly a Carlebach early record listening to the passion of a spiritual persona. This was a significant reminder of heartfelt Jewish experiences in alien Arkansas country.

Knowing Shlomo's capacity to captivate and inspire Jewish youth, some time later I invited him to Pittsburgh for "An Evening with Shlomo Carlebach," celebrating Chanukah, which was sponsored by B'nai Israel's United Synagogue Youth (USY). Some two hundred young people were arranged on three tiered stands facing each other with Shlomo on a platform in the center. He had only a microphone and a guitar. He slowly strummed while telling some of his signature Hasidic stories, tales of humor and mystic spirit the young people had never heard.

Suddenly, Shlomo started to sing accompanied by his guitar. Gradually the beat became stronger and Shlomo started to dance on the platform. The sound became louder and the beat more and more intense.

He then invited the audience to get out of their seats and dance hand-in-hand, or arm-in-arm with him in the lead. The linked line of people threaded its way around the auditorium singing and dancing while Shlomo urged them on as he now stood on his platform singing, strumming and his feet jumping up and down.

I looked in astonishment at this phenomenon as it went on and on for what seemed like an eternity. When the "concert" was over, the young people left the auditorium exhausted—and inspired.

When at the University of Judaism, I, along with Max Vorspan engaged Shlomo to play the leading role in a musical we were producing about Sholom Alekhem. Shlomo was on a plane as he shuttled between Los Angeles and New York. Alas, on one such flight, Shlomo suffered a heart attack and from that plane ascended to the great beyond.

EDWARD KOCH: MAYOR

During a visit in his New York office, I had invited Edward Koch, the famed former mayor of New York City, to the University of Judaism platform on two occasions, once to discuss "Israel and American Interests: Conflict?" And a second: "Race Relations" with Rev. Cecil Murray, the prominent pastor at Los Angeles' African Methodist Episcopal Church.

On both occasions he captivated our massive Southern California audiences with his signature dynamic, stimulating presentations, rich in candor—the characteristics with which he governed his great city for twelve years. Outspoken and fearless to an extent rarely seen in public life, Mayor Koch was also, in the words of the *New York Times*, "a man of kindness, humor, vigorous fairness, and incisive intelligence." In sum, Edward Koch was one of the country's charismatic figures.

What I found especially noteworthy of the Koch visit was the nature of the reactions to him personally. When I picked him up at the airport, for example, as we were walking to the luggage area, a number of people recognized him and called out to him: "You did good, Mr. Mayor...You're a smart man...I like the way you talk...keep those guys in line." This all, and more, with a tone of affection and respect, from people in another city three thousand miles away. I realized yet again the village-like character of our world due to modern technology and the personal charisma of Edward Koch felt by so many.

Koch's "Jewish" self-awareness was apparent. During one of our visits, I took him for a walk through the posh streets of Beverly Hills. I mentioned the taxi driver who told one of his passengers that Beverly Hills had a population of thirty-four thousand, thirty-two thousand of it being Jews and the other two thousand who worked for them! I then pointed to the numerous *mezuzot* on the doors of the push homes we sauntered by...to which he reacted with his signature skepticism: the mezuzas are their way of warding off the evil spirits!

And then during one of the lecture programs, I served as a discussant as a member of the school's faculty. I apparently prefaced my remarks with an apologetic tone which hinted at controversy, to which Koch shot back, "Rabbi, don't you have tenure?"

Charisma: *A personal magic of leadership arousing special popular loyalty or enthusiasm for a public figure.*

—*Merriam-Webster Dictionary*, p. 192

THE VISHNITZER REBBE:
ON BEING IN ONE'S PRESENCE

It was during the period between *mincha* and *maariv* (late after-noon and evening), Shabbat services at the "court" of the Vish-nitzer Rebbe in B'nai Brak, Israel. Several hundred Hasidim were seated on wooden stands arranged horseshoe-like, with the Rebbe seated at a table at the opening of his arrayed followers. The back benches were a good distance away from the rebbe. There I climbed up the stands and stood precariously holding on to a pole which anchored the seating structure.

Everyone listened in hushed silence as the rebbe expounded Torah. The distance from where I stood along with the seated Hasidim next to me was so removed that the rebbe appeared like a large black dot, and it was impossible to hear him except for a quiet murmur. Yet the Hasidim near me reacted with awe, with "oh" and "ah," with various other expressions of appreciation for the wisdom of this rebbe's words. They were moved, in-spired, indeed, even though they could not hear a word their teacher was uttering!

At the time I remember going away from that experience with a smirk and a little ridicule. Later I began to speculate that per-haps simply being in the presence of a special persona, or merely hearing the voice of a wise man is perhaps sufficient at times when also surrounded by people of spiritual sensitivity. This all made extraordinary by focused attention and genuine disciple-ship can become an occasion for glimpsing the profound.

The basis for the rumination: on *seeing* a wise man distin-guished by sacred knowledge? The rabbinic sages established the following blessings:

בָּרוּךְ אַתָּה ה' אֱלֹהֵינוּ מֶלֶךְ הָעוֹלָם שֶׁנָּתַן מֵחָכְמָתוֹ לְבָשָׂר וָדָם

Blessed are You, O Lord our God, King of the universe, who has given of Your wisdom to mortals.

About this matter Israel Levinthal comments:

I often think of the greatness of our ancient sages who appreci-ate the psychological value of merely meeting or even seeing a geat personality, and who enjoined us to recite a blessing at such an experience...

Judah Magnes was a great leader of our people. He was a handsome figure; his was a handsomeness of a sculptural Greek god that one admired in museums. There was a sympa-thetic expression on his face that just won you to him. I was so fascinated by the youthful Dr. Magnes that, when I was a stu-dent at the seminary and saw him walking in the neighbor-hood, I would follow him for blocks, just to stare at him.

A number of the seminary professors were as yet new to the English language, and I must confess that it took many of the students some time before we could easily follow the lectures of the sainted professors Louis Ginzberg and Alexander Marx, both of whom spoke with a heavy German accent. But to sit in the presence of these two great figures made you feel that you were sitting before the great scholars of the ancient Babylonian and Palestinian academies of learning.

—Israel Levinthal, *The Message of Israel*, p. 14

MR. GRONER: MODELING PRAYER

הַמַּעֲשִׂים הַנִּרְאִים יִתְפָּעֲלוּ הַלְּבָבוֹת
מֵהֶם יוֹתֵר מַהַדְּבָרִים הַנִּשְׁמָעִים

Things seen will move the heart more than things heard.

—Abravanel

When I was a youngster (age eight to sixteen) I used to sit opposite a man of deep piety; he was Mr. Groner, whom I watched at prayer. This was in a Hasidic *shtibel*, a small prayer hall in Brooklyn, New York, where I grew up. This special man was the father of Label Groner who served as the secretary/aide to the Lubavitcher Rebbe himself. Mr. Groner prayed with earnest fervor, his *tallit* (prayer shawl) over his head, his eyes closed, his hands outstretched, his body swaying from side to side, his voice alternately loud and quite—this all with a passion that is etched in my system to this day still.

What was so gripping to my young eyes? Before me was someone who appeared connected with the "Transcendent." I watched an adult praying with the unrestrained innocence of a child. Indeed, to my young eyes and receptive heart, his was a piety and intimacy with God that appeared so very real.

When we wonder about how to educate our children and ourselves, what will make them and us faithful and at home with the art of prayer, we need to expose ourselves to the likes of a Mr. Groner. Do we take our children and ourselves to places where we witness reverence? Have we seen men and women in earnest prayer? If not, we are missing one of the profound and lasting impressions religious life has to offer.

לְמַנְהִיג נַעֲשֶׂה עַל פִּי רֹב לֹא מִי שֶׁיּוֹדֵעַ אֶת הַדֶּרֶךְ, כִּי אִם מִי
שֶׁסָּבוּר שֶׁהוּא יוֹדֵעַ אֶת הַדֶּרֶךְ

Most often, the man who becomes a leader is not the one that knows the way but the one who behaves as if he does.

—David Shimoni, Hebrew poet, 1886-1956

BERYL BAUMGARTEN:
A HASID AT THE SEMINARY

Beryl Baumgarten was a fervent *Habadnick,* a member of a Hasidic group (also known as Lubavitch) dedicated to disseminating to others its approach to Jewish religious life. His approach to Jewish ritual and thought could not have been more removed from that of the students of the Rabbinical School at the Jewish Theological Seminary where I was a student.

Beryl, with his flowing beard and unmistakable Hasidic garb, would visit the seminary dormitory every Wednesday evening without fail throughout the four years of my student days. Armed with the *Tanya,* the magnum opus penned by the founder of Habad, Shneir Zalman of Liadi, Beryl would knock on door after door, urging the students to study *Tanya* with him. Here and there, a reluctant student would agree. He would study the Hebrew text with Beryl and more often than not argue about its relevance and its "outdatedness."

Most of the students closed their doors gently after Beryl knocked. He averaged one, maybe two, "takers" each Wednesday. Most of the time, the takers were either actively or passively resistant to Beryl's efforts. Cool invaded the dormitory hall as Beryl strode down in search of his *Tanya* customers. Yet Beryl Baumgarten never stopped coming to the seminary dormitory every single Wednesday. And I knew that such was the case in the years before and after my studies at the decidedly non-Orthodox institution.

In those days it was quite unusual for an Orthodox rabbi to walk through the portals of a non-Orthodox theological seminary, the bastion of Conservative Judaism in America. On one such rare occasion, Emmanuel Rackman, a prominent modern Orthodox rabbi, addressed a gathering of seminary rabbinical students. I was among them. He made an articulate and persuasive case about the importance of the traditional halakhic methodology.

Rabbi Rackman was roundly condemned in Orthodox circles for his single appearance at the seminary. Beryl Baumgarten never was.

THE QUINTESSENTIAL CHARISMATIC:
THE LUBAVITCHER REBBE

The palpable charismatic leadership of the Lubavitcher Rebbe has long resulted, amongst many other things, in a program of outreach to the non-Orthodox. I decided to welcome his outreach.

Thus some two dozen Habad Hasidim were invited to congregation B'nai Israel for a weekend of prayer, study, song and dance, fellowship and one-on-one interchange. The program was sponsored by the synagogue's United Synagogue Youth (USY) organization. Some one hundred teens along with another some one hundred adults attended the marathon event which turned out to be a major spiritual and human experience.

What follows is a description of the event by Jacob Spitz, B'nai Israel's education director, followed by my own reflections about it, both published in the synagogue bulletin.

The activities were centered in our new Youth Lounge that Rabbi Shechter persuaded the Perilsteins to build and furnish when he first came to our congregation. The lounge was set up as an Orthodox *shul*, with a *mechitza* (divider) separating the males from the females. Other activities took place in the social halls, chapel and classrooms. Twenty-four young Hasidic men and women—clearly talented and carefully chosen—came from Pittsburgh itself, New York and Boston.

The conclave opened with *Kabbalat Shabbat* services enlivened by lusty singing of the prayers. As prelude to the festive meal that followed, all washed their hands in the traditional religious fashion accompanied by the appropriate blessings. The ample food was spiced with *z'mirot* (table songs) and the full grace after meals.

The keynote speaker following dinner was Professor Avraham Hasofer, chairman of the Department of Statistics and head of the School of Mathematics at the University of New South Wales in Sydney, Australia, and currently exchange professor at M.I.T. in Boston. Dr. Hasofer set the theme of the weekend by explaining aspects of the teaching of the Baal Shem Tov, founder of the Hasidic movement: love of the Jewish people, love of the Torah, and love of God. It was a lucid and passionate presentation. A lively confrontation between Mrs. Hasofer, a clinical psychologist, and members of the audience about "women's lib" ensued. The differences of opinion on the role of women in Jewish and religious life were apparent.

Rabbi and Mrs. Shechter told me about their experience with the fifteen young Hassidim who spent Friday and Saturday as guests in their home. They slept in the basement on cots; however, not much sleeping took place. Far into both nights, until about 3:00 a.m., they kept the Shechters and their three sons engrossed in storytelling. Especially riveting were their enthusiastic descriptions of the Lubavitcher Rebbe's "miraculous" deeds, his uncanny intuition, his towering stature, his vast authority, and his visions of the future. Rabbi Shechter indicated that aspects of this storytelling were taken by him with a "grain of salt." However, it was these young people's passion in the telling that was gripping.

Shabbat morning services, predominantly in Hebrew and highlighted by vigorous chant, featured the sermon of Rabbi Ephraim Rosenblum, one of Pittsburgh's charismatic Hasidic leaders. He stressed that we Jews are "slaves" to our environment and that we should seek freedom from it and be true to our inner selves as Jews. Then Shabbat luncheon with the young people was followed by group discussion, with the participants divided into various subgroups that dealt with specific topics of contemporary concern.

Exploration of Jewish ideas, singing and dancing, fellowship and one-on-one interchange took place throughout the afternoon. Our young people were particularly intrigued by the Hasidic precepts transmitted through the medium of popular catchy tunes, led by Yossi Baumgarten and Yisrael Shusterman,

Yeshiva students from New York. They explained with characteristic verve the various prayer customs and sections of the services.

Some two hundred teenagers and adults attended the *mincha, shalosh seudot* (third meal), *maariv* and *havdalah* services. A *Melaveh Malka event* ("escorting the Queen" out of Shabbat) on Saturday evening followed with stories, singing and dancing to the accompaniment of one of our USYers on his guitar. The evening culminated with a basketball game in the B'nai Israel gymnasium, which had been reactivated at Rabbi Shechter's urging, with the young Hasidim and the USYers the players.

On Sunday morning our visitors met with hundreds of our youngsters attending Sunday school explaining religious ideas through animated storytelling and discussion and again through song and dance.

While the younger visitors met with the children, Dr. and Mrs. Hasofer addressed the B'nai Israel Men's Club Sunday breakfast convened for the occasion. The meeting, which stretched into lunchtime, featured a vigorous interchange about the spiritual underpinnings and purposes of Jewish observances. It also focused on the need for a gradual and incremental approach to Jewish observance, but that the ultimate goal of Jewish living must ever be kept in mind. It was an illuminating session and, as Rabbi Shechter has often observed, the incremental methodologies of the Habad and Conservative Movements have more in common than meets the eye.

The success of this weekend experience for our young people can best be summed up via the reaction of one of our USYers, who said, "The atmosphere of the experience made everyone happy because the Hasidim were happy. They taught us a lot about being good Jews. They put a lot of enthusiasm into everything. I liked the whole thing very much. When are they coming back?"

The reaction of the adults was more tempered. Clearly they were enamored by the visitors' warmth and enthusiasm. They were less enamored by some of the intellectual substance presented. They did not appreciate the *mechitza* and what some considered the absence of "dignity" in some of the activities. Nonetheless, the adult consensus was that the weekend was stimulating and provocative, and a creative and undertaking.

Rabbi Shechter:

Mr. Spitz's report above details the extraordinary weekend experience we at B'nai Israel had with Hasidim of the Lubavitcher/Habad movement. Here I want to add some personal observations and indicate what I believe we need to learn from the experience as it applies to us as principled non-orthodox Conservative Jews.

The intensive religious environment of my youth fostered for this experience that Judaism was a warm and enriching way of life, that religious expression was not primarily somber, sober and sad, but full of joy and enthusiasm, suffused with vigor and excitement, replete with spontaneity and informality.

I was reminded that Judaism was not only for the mind, but for the heart and soul as well, that it was not an ascetic abstraction but a vigorous affirmation of life in all its manifestations, that the Jewish way of life was not a "sometime thing" but an everyday thing and that to gain the fullest measure of inner satisfaction, all of a person's senses must be brought into use. And I was again reminded that the synagogue, next to the home, was a setting in which this spiritual beauty was to come to fruition.

I have, of course, since moved out and away from the Orthodox Hasidic realm into that of the Conservative Movement and have done so with strong commitment to its non-fundamentalist ideology and practice. I've long since become aware that many of the Hasidic forms—its garb, its rigid ritualism, as well as ideology rooted as it is in eighteenth century thought processes epitomized by Habad's founder, Shneur Zalman of Liadi whose opus, the *Tanya*, remains the group's "bible" to this day—are neither appropriate nor workable in the modern American milieu.

And yet, I am convinced that the essential spirit of that "old time religion" remains relevant, that its message of love and joy is as vital to the Jew today as it ever was. As a matter of fact, Conservative Jews—young and old—sense that something vital is missing from their lives, and thirst for full-hearted and genuine religious conviction and expression. The warm and positive response of our people to our Hasidic friends over the January weekend testifies to that yearning.

For us, the essential lesson and challenge which I believe has emerged from this weekend is this: how can we contemporary Jews, within the necessary and indispensable context of the Conservative Movement, incorporate the spirit of Hasidism in our midst? To use Martin Buber's distinction between spirit and form in the religious enterprise: how can we incorporate the "religiosity" (i.e., spirit) of the "religion" (i.e., forms) of our Hasidic brethren into our lives? I believe we need to come up with an answer to that question, along with a pattern of action, lest we modern, staid and "sophisticated" Jews wither on the vine from spiritual apathy and sheer boredom.

A Letter from the Lubavitcher Rebbe

After this edition of our bulletin appeared with Mr. Spitz's report and my observations about the weekend, I sent the bulletin to the Lubavitcher Rebbe in New York with a letter of thanks and with commendation of his wonderful Hasidic followers who had spent the weekend with us.

The Rebbe, a busy man as the worldwide leader of the Habad movement, wrote back to me personally and at length. The letter was carefully typed, written with characteristic passion, though, from my perspective, with a somewhat "fundamentalist" caste. Among other things, he insisted that the "forms" I claimed were outmoded were necessary as distinctively Jewish ones and that they encase and nourish the "spirit" of which I spoke. When, for example, a Habad follower appears in this garb in public, he is making a statement, "Here is a Jew." The forms were needed, he insisted, in order to get the Jewish way to work in our day as they did in the past. Thus, for example, to appear in public in distinctive Hasidic garb demonstrates "here is a Jew."

Note: I had told my Pittsburgh Habad friends about the Lubavitcher Rebbe's personal letter to me. As fervent followers of their leader, they urged me to show them his letter, for to receive a letter from the Rebbe and especially about their activity was somewhat of a "happening" for them. I had misplaced the letter. They kept urging me to locate it. Try as I might, I couldn't and, alas, never recovered it. I had to repeatedly "swear" to the Habadnicks that I really received that letter. Truly I did. I always hoped they believed me.

When I showed this vignette to Dr. Jonathan Sarna, he said to me, "I hope you find the Rebbe's letter." To which I responded that over the years many substantial "offers" were made to find and turn over the letter. I could have reaped a fortune and enjoyed retirement on a luxurious level. Alas.

The Lubavitcher Rebbe Lays Out His Approach to Jewish Outreach

This is a translation of a discourse in Yiddish delivered by the Lubavitcher Rebbe at a Farbrengen (an assembly) with his followers at the Habad headquarters in Brooklyn, New York. The translation is taken from the screen of the live video and is that of a Habad translator.

…to strengthen Jewish observance in a given place one needs to take into account its particular circumstances and will need to

consider the context, the character and milieu of the specific place and time. When you have an opportunity to approach a fellow Jew, you need to do so with love even though the fellow might not share your spiritual outlook, and you seem to have nothing in common that binds you. Yet, given that he is your fellow Jew who the Torah describes as a child of the same God, a descendent o Abraham, Isaac and Jacob, it means that despite any lapses you see, he is still a Jew…

…Torah is "our life and the length of our days." This applies to every Jew, however he may affiliate. This is the point: there needs to be a resurgence of Judaism through the Torah and so, one should not be satisfied with working only in one's immediate environment, or be content staying where it is familiar, a place he likes.

Rather, he must go wherever he can; wherever he has information that there might be other Jews. He cannot demand of them that immediately upon meeting them, they transform their lives to be like his, or anyone else's. Rather, he must reach out to them. And bring them closer to the Torah in a way which they can relate to. Then he will succeed in strengthening their Judaism.

A "Polemical" Note

I have always felt there is a remarkable similarity of the methodical approach to religious actions between Habad and the Conservative Movement. That is to say, *the context of life in the present and the incremental methods* of both of them.

- "The need to take into account the particular circumstances"

- "The need to consider the context and milieu of the specific place and time"

- "If you begin with deep Hasidic discourse or a Talmudic tractate (translate profound contemporary Jewish theology or literature) he won't understand you, it won't bring him any closer to Judaism"

- "The way to teach them 'within the context' is: for those who are unaware of Alef, begin with Alef, proceed to Beis and so on."

Note the following guiding principle for the Conservative Movement articulated by Rabbi Simon Greenberg, vice chancellor or the Jewish Theological Seminary, an authoritative spokesman of the Movement. The context of this statement is the approach the rabbi is to employ when dealing with congregants with minimal knowledge and practice of the Jewish way:

I think it is good to remember that our duty in the rabbinate is to bring others to a maximum observance of the Torah, and not merely to enable ourselves to save our own souls. Effective, democratic leadership, whose only weapon is persuasion, always entails a certain amount of compromise. The main difference between one democratic leader and another is the ability of one to keep his eye on the essentials, and compromise on the peripheral.

Some contend that the difference between Habad and the Conservative Movement is the former's eventual goal being a full Jewish religious life whereas the latter posits an eventual "watered-down" religious life. To this the Movement responds that, in fact, it posits a far more substantive religious life of thought and practice than when it starts with its constituents. It sees itself as commanded by God in this direction, but that it employs an incremental approach toward its realization, guided by "the context and milieu of the specific place and time." This is precisely the Habad practice with its characteristic acceptance of quite partial religious observance om the part of those with whom it deals.

What else is compromise when Habad worship locales everywhere allow, in effect, encourage, its followers to drive to their locales on Shabbat, festival and High Holy Days for prayer? When it invites congregants who openly disregard Shabbat and holiday observance and/or kashrut in even minimal fashion, to be its congregation's Torah readers on Yom Kippur before hundreds of worshippers? Numerous examples of this tolerant, accepting, compromising methodology could be cited. This, by no means, is meant to be critical. Indeed, without this approach, the Habad outreach enterprise could not begin to exist. Its incremental approach would simply not be possible.

An unbiased examination of the two movements will, indeed, show a remarkable similarity of the incremental approach to their constituencies, i.e. begin with the minimum and gradually proceed toward the maximum possible. The only significant difference between Habad and Conservative in this context are the theoretical notions of what religious observance and ideology *ought to be,* in an ideal world, or as Habad puts it, in the Messianic era. And this is a matter for discussion at another place and time.

I rest my case.

– Chapter Five –

THE ESPECIALLY WELL-KNOWN

One of the "perks" as producer of various public lecture series and continuing education endeavors over the years was coming into direct contact with prominent persons—lecture platform, Sunday and weekend institute guests. These personal encounters provided insights about Judaism, the Jewish people, the perils and rewards of public and professional life and the often stormy inner life so characteristic of the human condition.

LEON URIS: EXODUS

Leah and I had been vacationing in Aspen, Colorado for a number of summers. We learned that the famous novelist, Leon Uris, lived in a mountaintop home with a panoramic view of the city. His novel *Exodus* had become one of the all-time successes in American publishing history and, along with the movie adapted from it, made a positive impact on behalf of the State of Israel and the image of the Jew. And so, I thought he would be a natural candidate as lecturer at the University of Judaism. If I could visit him at his Aspen home, I would suggest the idea.

I managed to locate his unlisted phone number, called, told him who I was and what I had in mind. "Okay, come to see me," he said. Following his detailed instructions, I wended my way up the circuitous road hugging the Aspen mountain and finally reached the gate of the Uris home. Forged onto the iron gate was the *Exodus* logo that appeared on the novel's cover and in various places in the movie.

Greeting

I knocked and entered through the inner door of the home to a greeting from his stunning wife, two barking dogs and a twelve-year-old son. They ushered me into Mr. Uris' study. A diffident man, his voice soft and hands a bit shaky, he welcomed me somewhat quizzically and warily, but warmed up as we discussed an extensive and profitable lecture tour in Southern California.

We also talked about his life in Aspen, about his son, who was studying via phone and mail in preparation for his Bar Mitzvah with a rabbinic tutor in Denver. He was concerned about the process and asked my advice about it. We talked about the writing projects he was engaged in, including a table-top book about Jerusalem with text by him and photographs by his wife, Jill, who was an accomplished photographer. We then reached agreement on the dates, terms and other details of the lecture tour.

The Library

What struck me most about the meeting was Uris' library. It was jam-packed with books about the history of the Middle East, about Jewish life and religion, about biblical times, about Muslim history and doctrine, and the character of warfare. A volume of the Jewish encyclopedia was opened on his desk; the *Encyclopedia Britannica*, and numerous other reference works occupied the shelves which practically circled the entire room. It was an impressive library, indeed.

As I thought about Leon Uris' library, it became clear to me that the literary creations this man was engaged in were not merely the imaginings of a fertile mind and a facile pen; they were the fruit of extensive research, absorption of a host of specific data, knowledge of the motion of history, awareness of physical settings in specific locales, of the ways people interact, and much else. All this flows from painstaking research akin to the kind professional scholars engage in. I then realized the power not only of Exodus, but of *Uris' Battle Cry, Mila 18, Armageddon, Topaz, QB VII, Trinity,* and *The Haj.*

The lecture tour was a mild success; often public lecturing does not quite match extraordinary writing skill.

My son, make your books your companions, let your shelves be your treasure grounds and gardens. If you are weary, change from garden to garden. Your desire will renew itself, and your soul will be filled with delight...Arrange your library in fair order so as not to weary yourself in your search for the book you need.

—Judah Ibn Tibbon, twelfth century

CHAIM POTOK: NOVELIST

Chaim Potok was a leading Jewish novelist of his generation, having written such landmark works as *The Chosen, The Promise,* and *My Name is Asher Lev.*

We were fellow students at the Jewish Theological Seminary. Once while eating together in the Seminary dining hall and exchanging ideas about our various preoccupations, Chaim told me that he was in the midst of writing a novel. Now, rabbis, let alone rabbinical students, in those days hardly ever wrote novels (Milton Steinberg was the exception with his work, *As a Driven Leaf,* and that was two decades earlier as a long-practicing rabbi). And so with a skeptical, even mocking tone, I said to Chaim, "Oh come on!"

Fast forward. During the next decade, two of Chaim's novels appear to acclaim. In addition, he becomes the editor of the prestigious Jewish Publication Society.

Chaim is now famous; he's illuminated the tension in which the contemporary Jew lives in an open American society. He's a perfect person for the lecture series I've been conducting in my Pittsburgh congregation. How can I now invite him?

I plunged ahead and, with some trepidation, placed the phone call:

"Chaim, I'm a little embarrassed."

"What's up, Jack?"

"I'd like you to lecture at my shul."

"When?"

"On November 15."

"Okay. Jack, do you remember our lunch conversations at seminary?"

Chaim came to Pittsburgh and delivered a memorable address to a huge assemblage!

"Reticent" Dinner

At the Pittsburgh lecture visit, Leah and I invited Chaim to dinner at our home prior to the lecture along with a number of our lay leaders. As we sat around the table, Chaim was strangely silent. When one of the guests asked him to explain the meaning of the theme of "silence" which pervades his novel, *The Chosen*, Chaim was cryptic, saying, let the reader ponder its meaning, and again retreated into silence. Our guests were puzzled by Chaim's behavior and later told me how "put off" they felt.

Years later I came across a passage in a "SparkNotes Study Guide" about the theme of silence in Potok's *The Chosen*:

> There are many other instances of silence within the novel, which reinforce the complexity and subtlety of the relationship between silence and communication. When Danny reveals that he has learned to hear silence, he strengthens the idea of silence as a means of communication. Danny's paradoxical statement perplexes Reuven, because it implies that a lack of sound need not entail a lack of knowledge and information. Danny's statement shows us that silence is a complex concept, that it can have form and function, and that it can affect a person as much as words.

My own speculation: perhaps Chaim was seeking to illustrate this silence phenomenon via his strange behavior at our home that night.

When we had moved from Pittsburgh to Los Angeles, I encountered Akiba Potok, Chaim's son. Akiba was pursuing a writing career and seeking entry into the screenwriting scene in Hollywood. He had moved into an apartment in Beverly Hills. Our house was across a back driveway from his apartment.

One day Akiba knocked on our door. In his hand was a folder containing research material about the land of Israel in biblical times I had been using for my dissertation work. He explained that as he was putting his trash in an adjoining bin located in the back of our homes, he found the folder on the ground. He saw my name on the folder and address inside on a letter of correspondence. He thought I might well need the folder. Yes, indeed, I reacted with grateful thanks. I had accidently included the folder with the items of trash.

Chaim's son appreciated the value of Jewish writings; "like father, like son."

ADMIRAL HYMAN RICKOVER:
"THE FAITH OF THE FALLEN JEWS"

Father of the nuclear-powered navy, developer of the world's civilian nuclear power plant for peaceful means, educator who has both practiced and preached high standards of excellence in both military and civilian life, Hyman Rickover was manifestly one of the outstanding men of our time.

Because Rickover authored three acclaimed books calling for high attainment in America's educational system and demanded basic reform of school learning practices in the country, both in the sciences and humanities, I though it appropriate that he occupy the lecture platform of the University of Judaism. Another reason: I speculated that his especially emphatic stress on education might be rooted in his Jewishness. When I asked him about this, he told me how wholly peripheral Jewishness was in his life. No matter, I offered and he accepted our invitation.

His lecture subject: *Striving for Excellence in Education: Why? How?* Emblematic of Admiral Rickover's stature, Dr. Richard Atkinson, a disciple and at the time chancellor of the University of California in San Diego, and Stanley Sheinbaum, vice chairman of the Board of Regents of the system-wide University of California, both accepted our invitation to serve as discussants in the program.

A Fall on the Bimah

It was Sunday evening. A thousand people gathered for the lecture at Valley Beth Shalom in Encino. Rickover was holding forth; suddenly, he fainted and fell to the floor on the platform; the audience sat in a stunned hush, murmuring concern. I rushed to his side, called for a doctor, and as I gently lifted his head, he opened his eyes and said quite calmly, "I always thought I would die in a synagogue." Then he got to his feet, took out a comb from his pocket, smoothed his ruffled hair, proceeded back to the lectern, and completed his lecture as if nothing had happened.

"Striving for excellence in education"..."I always thought I would die in a synagogue"...This from a *peripheral* Jew. I could not help but feel that planted in this man's inner psyche was the Jewish passion for learning, which was a basic guideline of his life and career and that at that moment in a synagogue, Hyman Rickover's Jewishness flared.

While recording this vignette, I came across a transcript of a lecture delivered by Rabbi Israel Levinthal of the Brooklyn Jewish Center. It was a tribute to the recently deceased Rabbi Abraham Isaac Kook, the great chief rabbi of the pre-state of Israel in the 1920s and 1930s.

Rav Kook had an overpowering love for all his people. This was illustrated by a sermon Rabbi Levinthal heard him preach in the old Hurva synagogue on Passover about Jews who were returning home to Eretz Yisrael. They were quite lax in Jewish religious observance and thought.

This is how he summarized Rav Kook's sermon: "Twice the Jew is enjoined to eat matzoh at the Passover seder: at the beginning of the meal, and at the end, when he tastes the Afikoman, known in rabbinic language as tzafun, 'hidden.' Which of the two mitzvot or duties is the more important?"

Thus he began with a discussion of Jewish law, and after a display of legal reasoning he proved that the latter, the mitzvah of *tzafun,* was the more important. *"These two matzot represent mystically two types of Jews: the Jew whose Judaism, like the first matzoh attractively displayed on the Seder table, is always visible and always to the fore, and* the Jew whose Judaism, like the *tzafun* matzoh, is hidden and almost unknown.

We often think disparagingly of that type of Jew, because he seems to us to be lost to Jewish life. But there is no lost Jew. Times come when that hidden spark suddenly appears..."

Rav Kook's homily has re-enforced my theory that the hidden spark of Jewishness suddenly appeared on that lecture platform on which Admiral Hyman Rickover fell and arose.

WOLF BLITZER: TELEVISION JOURNALIST

One of the outstanding newsmen in America, Wolf Blitzer is cable network CNN's pervading presence in the world as anchor, reporter and commentator. Many millions hear the news and its interpretations daily. Blitzer and CNN are indeed a phenomenon.

Prior to this prominent role Wolf was the Washington correspondent for the *Jerusalem Post*. Israel, the Middle East. The Jewish condition has been at the root of his life and work.

When I brought him to the University of Judaism lecture platform in Los Angeles, Wolf told us about his Jewish upbringing in Buffalo, New York, and what was for so many of us within the Conservative Movement significant: he had attended Camp Ramah for a number of summers, which helped in significant measure shape his Jewish consciousness and commitment.

As I thought about our conversation, a notion occurred to me with which I think Wolf would agree. It is contained in the nature of the shofar: from its narrow aperture, the sound reverberates into the larger surroundings. Wolf Blitzer, rooted as he is in a particular ("narrow") Jewish matrix, has succeeded in widening his concerns to encompass the larger world.

HANS KUNG: CATHOLIC RENEGADE

One of the major Christian theologians of the twentieth century, the author of some two-dozen important theological works that have sold in the thousands, Hans Kung was professor of ecumenical theology at the University of Tubingen, Germany.

World-renowned, Dr. Kung was avidly read, listened to and respected by thinkers of all denominations around the globe. He was the author of *Does God Exist?, On Being a Christian, Eternal Life,* and *Infallible?* In addition to his professorship at the University of Tubingen, he was director of that institution's Institute for Ecumenical Research.

Hans Kung personally knew the struggle of one who works to reform existing religious institutions and doctrines. From Rome on December 18, 1979, the Roman Catholic Church's "Sacred Congregation for the Doctrine of the Faith," with the approval of Pope John Paul II, issued this statement:

> This Sacred Congregation by reason of its duty is constrained to declare that Professor Hans Kung, in his writings, has departed from the integral truth of Catholic faith, and therefore he can no longer be considered a Catholic theologian nor function as such in a teaching role.

Professor Kung's response to this condemnation by the Pope and church authorities: "I plan to continue as a Catholic theologian, in the Catholic church, to be an advocate for numerous Catholics."

A Lecture Tour

I brought Dr. Kung from Germany to lecture in various locales in southern California under the aegis of the University of Judaism. His topic dealt with the relations between Christians and Jews in the post-Holocaust era. He was received with profound respect yet with the still lingering memory of the pain that had been inflicted on Jews during that terrible era when many felt the Catholic church remained silent in the face of atrocity.

I had invited to the Kung lectures the leaders of the Catholic church in our area, including the then Archbishop Roger Mahoney. They all shunned him, citing the church's interdiction. A striking exception was the appearance of three nuns without their habits, except for a head covering.

This incident reminded me of the experience of Dr. Mordecai Kaplan, whose new and untraditional Passover Haggadah had literally been burned by a group of ultra-Orthodox rabbis in a public "ceremony." Kaplan should be shunned, not permitted to teach, they pronounced. Dr. Kaplan, as did Hans Kung in his church, continued to teach and function within the Jewish fold and at the Jewish Theological Seminary. Some of his faculty colleagues, however, avoided being in his presence whenever they possibly could. For some, such attitudes about dissenters linger.

HARVEY COX: CHRISTIAN THEOLOGIAN
AND HIS JOURNEY TO JUDAISM

It was in the 1960s when I served as director of the New England region of the United Synagogue of America, headquartered in Boston. We were on a plane headed for Selma, Alabama—a cohort of clergy of all religious denominations in support of Martin Luther King's planned march on behalf of civil rights.

Harvey Cox, then a young professor of religion at the Harvard School of Divinity, suddenly took to the plane's loudspeaker. He asked if there was a rabbi on the plane who would join him as a Protestant minister, a Catholic priest and a rabbi; we would compose a joint statement to be read upon arriving at the Selma airport in support of the civil rights cause King was deeply involved in. I answered Cox's call.

Already then Cox was a leading young theologian and avid supporter of the civil rights movement at the time. We became friends living as we were in the same New England city. In the years following the arresting Selma experience, Cox emerged as one of America's leading theologians having penned what became a classic, *The Secular City*, as well as several other volumes on the meaning and role of religion in contemporary culture.

Though remaining a Christian, Dr. Cox married a Jewish woman, Dr. Nina Tumarkin, a professor of Russian history at nearby Wellesley College who retained her strong ties to Jewish faith and peoplehood. Cox's book *Common Prayers* chronicles this fascinating experience and its ideological and Jewish fallouts.

———————————

This is what I wrote about why I invited Harvey Cox to occupy the podium at the University of Judaism's highly engaging Los Angeles lecture series:

> *Dr. Cox is a figure whose following transcends the*

limits of a single faith or belief and who represents, for many people, the voice of ecumenical faith at its most persuasive and deeply felt pitch.

Professor Cox himself, as a teacher, a minister, a social activist and theologian, is a charismatic figure; but his books and writings have a charisma of their own—a curious and potent mixture about the nature of the religious experience, and a profound determina tion to show that religion itself can be, must be, a source of pleasure and enjoyment, an aspect for our love for life.

YOSEF YERUSHALMI:
STUDENT, SCHOLAR, CHARISMATIC

My classmate in the Rabbinical School of the Jewish Theological Seminary, Yosef Yerushalmi, passed away on December 8, 2009, at the age of seventy-seven. This was part of his obituary:

> We mourn the passing of the pre-eminent Jewish historian Yosef Hayim Yerushalmi (1932-2009), who died today following a lengthy illness. Yerushalmi served as the Salo Wittmayer Baron Professor of Jewish History, Culture and Society at Columbia University from 1980-2008. Before then, he taught for fourteen years at Harvard University, where he rose to become the Jacob E. Safra Professor of Jewish History.
>
> His wide-ranging books—from *Spanish Court to Italian Ghetto, Haggadah and History, Zakhor,* and *Freud's Moses*—generated significant discussion and paved new areas of scholarly investigation. He also personally trained a generation of creative Jewish historians, most of whom contributed to the important festschrift in his honor, *Jewish History and Jewish Memory.*

During our student days at the seminary, the promise of this young man was apparent. Once, a number of the senior rabbinical students were seated before Professor Salo Baron, the distinguished historian at Columbia University, who was also teaching at the seminary.

We were taking an oral examination as part of our academic requirement in Jewish history. Joe was being queried by Dr. Baron. I remember listening in astonishment as Joe responded at length and in detail about the life and mindset of the Marranos. It was as if he was delivering an authoritative university lecture on the subject. Professor Baron simply sat back and listened intently and appreciatively. No wonder this talented student later succeeded our teacher as "The Salo Baron Professor of Jewish History" at Columbia University.

I once knocked on Joe's door to ask him something. As I entered the darkened room I was greeted by a provocative odor, shades drawn, and the music of a Bach recording. It had a kind of mystical feel, that room, clearly revealing an intense and sensitive spirit and, of course, his lifelong attachment to classical music.

When Joe was professor of Jewish history at Harvard University, I had invited him to speak in our public lecture series at B'nai Israel in Pittsburgh where I served as rabbi. At the dinner table in our house prior to the lecture sat a distant relative of mine who had joined a Christian cult in Davenport, Iowa, along with her mentor, the cult's leader. I had brought the two to Pittsburgh to try to dissuade the girl from her choice.

Her mentor was expatiating about the necessity of faith in Jesus Christ as the route to salvation, the resistance of the Jewish people to the truths of Christianity, and all the rest. Whereupon, Joe exploded in anger, saying that in the name of that kind of Christian talk countless Jews throughout the ages suffered humiliation, persecution and death. And to the astonishment of all of us sitting at the table, Joe got up from his chair and summarily walked out of the room. It was clear that Joe Yerushalmi took his history seriously—not just as an academic...and this was not how I planned the visit with the Iowans.

Joe, at times, could be a remote, even intimidating professor. His entrance into the classroom evoked a silent hush of anticipation. He had little patience with casual students. Dr. Benjamin Gampel, currently a professor of Jewish history at the Jewish Theological Seminary (the husband of a cousin of mine) had sought to come into Joe's academic orbit when he was a student. It was not easy, but eventually it came about. Joe explained: Benjy took the initiative to go to Spain for several months at his own expense and without Joe's prompting, to do some research on Spanish Jewry. Said Joe: "With that kind of attitude, that young man could be a student of mine."

A fascinating story about Joe appeared in the *New York Jewish Week* in August 2011. After his passing, a heretofore unpublished and unknown novel that Yerushalmi wrote was published in *The*

New Yorker magazine. It concerned a character simply called Ravitch who is a scholar of Jewish history with a restless spirit who
yearns for peace of mind. The article goes on to tell about
Yerushalmi's famous book, *Zakhor*, which was about the tension between Jewish memory and Jewish history—and more broadly between the ancient, spiritual and religious life versus the modern,
secular and academic one.

"Many Jews today are in search of a past," Yerushalmi wrote,
"but they do not want the past that is offered by the historian."

Yerushalmi, who taught at Harvard and Columbia, was never
quite sure he wanted the history he had to offer either. He was religiously observant in his youth and later ordained at the Jewish Theological Seminary, but then abandoned the life of the pulpit for one
of the professor's podium. The dilemma he faced was similar to
Ravitch's: should he embrace the emotional pull of faith? Or should
he dismiss it and risk finding comfort only in the facts?

"I think his life conflict was unresolved," Ophra, Yerushalmi's
wife, said of the Ravitch character. And how about her husband,
Yosef? Was the conflict unresolved too? Perhaps, she ventured:
"Like everyone, we all carry unresolved conflicts within us."

----

*After reading the scholarly works of Yerushalmi and his teacher,
Salo Baron, I was puzzled by the apparent problem Yerushalmi
expresses as recorded in the above story. His dilemma: should he
embrace the emotional pull of faith? Or should he dismiss it and
risk finding comfort only in the facts?*

*It appears that both Yerushalmi and his mentor from whom
he learned so very much hardly seem bereft of the emotional and
religious faith of the Jewish experience both scholars recorded so
very well. Witness the following three citations:*

*Yosef Yerushalmi has articulated the basic stance of the rab-
bis regarding the past bequeathed to them:*

Prophecy had ceased, but the rabbis regarded themselves

as heirs to the prophets, and this was proper, for they had thoroughly assimilated the prophetic world view and made it their own. For the rabbis the Bible was not only a repository of past history, but a revealed pattern of the whole of history, and they had learned their scriptures well.

They knew that history had a purpose—the establishment of the Kingdom of God on earth and that the Jewish people has a central role to play in the process. *Above all, they had learned from the Bible that the true pulse of history often beats beneath its manifest surfaces, an invisible history that was more real than what the world could recognize.*

—*Zakhor: Jewish History and Jewish Memory,*
Seattle: University of Washington Press,
1983; p. 21.

Salo Baron wrote this about the God idea:

God's realization in this universe as reflected in our mind comes through the endless flow of time. In this long historical process God may assume different shapes in the minds of men. He may divest Himself of one historical form and take on another to suit the new conceptions of the age.

So profoundly imageless is God in Judaism, however, these transformations have no effect whatever upon His eternally uniform substance...*Thus God, eternal and therefore indifferent to time, brooded over history and waited, as it were, for a clearer articulation when circumstances should favor or demand it.*

—*A Social and Religious History of the Jews, Vol. 1.*
New York: Columbia University Press, 1952; p. 14, 53.

And Baron wrote this about the survival of the Jewish people:

New leaders arose. A transcendent and holy God, they taught, has selected the people of Israel and His holy nation, for reasons known only to Him. Through a life of holiness and, if necessary, of suffering, this people will continue to make known the name of God until the end of days, when all nations will recognize their error and worship the One God.

In the meantime, Israel must keep aloof from these other nations, in order not to be contaminated by their errors and their unholy life. Such an aim can only be achieved by a full, specific, and peculiar law in all its ramifications. The life thus demanded is necessarily artificial and contrary to nature in many ways [i.e., a people without its own land and all that goes with it]. Thus the Jew has to live, if necessary, in defiance of nature.

—*A Social and Religious History of the Jews,*
Vol. 1. New York: Columbia University Press,
1952; p. 164. See also "Emancipation from
State and Territory," p. 16-25.

ISAAC BASHEVIS SINGER:
NOVELIST, VEGETARIAN

The famed Yiddish novelist who captured the inner life and spirit of his native Jewish Poland, Isaac Bashevis Singer had his works translated into English when he arrived in America to pursue his writing career. He authored *The Satan of Goray*, a mystical work about the false messianism of seventeenth-century Poland, *The Family Moskat*, a realistic novel of pre-World War II Warsaw, and numerous other works. These established him as a leading exponent of imaginative prose in Yiddish, and also as an important figure in contemporary world literature. He subsequently received the prestigious Nobel Prize and his story, *Yentl*, was adapted for a motion picture produced, directed and starred in by Barbara Streisand.

When Singer participated in our Pittsburgh lecture series. I asked him to tell us about the essential character of the Jew as he perceived it. A frail, elderly man with impish face, soft voice and hesitant manner, he read his lecture from the written text he had prepared, and mesmerized our audience. His response in essence: it was as if one was asked to unravel the inscrutable. (An aside: since he was also somewhat absent-minded, he left his prepared text on the lectern, which I subsequently mailed back to his New York residence.)

Leah had invited some of our lay leaders to dinner with Singer at our home prior to the lecture appearance. Two days prior to his arrival we learned that he was a vegetarian, and that he not only did not eat meat, but did not eat fish as well. Leah proceeded to figure out what kind of food fare to offer the man for dinner. I asked Singer the reason for his being a vegetarian. In his cryptic yet lucid way, he referred to the book of Genesis in which mankind is told to eat only fruits and vegetables and only specific animals after removing their blood. "You don't consume a being that lived and breathed," he said, and as far as he was concerned, that included fish. Singer's response appeared to grasp the essential spirit of Jewish teaching on this matter, which views eating meat as a Divine compromise to man's weakness and craving. And so, Singer decided to embrace the Jewish ideal about diet in his personal life. His explanation of his way of eating was simple, clear and compelling.

When I introduced Isaac Bashevis Singer to our audience, I prefaced my remarks about the vegetarian matter at our home. Whereupon someone burst out from within the audience of some five hundred people: "What did Leah serve him for dinner?"

ALEXANDER SCHINDLER:
REFORM LEADER AND COMPETITOR

For a five-year period in the 1960s, I served as the director of the New England Region of the United Synagogue of America, the national association of Conservative congregations. My task was to help nurture our synagogue affiliates and to expand association with the movement as members of the network.

Rabbi Alex Schindler was my counterpart as the director of the New England Council of the Reform Union of American Hebrew Congregations (UAHC, since renamed the Union for Reform Judaism). A brilliant speaker, shrewd tactician, zealous partisan and indefatigable professional on behalf of his cause, he eventually became the distinguished national president of the Reform Union.

We competed for new affiliates for our respective movements.

Stimulated by the creation of the "Peace Corps" envisioned by President Kennedy, our United Synagogue Region launched a "Torah Corps." We brought together the rabbis, cantors, educators, executive directors and leading laymen of the Conservative Movement in New England for a joint and coordinated effort to guide and advise the so-called "underdeveloped" congregations in the region, the smaller ones unable to engage full-time rabbis, cantors or qualified teachers. The venture turned out to be highly successful—one factor in bringing some thirty new congregations into the fold of the Conservative Movement during that five-year period.

During the above time span, Rabbi Schindler, deploying his signature skills scoured the New England area seeking to bring unaffiliated synagogues under the Reform umbrella. Armed with our Torah Corps and other resources, I either preceded or followed Schindler's appearances with the Conservative alternatives. Alex, of course, had his successes. He was not averse of assuring potential affiliates for his movement that if they wanted more traditional practices than those currently offered by his movement, the latter would warmly welcome such traditions. In a word: he succeeded in some measure in blurring the distinctions between the two movements making his task of persuasion easier.

I remember vividly the frustrated praise of Alex on the part of Dr. Benjamin Shevach, the executive director of Bureau of Jewish Education, whose work covered Boston and environs. Shevach advocated a neutral bureau insofar as the denominations were concerned. Schindler (as I did for the Conservatives) pressed for a Reform-oriented approach to Jewish education and did so with "indefatigable energy; he traveled on a moment's notice; he was extremely convincing," moaned Shevach.

Years later, at the University of Judaism, when Rabbi Schindler was the national president of the Union for Reform Judaism, I invited him to occupy our popular lecture series platform. Alex had a more nuanced position with regard to the issues surrounding the State of Israel at the time, and candidly expressed them in his lecture.

Suddenly, a phalanx of Jewish Defense League zealots marched towards the lecture platform, jaws clenched, eyes flashing, and in loud voices hurled menacing epithets at Alex. This, all in the midst of the lecture. Alex was shaken, the audience was apprehensive as it watched the scene. Instantly, I jumped from my seat on the platform, proceeded to its edge and held my hands up in front of the Defense League phalanx, and insisted they retreat. They did. Calm ensued. Rabbi Schindler completed his lecture. We were all relieved.

GIDEON HAUSNER:
ADOLPH EICHMANN'S PROSECUTOR

Gideon Hausner was the famed prosecutor of the infamous Adolph Eichmann. Prior to his becoming Israel's attorney general, he was a prominent officer in the Israel Defense Forces. I was stationed in Fort Chaffee, Arkansas, as a chaplain in 1960 when Colonel Hausner was sent to the small neighboring town of Fort Smith to appeal for funds from its Jewish populace.

In conversation with him, he told me about the Jewish informality of the Israeli soldier at the time. He would move among the soldiers as an officer who was to be respected and saluted at all times. One soldier, a Holocaust survivor who was reared in a Russian Jewish family, walked by Hausner quite casually, minus the required salute. When Hausner demanded the gesture, the man responded in Yiddish:

Seren laybin, vos shpilt bai mir a salut!

Colonel, dear, what do I care about a salute!

Many years later, I had invited Mr. Hausner to lecture at the University of Judaism in Los Angeles. This was after the Eichmann trial that brought Hausner worldwide fame. When I picked him up at the airport in my modest car, Hausner was perturbed; he thought a more elaborate vehicle was appropriate. When I set him up in a relatively modest hotel, again, he was upset; he thought that more than such modest accommodations were appropriate for the man who prosecuted Adolph Eichmann. He was right.

He who is kind to a Jewish leader is rewarded as though he were kind to the entire people of Israel.

—Eliezer ben Jose, *Canticles Rabbah*, 2:5

MORT SAHL:
A COMEDIAN'S TAKE ON AMERICAN LIFE

I knew that Mort Sahl lived somewhere in the Hollywood Hills, about his fame as an arresting comedian with his own incisive perspectives about America's political and social life. And I knew that many of Sahl's perspectives as a Jew were rooted in his people's particular "psychology," even as was the case with America's leading Jewish comedians.

I searched and located his phone number. I called, and he responded with a quiet hesitancy; after "drilling" me about what I wanted, who I was, who did I represent and more, he agreed to meet me at a Beverly Hills coffee shop he frequented.

We sat and talked, again he was quietly probing from which conversation it was clear that this was an intelligent man and more: that he was Jewish at his core. His quiet and halting manner belied his famous "bombast" at his public appearances. Apparently, I passed his "testing" and he agreed to my proposal that he appear at the University of Judaism's public lecture series at two of the leading synagogues in Los Angeles. A generous renumeration helped secure the arrangement, no doubt as an assist to my own personal "persuasiveness."

The following appeared in the publicity for the occasions:

Probably America's most incisive, insightful and controversial comedian, Mort Sahl has created a new age of comedy in our time. His cutting commentaries about American political and social life—the people, the power, the trends, the fads, the foibles—have earned him such epithets as "The Thinking Man's Comedian" and "A Will Rogers with Fangs."

Lawrence Christon of The Los Angeles Times: "...indeed Sahl is an American town crier—with a comic mask. He's virtually alone among modern co-medians (and humorists) in both his outlook and his indifference toward being liked. He doesn't want an audience to love him as much as he wants it to listen to him develop his picture of the American social and political landscape. It's always been a complex pic-ture, delivered by a complex, smoldering, even obses-sive man whose metier in comedy is political com-ment, but who at center remains beyond categoriza-tion..."

Note: Well over two thousand people attended these two occa-sions and were thereafter talked about, and talked about...

MARTIN LUTHER KING

Clergymen throughout the country had been summoned by Dr. Martin Luther King to join him in Selma, Alabama, to march on behalf of the civil rights of the black citizens of America. From Boston I joined fellow ministers and priests in a plane en route to Selma. Harvey Cox, then a professor at Andover Theological Seminary in Newton, who later became the famed author of the seminal book of contemporary religious life, *The Secular City*, and professor of Divinity at Harvard University, was on the plane. On the flight he called through the plane's microphone for a rabbi who might be aboard to join with fellow clergy to compose a statement to be read upon our arrival at our destination. I joined the group.

When we landed, we were ushered into a huge tent used as a staging area for the march. There we heard Dr. King speak. We then were brought to a black church for a rousing religious service and proceeded to the unforgettable march.

Following the march, a group of us were invited to a house of one of the black leaders to meet Dr. King personally. Surrounded by reverent, supportive and determined followers, Dr. King greeted each of us with words of deeps appreciation for our support in the difficult struggle. This was experienced personally by me as Dr. King firmly and warmly took my hand in his along with his intense eye contact—this for one of his rabbinic sympathizers.

Two years later I remembered the overwhelming emotion I felt following Dr. King's uplifting and inspiring oration at the National Convention of the United Synagogue of America. The following year, this towering man was assassinated.

Now, I need to note that I've never been a civil rights activist. My ambivalence has been rooted in thoughts about the black man's apparent lack of drive for self-improvement, his tendency to shift the blame for his negative lot primarily on society's prejudices rather than looking to himself. However, my sympathy for the black cause in America has remained because of the dream of Dr. Martin Luther King, who pointed to freedom and equality for all Americans, the black man and woman and child being litmus tests for its realization. Indeed, I've viewed this matter through the prism of Dr. King's soaring vision.

בָּרוּךְ אַתָּה ה' אֱלֹהֵינוּ מֶלֶךְ הָעוֹלָם זוֹקֵף כְּפוּפִים

Blessed are You, Lord our God, King of the Universe, who raises up those who are bowed down.

Because of the wondrous way you have designed the human body, I can uncoil a bending spine, lift up slumping shoulders and drooping neck. Yes, I can straighten myself out physically—and mentally—so that I can go about my life proudly and confidently. How good and satisfied I feel about myself when I add my own earnest effort to your design. Thank you, God, for giving hope to the oppressed, the downcast, those who are bent over in spirit. Amen.

—One of the fourteen daily morning blessings
amplified by JS

HAROLD KUSHNER: "AMERICA'S RABBI"

Harold Kushner became famous as the author of *When Bad Things Happen to Good People*, who was once pronounced "America's Rabbi." We were fellow students in the rabbinical school of the Jewish Theological Seminary. Kushner grew up under the tutelage of one of American Judaism's outstanding preachers, Rabbi Israel Levinthal of the Brooklyn Jewish Center. His father was an active leader of the congregation and the family longtime members. This is where Harold attended Shabbat morning services.

As a senior rabbinical student, I was assigned to deliver a sermon at a synagogue located where I lived in Brooklyn. It was designed to orient future rabbis for eventual sermonizing. The Brooklyn Jewish Center, the prominent Conservative congregation, was the setting for me. Rabbi Levinthal was instructor of homiletics at the seminary, and so one summer at Camp Ramah where I worked and where he and his wife often spent their vacation time, this consummate homiletician prepared me for my presentation at his synagogue.

A Student Sermon

The sermon was based on a *midrash* that described the contrast between the windows of an ordinary dwelling and those of the *Bet Hamikdash*, the temple in Jerusalem. The windows of the ordinary dwelling were *bullhorn-like*, that is, narrow on the outside of the dwelling and wide on the inside; the reason: the narrow aperture on the outside minimized dust and heat, while projecting a maximum amount of light into the house interior.

On the other hand, the windows of the temple were fashioned on the opposite way: they were wide on the outside (*atumim*) of the structure and narrow (*shkufim*) on its inside; the reason: the temple, i.e., the "light" of its religious teaching and spiritual radiance, was to be projected to the outside world. The message of the sermon then flowed naturally from this midrashic text.

When I served as director of the New England Region of the United Synagogue in Boston, I advised Harold about the open pulpit position in Natick, a Boston suburb, which he sought and accepted. I brought him to the platform of the University of Judaism as a lecturer during his golden years of prominence as an insightful writer and guide for people unnerved by life's difficulties.

Later at a convention of the Rabbinical Assembly where my 1957 rabbinic classmates and I were honored for our fifty years in the rabbinate, Harold approached me and said, "You know, Jack, I still remember your *shkufim-atumim* sermon at the Brooklyn Jewish Center!" Not having heard this from him during our early encounters, I was startled—not only because I had no idea he was present so long ago in the sanctuary of the Brooklyn Jewish Center where he heard that sermon, but also because he remembered with precision the sermon's contents a half-century later.

The Bible's Kohelet (11:1) teaches:

Cast your bread upon the waters, for you will find it after many days.

I have always understood this dictum to mean one must be careful about what one says or does, for one never knows if one's own words or actions will come back someday to either affirmation or negation.

YIGAEL YADIN:
SOLDIER, STATESMAN, ARCHAEOLOGIST

Yigael Yadin was one of the State of Israel's outstanding person-alities. He served as Chief of Staff of the Israel Defense Forces during and after the war of independence, and as Deputy Prime Minister of the State of Israel. He later immersed himself in pio-neering archaeological work, including the Dead Sea Scrolls, the excavations of Hazor, the caves of the Judean desert, the excava-tions of Masada and Magiddo, and other digs. As a soldier, pol-itician, statesman and scholar, Yigael Yadin was an historical persona indeed.

During a speaking engagement at the University of Southern California (USC), I approached Yadin on behalf of the University of Judaism and asked if he would consider an extended speaking tour in southern California the following year. Yes, he'd consider it, and invited me to come see him in Israel during a trip I told him I planned in the Holy Land.

Yadin's "Doctor"

Later, when in Israel, I called and made and appointment to see Yadin at his home in Jerusalem. He greeted me warmly; we dis-cussed the nature, length and terms of a proposed tour. There was an important stipulation he set forth: he needed to bring his doctor along to monitor his health during the lengthy foray. I said that seemed doable. Whereupon, he picked up the phone and summoned from an upstairs room an attractive female whom he introduced as his "doctor." The woman was not his wife. Since I was so eager to arrange a tour for our school with such an historic person, I agreed to the "doctor" stipulation. Agreement was reached during which Yadin pounded the top of his desk, proclaiming *gemacht*, it's settled, it's a deal.

Yadin's speaking tour at and for the University of Judaism throughout southern California the following year drew thou-sands of eager listeners who learned about his dramatic and exciting archaeological discoveries which he described and explained in lucid fashion. The tour turned out to be an educational and cultural experience of major proportion.

When Yadin and his "doctor" were slated to room together at Camp Ramah in Ojai for his weekend lectures, the camp director opposed the idea of their being together in the same quarters overnight; it was not proper or appropriate, he argued, not a good example for our young people and various other constituents. The director eventually let the matter alone. Yigael Yadin and his "doctor" roomed together, and we had another outstanding cultural and educational experience with an historic personality, a person of singular distinction. As for his "doctor," well…

CARDINAL ROGER MAHONEY AND ELIE WIESEL

Elie Wiesel was scheduled to lecture for the University of Judaism at Temple Sinai in Los Angeles. We expected an audience of over one thousand people. I had invited Cardinal Roger Mahoney, the distinguished leader of the Catholic church in the widespread five-county area of greater Los Angeles, to serve as respondent to the Wiesel presentation.

I brought the two prominent guests together at a small gathering prior to the lecture to meet and greet and discuss what was in the offing content-wise. When the Cardinal encountered Wiesel, he greeted him with "Welcome to Los Angeles," for, after all, Los Angeles was the Cardinal's domain.

What was especially striking about their interchange was the palpable, respectful, even reverential demeanor Mahoney displayed in Wiesel's presence. Here was a prince of the church known around the world, showing deference to a man who was in a sense the voice of conscience about the Catholic church's passive role during the Holocaust period.

Cardinal Mahoney displayed penetrating insight as he reacted to Elie Wiesel's presentation. Indeed, the Cardinal was a man of native intelligence, very well informed, a born leader, a wise manager and a counselor of his widespread and diverse flock. I have always wondered about the sad fact that the stellar qualities of this man will never be transmitted to future generations via progeny of his very own.

————————————

This reflection was written some considerable time before the revelations about child abuse on the part of Catholic clergy in Los Angeles during the Mahoney era.

– Chapter Six –

THE HOLOCAUST

The literature of the Holocaust is, alas, vast. What follows in this section is a series of vignettes about people who had been affected in one way or another by the cataclysm. They are based on my personal encounters with personalities who either successfully weathered the storm, wrenched vital lessons from the catastrophe, or remained numbed by it. For me, these accounts testify to the fortitude, tenacity and nobility of the Jewish spirit.

ELIE WIESEL: VOICE OF THE SHOAH

Elie Wiesel's stature and fame as a seminal chronicler of the searing import of the Holocaust on the hearts and minds of Jew and gentile alike needs no elaboration by me. Here is but a small observation about this man's approach to people.

I had invited Wiesel to participate in the University of Judaism's public lecture series on a number of occasions. Thousands came to hear his quiet, powerful, and evocative presentations. Yet he was always conscious of individuals and small groups who insisted on personal contact with him. He urged me to facilitate such meetings.

On one such occasion, I brought him to a meeting in a room at a hotel to meet with a group of some twenty second-generation children of Holocaust survivors. They gathered in a circle around him; they each leaned forward, their focus intense, their eyes glistening as Wiesel quietly spoke to them about the trauma of their parents. He told them that as their progeny, they had the sacred obligation to preserve their parents' memory, to honor their sacrifice, to carry on their legacy, and to realize their dreams and ambitions for them.

The reverence the group evinced as they sat in attentive silence in the presence of Elie Wiesel was palpable. I can never forget that scene.

Reverence is due to a person who embodies a high cause, who's very self and voice point to an experience not to be forgotten...The rabbis composed a blessing to be recited when one comes into the presence of such a person:

בָּרוּךְ אַתָּה יְיָ אֱלֹהֵינוּ מֶלֶךְ הָעוֹלָם שֶׁנָּתַן מֵחָכְמָתוֹ
לְבָשָׂר וָדֶם:

Blessed are You, King of the universe who, from His own wisdom, has bestowed such wisdom on human beings.

RICHARD RUBENSTEIN: THEOLOGIAN

Richard Rubenstein was the director of the Hillel Foundation at the University of Pittsburgh during the years of my rabbinate in the city. He was the controversial, incisive and illuminating author of the famed theological work *After Auschwitz* and other trenchant writings; he was also a compelling lecturer. Year after year I had invited him to occupy the popular lecture program of our congregation. His appearances invariably constituted an "experience." A perennial preoccupation of his and of his audience was the fallout from the Holocaust. On one such occasion he came right out with his view. His Auschwitz book's *Chapter Eleven*, summarized it in words of which the whole theological world took notice:

> I believe that the death of God is a cultural event. It has been experienced by millions of men and women who have had to face the collapse of religious faith and authority discussed in this book. It is also part of the experience of those who can no longer believe in the biblical God of history after Auschwitz. Belief in the biblical God entails interpreting events such as the extermination of Europe's Jews as exemplifications of the divine plan for human redemption.
>
> After Auschwitz, many of us find it impossible to believe in an all-wise, all-powerful God who acts decisively in human history. If there is such a God, the death camps were ultimately his handiwork. This idea places too great a strain on our credulity. Our death-of-God experience rests on loss of faith in the God-who-acts-in-history.

"On the Other Hand"

However, Rubenstein did not stop in the search for "God After the Death of God," the title of the chapter in his book *Morality and Eros*. Here God is conceived of as the ground and source of all existence. In speaking of God this way, he avers, we formulate an explicit judgement concerning the nature and the limitations of the human condition, and he then writes this:

> Perhaps the best available metaphor for the conception of God as the Holy Nothingness is that God is the ocean and we are the waves. In some sense each wave has its moment in which it is distinguishable as a somewhat separate entity. Nevertheless, no wave is entirely distinct from the ocean which is its substantial ground. The waves are surface manifestations of the ocean. Our knowledge of the ocean is largely dependent on the way it manifests itself in the waves.

To penetrate the full meaning of Rubenstein's metaphor requires examining the rest of that chapter. For me the notion that God is conceived of as "the ground and source of all existence" is the central affirmation notwithstanding Rubenstein's tortured metaphor. And so, no matter how much our theologians try, they cannot put God to death. God forbid.

WIESEL AND RUBENSTEIN MEET FOR DINNER

Richard Rubenstein held the position as Hillel director at the University of Pittsburgh during the same period of my tenure as rabbi at Pittsburgh's Congregation B'nai Israel. He was a frequent lecturer at the synagogue's public lecture series.

Elie Wiesel was the featured lecturer at one of the series' events. I designated Rubenstein as the "discussant" following Wiesel's presentation.

As was my and Leah's practice, we invited the program's participants to dinner at our home prior to the evening's event. Since Rubenstein was a Pittsburgh resident and participant in the evening's program, we thought it appropriate to have Rubenstein at dinner with Wiesel. (An aside: at each of these dinners we always had our sons, Reuven, David and Judah, present for the meal and so they could imbibe the presence of such major Jewish personalities.)

Picture the scene: Elie Wiesel, a frail man with piercing eyes, resonant but quiet voice, sitting in his chair a bit uneasily yet pleasant in demeanor. Richard Rubenstein, a robust figure, with strong voice, sitting confidently and jovial in demeanor. Rubenstein was emphasizing his views about the Holocaust. Wiesel did not choose to engage. Both men fell silent for what seemed minutes as did the others at the table. All that could be heard was the soft clanging of silverware on the dishes. It was a strange experience. I always thought that dinner significant simply because it brought together two seminal personalities well known throughout the Jewish world for their differing responses to the major tragedy of our time.

There was an oppressive silence…Only man speaks, said I to myself. Graves and stars are still. For a short while I sat, awake and not awake, then thought to myself again: Only man is silent; graves and stars speak.

—Rachel Shenberg, *Like a Lengthening Shadow*

DAVID WEISS-HALIVNI: TALMUD SCHOLAR

David and I attended the same high school in the Brownsville section of Brooklyn, New York, the Mesivta Rabbi Chaim Berlin. He was no ordinary student. He had already displayed Talmudic brilliance and so, instead of being placed in the usual Judaic studies class, he was assigned the highest grade—the *Shiur*, the teaching unit of the *Rosh Yeshiva* (the school head), Rabbi Yitzhak Hutner.

Due to David's recent experience as a Holocaust survivor and his exposure to the open American milieu, he decided, upon graduation from Chaim Berlin's general high school to attend Brooklyn College despite efforts to persuade him against such a move which, it was argued, would divert full attention from his advanced Talmudic studies. The jacket of his fascinating book, *The Book and the Sword: A Life of Learning in the Shadow of Destruction*, explained this move:

> Adherence to the fundamentalist world view that insists on recording and reconciling every apparent contradiction in the Talmudic text—troubling to him even as a youngster—had become impossible for him now.
>
> When he arrived in New York after the war, he began struggling toward the "window" of secular learning. From the synthesis of a traditional approach to Talmud study with the modern critical study of the Talmudic text, there emerged his original take on Talmudic study which characterized his distinguished later career.

After college, David came to the Jewish Theological Seminary as a student in its Rabbinical School, having moved in the direction of critical Talmudic studies. We became friends. I recall David sitting alone in the seminary library, focused on a Talmudic page; when he saw me, he looked up and, with worry in his eyes, spoke of his concern for his future upon graduation. When Leah and I were married during my senior year, David and his wife,

Zipporah, gifted us with a set of beautiful glasses that remain in the breakfront in our dining room to this day. The Seminary Rabbinical School class of 1957 picture shows me standing next to David, who was smiling benignly.

A star student of the great Talmudist professor Saul Lieberman, David realized his dream of joining the seminary faculty and eventually rose to a full professorship. He authored a number of seminal Talmudic volumes. His latent traditionalism did not allow him to accept the seminary's decision to ordain women as rabbis; and so, with the crucial intervention of another 1957 classmate, Yosef Yerushalmi, a professor of history at Columbia University, David joined the Columbia faculty as professor of Talmudic literature.

He also went on to found and serve as head of a rabbinical school which positioned itself as a "right wing" Conservative institution that combined firm adherence to halakhic discipline with halakhic elasticity. David emerged as one of the world's leading modernist Talmudic scholars.

The following story of an experience of David Weiss, Holocaust survivor, has been told in various versions. This is the one I know:

In the concentration camp David was assigned the task of lugging huge boulders from a quarry to a construction site. A German supervisor during a break was sighted munching a dripping sandwich that was wrapped in a torn page of the *Shulkhan Aruch*, the code of Jewish law.

Having been deprived of his precious sacred books and disturbed by the desecration of one of its pages, David hesitantly approached the German and asked him for the torn page; contemptuously, the German handed it to him.

For the next several weeks David and a group of his concentration camp fellows immersed themselves in study using the rescued page.

The sword and the book came down from heaven tied to each other. Said the Almighty, "If you keep what is written in this book, you will be spared this sword; if not, you will be consumed by it" (Midrash Rabbah Deuteronomy 4:2)

DWH: We clung to the book, yet we were consumed by the sword.

JS: No! Not entirely consumed. You did not forget yesterday but forged ahead and fashioned a creative today and tomorrow.

SHMUEL POSNER: HAUNTED PICTURE FRAMER

Following the Bar Mitzvah of each of our three sons, I decided to frame as memorabilia the invitations, pictures and bulletin articles that emerged from the occasion.

I engaged a man who was expert in the field of framing such items. He was a middle-aged man, bald, thin, fragile in appearance, soft-spoken, along with a permanent cast of sadness in his eyes. He was a survivor of the Holocaust.

In various conversations I asked him about his life in general and about his experiences in the concentration camp. He once described the horrors—the stench of burning bodies, the anguish and starvation, the indignities and separation from loved ones—and the rest.

And then he said, "For the last thirty years I haven't slept uninterrupted for a single night. I just cannot forget."

After hearing my picture framer telling of his sleeping ordeal, I thought about the passage in Deuteronomy 25:17-19 concerning the action of the Amalekites in the desert as the Israelites sought to pass through; they had attacked the weary wanderers. The text then tells us:

תִּמְחֶה אֶת זֵכֶר עֲמָלֵק מִתַּחַת הַשָּׁמַיִם לֹא תִּשְׁכָּח

Wipe out the memory of Amalek from under the heavens. Do not forget.

This verse appears to contain a mixed message. On the one hand, Israel is told to forget Amalek, erase the memory of him from their consciousness. On the other hand, Israel is told, "Do not forget," which usually has meant that Israel was to remember Amalek and the wickedness perpetrated. (Could it also mean: don't forget to forget Amalek?!)

And so, we may ask, which is it? Is it better to remember or to forget?

In his classic work on memory in Judaism, *Zakhor*, Yoseph Yerushalmi refers to a story told by the Argentine writer Jorge Luis Borges called "Fumes el Memorioso." It concerns a man who, due to a riding accident, has become incapable of forgetting anything. Every minute of every day in his past, all the conversations and all his thoughts about them, remain vivid in his memory. He can only go over them time and again, grinding them into ever smaller pieces, then remembering even the grinding process. How unnerving such a condition can be.

When I read this in Harvey Cox's *Common Prayers* (p. 162), I thought of the actress Ingrid Bergman's "memorable" response to the question about the secret of her longevity. She responded, "Good health and a bad memory."

In the case of Mr. Picture-Framer, haunted as he was by the horrors of the Holocaust, perhaps it would have been better if he could forget — and sleep through a night in peace at long last. On the other hand, inhuman behavior inflicted upon others must never be forgotten so that it will not ever be repeated. Which is it?

These are memories...stored below the scene illuminated by consciousness. Yes, I believe that all our past life is there, preserved even to the most infinitesimal details, and that we forget nothing.

—Henri Bergson, *Dreams*, 1914, p. 33

SIMON WIESENTHAL:
STAMPS AND ABRAHAM JOSHUA HESCHEL

One of the great Jewish figures of our time, Simon Wiesenthal, hunted down hundreds of former Nazis who perpetrated atrocities on Jews during the Holocaust period. He was instrumental in bringing the notorious Adolph Eichmann to trial in Israel.

I invited him to lecture at B'nai Israel in Pittsburgh. When I picked him up at the airport, he said he had a special request to make. Later in the day, would I take him to downtown Pittsburgh to a major stamp collection dealer he knew about. He wanted to fill in gaps in his collection with stamps issues in various European countries. The stamps located areas occupied by Jews once, but no more. This was important to him; it helped him in his life's work, he said. I agreed and took him to the stamp dealer.

As he perused the collection, I observed how focused he was; each stamp was examined with a magnifying glass the dealer provided; each was carefully studied; some were lovingly handled and selected; exclamations of quiet delight came from Wiesenthal as he located a stamp that would fill one of his gaps. It was a true voyage of discovery on the man's part.

At dinner I had occasion to mention that Abraham Joshua Heschel had been a teacher of mine at the Jewish Theological Seminary. When I mentioned Heschel's name, Wiesenthal erupted with a burst of enthusiasm: how great a theologian of our time was Heschel, he exclaimed; he has revealed the *neshama*, the soul, of the Jewish people; he has given our people inspiration and hope through an unforgettable prose-poetry that uplifts the sad—and there are many who are sad because of the evil inflicted on our people. He went on...and on, with tears welling up in his eyes.

What poetry there is in human tears.

—Heine, *Poetry and Prose*, F. Ewen, p. 646

EMIL FACKENHEIM:
ENCOUNTER WITH CHRISTIAN THEOLOGIANS

I had engaged Dr. Emil Fackenheim, the trenchant thinker and consummate theologian, to lecture in our series at Congregation B'nai Israel in Pittsburgh. I also invited the Christian Bible scholars who were my doctoral studies teachers, members of the faculty of the nearby Pittsburgh Theological Seminary, to the lecture.

One was Dr. Eberhardt von Waldow, professor of Bible, and the other Dr. Markus Barth, professor of New Testament. Both strong advocates of rapprochement between Christians and Jews based on their intensive studies of Biblical literature. They knew about Emil Fackenheim and were eager to be in his presence.

At an informal gathering in my office prior to the lecture, I brought the German-born seminarians and Dr. Fackenheim together to meet and greet and engage in conversation. What I remember vividly about the encounter was Dr. Fackenheim's decided unease in the presence of the Christian scholars. I was also struck by the equal unease of the seminarians in Fackenheim's presence.

I think I understood: profound pain on the one hand and bad conscience on the other hand.

The mantra long-since introduced into the vocabulary of the Holocaust by Emil Fackenheim:

We cannot grant Hitler a posthumous victory.

A "FRUM" FAMILY ON YOM HASHOAH/ HOLOCAUST REMEMBRANCE DAY

We received an invitation to a wedding scheduled for the twenty-eighth of Nisan, 5770 (April 11, 2010). The calendar indicates that this is Yom HaShoah, the day that commemorates the destruction of some six million Jews by Nazi Germany. Since in the year 2010 the twenty-seventh of Nisan fell on Saturday night and Sunday, Yom HaShoah was postponed one day until the twenty-eighth of Nisan, Sunday evening, April 11, and Monday, April 12; this was mandated by the Israeli Knesset, which originally established the day in 1952. And so, a wedding of religious Jews was scheduled to take place on the Yom HaShoah of the year 2010!

Observance in Jerusalem and Israel

The heading of the above invitation proclaims in Hebrew: "Let us go up to Jerusalem as our chief joy." Here is how Holocaust Day is observed in that very city of Jerusalem:

Since in the Jewish calendar the day begins in the evening and ends the following evening, in 2010 Yom HaShoah begins in Israel at sundown in a state ceremony held at the Warsaw Ghetto Plaza at Yad Vashem, the Holocaust Martyrs' and Heroes Authority, in Jerusalem. During the ceremony the national flag is lowered to half mast, the president and the prime minister deliver speeches, Holocaust survivors light six torches symbolizing the approximately six million Jews who perished in the Holocaust, and the chief rabbis recite prayers.

At 10:00 a.m. on Yom HaShoah day, sirens are sounded throughout Israel for two minutes. During this time, people cease from action and stand at attention; cars stop, even on the highways; and the whole country comes to a standstill as people pay silent tribute to the dead. Ceremonies and services are held at schools, military bases and in other public and community organizations.

On the eve of Yom HaShoah and on the day itself, places of public entertainment are closed by law. Israeli television airs Holocaust documentaries and Holocaust-related talk shows, and low-key songs are played on the radio. Flags on public buildings are flown at half-mast.

Observance in the Diaspora

Since the Jewish people as a whole experienced the trauma of the Holocaust, Yom HaShoah is observed by Jews throughout the world. Here is how it is observed in the Diaspora:

On Yom HaShoah eve, memorial candles are lit and there are public gatherings at which *kaddish* is recited. A Holocaust survivor or a direct descendent speaks; psalms, plaintive songs and readings are heard; a Holocaust-themed film is shown. Some communities choose to emphasize the depth of loss that Jews experienced by reading the names of Holocaust victims one after another—focusing on the unfathomable notion of six million deaths.

And during the day thousands of Jews—young and old—from around the world hold a memorial service at Auschwitz, in what has become known as "The March of the Living" in defiance of the Death Marches.

Such is the time a Jewish religious family schedules the wedding of their children!

Appropriate Such Celebration?

When initially questioned about the appropriateness of celebrating such a joyous occasion on that very night, a member of the family responded that Yom HaShoah has no *halakhic* authority since it was proclaimed a Jewish national day by the Israeli Knesset, and who says its actions have any authority for religious Jews? The response was, no doubt, buttressed by the family's rabbinic authorities.

And so, it is quite acceptable for this Orthodox family to have a religious wedding celebration, with its vigorous and joyous singing and dancing and prancing and picture-taking and choice food, on an evening marked by searing tragedy. For, after all, it was *halakha* that determines legitimacy on such matters, not Is-raeli-secular-Zionist institutions.

Quite aside from the *halacha*, as some religionists apply it, would not a measure of sensitivity be called for as the Jewish people recall the pain and anguish, the slashing and slaying of millions of Jews—non-Orthodox and staunchly Orthodox alike? How very sad.

The inexorable intertwining of Jewish religion with Jewish na-tionhood/peoplehood has been at the heart of the Jewish experi-ence throughout the ages. To sever one from the other is to en-danger the very survival of the Jewish people.

The above vignette does, indeed, limn such a severance.

—"The Miracle of Jewish Survival" in
In Search of The Religiosity in Religion, p. 79-88

– Chapter Seven –

ISRAEL

A Rabbi and Congregants Set Forth for the Holy Land

As you read these lines, your rabbi, along with some fifty members of B'nai Israel, will be experiencing the sights and sounds, the spirit and sanctity of the Land of Israel. This small piece of space has always been embedded in our imagination. To think that soon we will have the opportunity to walk on this very soil, to see with our own eyes these sights, to hear the echoes of the prophets of the land is an exciting prospect indeed.

—Bulletin, Congregation B'nai Israel
Pittsburgh, PA

AN ARAB GUIDE ON THE TEMPLE MOUNT

All peoples have religious places that are the locus of their most fervent spiritual convictions and aspirations. For Jews, the Temple Mount in Jerusalem is such a place. On that high hill there once stood the Temple of Solomon, rebuilt in the time of Ezra and Nehemiah, expanded later by the Hasmoneans and then in the first century C.E. reconstructed in impressive fashion by King Herod. Partial remnants of the wall that surrounded and reinforced the Temple Mount are what exist today—for all to see and conjure with in reverence and in recollection of great periods of Jewish history.

Jews are admonished by the Israeli Orthodox rabbinate to beware of walking on the Temple Mount lest one tread on the very ground upon which the ancient temple stood—a desecration. Not all traditional Jews adhere to this warning; neither do I. And so I located the sole entryway to the Mount and reverently walked about the sacred area for hours.

The Tour

A short, dandy and smooth-talking Arab guide, spotting three lone tourists, approached and invited us to join him and one of his "customers," a well-spoken black American from the South, in order to get a "first rate" tour of the Mount. We agreed. He proceeded to point out in obviously well-rehearsed rapid-fire talk the various medieval and more recent shrines, their origins, traditions, associated personalities, etc. Notice the numerous circles of Arab men fervently reading or chanting sections from the Koran; he told us to observe the prancing Arab children on recess from the *madrasa* (Muslim religious school) permanently located on the Mount…these details and much else.

Our guide then took us to a tree-shaded area at a corner of the Mount containing several conveniently placed benches. He invited his three customers to sit down and rest. He then requested we give him the one hundred *shekalim* fee for his services. We did. Whereupon he launched into a lecture about the superiority of Islam over Christianity and Judaism.

To my Christian fellow tourist he said that Jesus was such a good and holy man that God would not possibly have allowed him to be crucified; the Koran said this and holds that Jesus never, in fact, was crucified. To me, his Jewish tourist, he emphasized that Muslim law was far superior to Jewish law and that Mohammed was a higher prophet than Moses of the Old Testament.

We were taken aback by our Arab "guide" who in this setting "guided" us into the realm of Muslim theology. As soon as he finished his monologue he peremptorily walked away, with his two hundred *shekalim* safely in his pocket, leaving his three (now former) customers sitting on our benches. Our guide not only got his good fee but also got in his "superior" theology.

As I continued to walk about the Temple Mount, I spotted our Arab guide from a distance plying his trade and was tempted to confront him with *my* theology. I didn't. In retrospect, I'm thinking I should have. At the time, I figured who needed yet another argument with Muslims?

Zvi Hirsch Chajes, the Galician Talmudist and historian, once remarked, "Just as faith in its highest sense is what unites people, so religion is what divides them. If this is so, why is it so?

Religion deals with the area of man's deepest concerns, with *his attempt at relating himself to the most ultimate reality he can find, i.e., God, the Transcendent, the Divine, the Ultimate Power of the universe—however the believer may choose to express the object of this yearning. Thus* everything attached to that relationship partakes of great seriousness. This is religion's vital nerve; whatever touches it touches religion at the core of its being; *it is instantly alert to any threat in this area. This is what religion signifies by marking off certain things with the mark of "holiness" or "sacredness." It is saying of such things, "These have to do with the most vital concerns known to man; beware how you handle them!"*

To our Arab guide, the numerous details in the Koran which tie the Muslim follower to his "ladder" reaching for Allah are of ultimate importance. To differ with or dismiss any of these details is to endanger the climb "upward."

— "Religion Can Engender Rage as Well
as Rapture" in Jack Shechter's book
In Search of the Religiosity in Religion, p. 117-125

A MUSLIM GUARD AT THE DOME OF THE ROCK:
A SACRED LOCALE

Because the Temple Mount in Jerusalem is in full control of the Muslim authorities, Jews who do choose to explore the place do so warily as I did when approaching this special Muslim sight...

I circled the massive circular Dome of the Rock, which encloses the rock upon which Abraham reportedly prepared to sacrifice his son Isaac, which sits on the spot of the Temple of old, and which houses a huge mosque.

After circling the dome seven times (with no biblical consequences!) I paused at the entrance and sought to go inside, whereupon I was stopped by a menacing Arab guard. "No non-Muslims allowed," he emphasized. "How do you know I'm not a Muslim?" I asked. "In three ways," he responded. "You don't look like one...your passport will tell...you'll need to recite several verses by heart from the Koran." So much for entering the Dome of the Rock.

A significant facet of study about the sanctity of space has projected the notion that the "holiness" of concrete place is a cultic one with mythological characteristics: God Himself lives in the land, as it were, and it is that which renders it "holy." It is inherently so.

Another facet of study about the subject views it differently: it is human beings' "holy action" which renders sanctity to land. That is, man's behavior on the land in response to divine moral and religious dicta is the determining factor. Land is not inherently holy. It is conferred on by religiously faithful human beings.

For a full analysis of this double perspective, see this author's essay in In Search of the Religiosity in Religion *(p. 43-78). Indeed, what is the normative Judaic notion about that which renders a locale "holy"?*

ROAMING THE KOTEL AREA

I was in the habit of roaming around the western wall area for hours observing the scenes of constant prayer and study and often participating myself in the proceedings. During this roaming and just sitting in the provided chairs observing the scene, I was repeatedly approached by bearded, side-locked, black-hatted Orthodox men—young and old and in between—asking for charity.

As was my wont, I struck up a conversation with one such man in his mid-twenties. The interchange was in Hebrew. "Did you work today?" I asked.

"Yes, I did," he responded. "I prayed and studied Torah; you think that's not hard work?"

Then I asked, "Did you serve in the *Tzavah*, the army?"

"I serve in God's army; my prayer and study is as good as the service of any soldier."

Another question: "Where does the money to support you and your family come from?"

He answers, "Government stipends and people like you."

I persist: "But you don't think much of the Israeli government, do you?"

"No, I don't. It tramples over the Torah."

Provoked by the young man's comments, I proceeded to say to him, "So you don't work to support yourself, your family and others in need financially; you don't pay taxes; you don't defend the country you live in in a concrete way; you live off the largess of a government you don't really believe in; and worst of all, you maintain your lifestyle by soliciting handouts from tourists. Don't you have any self-pride?"

Exasperated by my lengthy and provocative talk, the young man said to me: "*Adoni Hayakar*, my dear sir, I don't need your approval, I have God's approval. Will you contribute or not?" I couldn't and didn't.

The next day, I saw the same young man, this time with a talis over his head, moving about the Kotel area, stopping and talking with potential customers/contributors.

In the Laws of Torah Study, *in Maimonides' Mishna Torah (Chapter 3:10) the great sage wrote this:*

כָּל הַמֵּשִׂים עַל לִבּוֹ שֶׁיַּעֲסֹק בַּתּוֹרָה וְלֹא יַעֲשֶׂה מְלָאכָה וְיִתְפַּרְנֵס מִן הַצְּדָקָה הֲרֵי זֶה חִלֵּל אֶת הַשֵּׁם וּבִזָּה אֶת הַתּוֹרָה וְכִבָּה מְאוֹר הַדָּת וְגָרַם רָעָה לְעַצְמוֹ וְנָטַל חַיָּיו מִן הָעוֹלָם הַבָּא.

> *Whoever sets his heart to pursue the study of the Torah but does no secular work at all, and permits himself to be supported by charity, behold, he blasphemed the Name, and degraded the Torah, and shadowed the light of religion, and caused evil to be bought upon himself, and deprived his own life from its share in the world to come.*

ENCOUNTER WITH A SHEPHERD

City folk in the twenty-first century don't know of shepherds—
except in the blurred images of biblical personalities such as the
young lad David who became king of Israel. Indeed, for the student of the Bible, shepherds tending their flocks conjure up visions of the open spaces of the ancient Near East, which has become our mental image of the biblical landscape.

Such an imagined shepherd became a real flesh-and-blood
person for Leah and me during a torturous jeep ride over the
steep rock-strewn hills on the outskirts of Moshav Amirim
where we stayed for five days. Amirim is located several miles
south of Safed in the Galil. Our guide had taken us to rest on a
level opening in the hills near a gushing rivulet. We sat down on
a flat rock, drank from water jugs and ate some seeds from a
pomegranate.

We Meet

There he was—an Arab shepherd with his staff and dog ma-
neuvering a bevy of some twenty-five goats along a short hill,
pausing as they grazed for the sprouting greenery on the ground
or stood on their hind legs plucking fruit from the trees.

"What are you up to?" I asked the shepherd. He replied in a
combination of halting English but fluid Hebrew. He shepherds
the goats all day for grazing, keeping snakes and other land creatures away from them. The staff in his hand helps navigate the
steep and rocky terrain, and with the help of the dogs keeps the
goats together and, when necessary, is used to kill the snakes
that would otherwise bite the animals to death.

He then leads them up the steep hill to the caves he pointed
to, way up there where the goats stay comfortably overnight.
The smoke coming from the cave area he pointed to was from
the dung being burned to later serve as fertilizer for the fig and
date trees in the area, which are staple foods in the region. The
next morning the shepherd and his "boss" escort the goats out

of the caves and resume the daily regimen. Finally, when the goats are fat and ready, they are sold to neighboring farmers for their milk, cheese, and meat.

This is how they eke out a living. Why eke out a living? I asked. Well, he said, he once had some two hundred goats when a plague broke out due to a careless borrower of some of his goats, leaving him with the meager twenty-five we saw.

I asked the shepherd about his life on these Galilean hills. He said he was tired of it all. He was divorced and his wife and two children moved away to nearby Carmiel. Why divorced? Because he drinks beer all the time, which consumes his meager earnings; his wife could not take it any longer, so they separated.

He was lonely, he said. "Take me to America with you," he exclaimed with a wry smile. I said that my backyard in America was too small for him to tend; besides, my plaster and wooden "animals" in the yard don't move, and even an expert mover of animals like him couldn't get my "animals" to move.

We parted with a handshake. The shepherd in the Galilean hills of Israel made vivid for Leah and me the life of the shepherds of biblical Israel.

Abraham and Jacob, David and Saul, Rachel and Jeremiah, Abel and Amos—shepherds all.

A YOUNG MAN STUDYING IN A YESHIVA:
HOW TO CUT BREAD

Yonasan ben Uziel was a star pupil of the great sage Hillel who lived during the first century BCE. We visited his tomb in the Golan Heights north of Safed in the village of Amuka, due east of the Hula Valley. Across from the cave compound I saw a two-story building from whose windows I could hear the animated voices of study—a Yeshiva I surmised. I climbed the stairs and entered a well-appointed study hall in which some two dozen bearded, long side-locked young men were pouring over their talmudic texts.

I sat down next to one of the young men who was deeply engrossed in a rabbinic text.

We talked. I asked him what was the עִנְיָן, *the subject,* he and his students were engaged in. He enthusiastically responded that the issue was the following: *if a person had a bread roll before him, does he cut the roll from the right side, the middle or the left?* I said that sounded like an interesting subject; could he show me the rabbinic sources preoccupied with the issue, whereupon he pointed to his Talmud text with its set of מְפוֹרְשִׁם, *commentators,* who deal with the subject in detail.

Clearly his learning expertise was manifest. I then asked him how much time he and his fellow students have been spending on the subject. He said that *they will have spent a full day dissecting the matter, exploring the various ramifications, and that exploration of the subject was likely to fill the week ahead.*

I asked him if he was confident that the abundance of time he was spending on how to cut bread would be useful preparation for his eventually working in order to support himself and his family-to-be.

The young man looked at me quizzically and, annoyed, turned away, lowering his face back to his Talmud page, and spoke not another word. I sat next to him for another minute or so; he remained silent; I got up and walked out of the Yeshiva study hall—taken by such admirable attention to detail.

———————————————

It appears I might have been a bit hasty in critiquing this young man. I took his study of bread out of its Talmudic context. Since penning this vignette and upon doing a bit of research on the subject, it turns out that the details of food preparation need to be done with sensitivity about the nourishment God provides for His children. A striking and detailed Talmudic passage about this subject can be found (among other comparable passages) in the Tractate Sofrim *3:14.*

OUR CHRISTIAN/ARAB/ISRAELI DRIVER

Victor Khoury became one of our frequent drivers. He took us from Jerusalem to Tel Aviv's Ben Gurion Airport to meet our son Judah and his son, Jeremy, who came to Israel for a weeklong visit, and ferried us back to our Katamon apartment. He brought me to the Tank Museum in Latrun and to its Mini Israel, a huge replica in miniature of the entire land of Israel today. He taxied us to Har Hamenuchot, the vast cemetery on the hills outside Jerusalem where Leah's parents lay in rest. He took us to the airport when we departed Israel for home.

A tall, robust man, yet gentle in speech, we learned much about Victor and even more about life in Israel. Victor was a Christian by religion, Arab in ethnicity, an Israeli by nationality, married to a woman reared in France, and the father of three children. He has a sister and brother-in-law who run a gas station in Ames, Iowa, a brother in Atlanta, Georgia who runs a car rental business, another brother who owns a restaurant in Omaha, Nebraska.

He has remained in Israel, he said, because he does not want to leave his aged parents, and for a practical reason: his father-in-law had been a career officer in the French army and thus entitled to significant stipends for the education of his grandchildren who were enrolled in a quality French-speaking school. (The school, Victor noted, had a large number of Jewish teachers, which accounted for its superior quality!)

Among the conversations during our time together, two of them revealed the "darker" side of life in Israel and of the Muslim world.

The First Conversation

Victor once drove a suspicious looking Israeli who gave the impression that he was on a serious mission in the Mea Shearim section of the city. Mea Shearim, as we know, is occupied by the ultra-religious in Israel what with their fur-capped headdress, flowing beards and uniformly black clothing reminiscent of Hasidic life in the old country. The man confided to Victor his objective: the acquisition of cocaine and various other profitable drugs.

His passenger got out of the taxi and entered what was, for Mea Shearim, an attractive building telling Victor to wait for him; he would return in about fifteen to twenty minutes. When the man returned to the taxi laden with a heavy package, he told Victor that *he gets the best drugs available in Israel from the Hasidic denizens of Mea Shearim.* "How come?" Victor asked. To which the man responded: the *haredim* have to live out their preferred lifestyle, pay their bills, support their yeshivot and rebbes. Besides, the authorities are inhibited from searching the *haredim* at key travel checking points.

The Second Conversation

In a discussion about Islamic extremism, I once mentioned to Victor that every seven years or so, President Murbarak of Egypt rounds up some of the country's prominent Imans who he feels were getting out of hand with their radical religious demands. He then places them in prison for a year or so until they and their followers retreated from their ways.

I thought I had told Victor something striking about how Muslim regimes treat their religious extremists. Whereupon Victor countered that Mubarak's action could not compare with what Syrian President Assad's father did in his time. As the need arose, he would round up Syria's key radical clergy, place them in an airplane, fly them high into the sky—and then have them fly out of the airplane down to earth.

Note the second paragraph of this vignette…the staggering variety of Israel's populace.

A TAXI DRIVER'S DVAR TORAH

One expects to learn Torah from a learned teacher or sage, or from a book or in a classroom setting. One usually doesn't hear a Dvar Torah from a taxi driver.

Leah and I did learn some Torah wisdom from a driver who was taking us to Ben Yehudah Street in Jerusalem. The traffic was congested and the cars doing their usual drive-up-in-your-face when, in order to avoid a crash, you make a sudden and quick turn-aside maneuver. It's Jerusalem's characteristic "danger confrontation—disaster avoidance dance." For America visitors, it is scary business indeed.

Sitting in the back of the taxi, Leah nervously comments about the traffic situation. The taxi man reacts in his easy, nonchalant manner and says to her, לֹא לִדְאֹג - אֵין צֹרֶךְ לִדְאָגָה, *Don't worry, there's no need to worry.* Then he continues in Hebrew and points out that the word for worry is דְּאָגָה — ד, א, ג, ה. If the letters were placed alphabetically, which letter would be missing? The answer is ב, right?

Well, now, explains our driver, the *bet* is the first letter of the word בִּטָחוֹן, which means "faith" or "trust." Worrying shows lack of faith, trust. So, admonishes our taxi man, have faith in God (and in him!) and you'll find that you don't have to worry so much.

I can't imagine listening to such a Dvar Torah from a New York City taxi driver.

At the YIVO Institute in New York, an organization which commemorates Jewish life in pre-World War II Eastern Europe, there is a volume of the Mishna saved from the Nazis and brought to the United States. On the front page of the book is stamped "The Society of Woodchoppers for the Study of Mishna in Berditchev."

That the men who chopped wood in Bertitchev, a job that had no status and required no education, met regularly to study Mishna, shows the pervasiveness of study in the Jewish community. It also helps explain the avidity for education among the grandsons and granddaughters of these woodchoppers wherever Jews reside today.

SHIMON PERES AND HIS "COMPANION"

As so many of the country's taxi drivers do, this driver evinced much familiarity and preoccupation with the politics and politicians of contemporary Israel. And they are quite frank and voluble with their views and assessments.

He's ferrying us past the residence of the State of Israel's president, Shimon Peres. Prior to becoming president, Mr. Peres, long married to the same woman, had a woman "companion" on the side through the years of his prominent political life. His wife knew about it and learned to live with the situation and continued to share the same home with her husband.

When Mr. Peres became president, he asked his wife to move into the president's residence with him—this for appearance' sake. She adamantly refused, telling him that if his extramarital way was okay through the years, let it be okay now as well—this time without her.

When I asked the driver how such a prominent leader of Israel could function so acceptably through the years (the public knew well of Peres' "companion"), he replied that the Israeli public takes such behavior for granted when it comes to their leaders; they separate public from private behavior and simply look away, making no judgements.

What about the religious orthodox who presumably are guardians of morality? His response: these religious just care about what they can get for their own purposes from their leaders.

Scripture harbors few illusions about the government officials who ruled the people, but did have ideals about what its leaders should be like. The book of II Samuel's second chapter tells us how displeased the Lord was with the heinous misdeed David perpetuated when he took another man's wife, Batsheva, for his mistress, and proceeded to have her husband sent to the front lines to face his demise.

Yes, King David was a great leader of his people; yet the prophet Nathan, at God's behest, condemned David in the most heated and emphatic terms. Even kings in ancient Israel could not hold themselves above the laws of morality.

AN ELDER IN A GREEK ORTHODOX MONASTERY: NO HANDS IN THE POCKETS

Some years ago Leah and I spent two months in Israel. Our home base was in an apartment in Katamon which is a Jewish neighborhood in south central Jerusalem.

"Katamon" is derived from the Greek, meaning "by the monastery." The neighborhood is built next to an old Greek Orthodox monastery, believed, from around the twelfth century, to be built over the home and tomb of Saint Symeon, the "god receiver." Symeon lived to an old age in order to see and hold in his arms the Messiah forty days after his birth, as recorded in the Gospel of Luke.

The monastery was part of a fascinating complex of structures, with worshippers streaming in and out of the compound's gates. Day after day I watched the scene and walked around the grounds. I then determined to enter the monastery sanctuary itself to observe the proceedings.

The grandly attired priests performed the ritual with automatic precision; some dozen nuns in full habit reverently followed the service in individual cubicles; some fifty congregants with focused eyes and outstretched arms watched the liturgical action which featured constant movement in and out of ornate doors. The colorful and plentiful iconography characterized the place. It was an altogether arresting scene.

Since the service was quite lengthy and I wanted to experience the place as much as possible, I took to walking back and forth along the aisles and into the alcoves. Unthinking, however, I did so with my hands in my pockets. When the service was over and the attendees beginning to disperse and gather outside the monastery courtyard for refreshments, a distinguished looking elder of the congregation approached me and quietly and emphatically admonished: "We do not casually walk around in this holy place with our hands in our pockets."

בֶּן־זוֹמָא אוֹמֵר   אֵיזֶהוּ חָכָם הַלוֹמֵד מִכָּל־אָדָם
שֶׁנֶּאֱמַר מִכָּל־מְלַמְּדַי הִשְׂכַּלְתִּי

Ben Zoma said: Who is wise? He who learns from all men, as it is said (in Psalm 119:99), "From all my teachers I have gotten understanding."

—*Ethics of the Fathers*, 4:1

– Chapter Eight –

JEWS IN A NON-JEWISH WORLD

I confess to a preoccupation with the notion of *golus mentality*. I do so with a degree of uneasiness, yet it persists and I must admit that it has persisted through the years. It has to do with the ever-present sense that the condition of Jews in the countries they inhabit is precarious; many seem to be always "looking over their Jewish shoulder" to consider, worry about, be conscious of what the gentile thinks about them. It implies a sense of questionable status of the Jew in the larger society, a lack of confidence and self-pride, of uneasiness about his own distinctiveness. For many this feeling about the Jewish self should be jettisoned in favor of a Jewish stance of full and equal status and standing in gentile society. Nevertheless, the "golus mentality" persists in me, try as I might to be rid of it.

Now, in America, a free, open and accepting atmosphere exists vis-à-vis its various religious, ethnic and racial subgroups and this is, of course, a good thing. Hence, a Jewish *golus* mentality may not seem to be called for. However Jews have a long and checkered history in the diaspora. It has been one of pain and rejection, jealousy and hatred, discrimination and worse.

When, therefore, one thinks about the Jewish condition through the wider lens of historical experience, it would appear to be natural to have been imbued with a *golus* mindset that is continually sensitive to what others think of the Jew.

The observations in this section seek to example this preoccupation.

ALAN DERSHOWITZ ON "CHUTZPAH"

I had brought Alan Dershowitz to Los Angeles to participate in the University of Judaism's public lecture series. The eminent lawyer and professor at Harvard University had penned this striking assertion in his book *Chutzpah*: "The byword of past generations of Jewish Americans was *shanda*, shame, fear of embarrassment in front of our hosts. The byword of the next generation should be *chutzpah*—assertive insistence on first-class status among our peers." This was the subject of his lecture, an obviously compelling position that I thought our audience ought to hear.

I have been examining the definitions and inner meaning of the work *chutzpah*. Louis Jacobs in his *The Jewish Religion: A Companion* (p. 81) writes this:

> **Chutzpah** Arrogance, impudence; a Talmudic word that made its way into Yiddish from which it was adopted into American slang and has now entered the English language and is recorded in the Oxford English Dictionary as an English word. It comes from a root meaning 'to peel' and hence 'to be bare'; chutzpah means barefacedness, sheer cheek.

Indeed, *chutzpah* is seen mostly as an undesirable human trait. Note this definition of the word in Webster's Collegiate Dictionary, Tenth Edition, p. 205: *chutzpah*: "supreme self-confidence, nerve, gall, temerity." In addition, the word connotes "conspicuous or flagrant boldness arising from rashness and contempt of danger" (p. 1208).

In addition to the etymology of the word and the dictionary definition, it seems apparent that the common popular usage of the word *chutzpah* harbors a decidedly negative connotation. Professor Dershowitz would, of course, emphasize that such connotation was not at all what he had in mind when using the word *chutzpah* in the title of his book and in his lectures.

Nonetheless, the word means what it means as per its etymology, the dictionary and in the popular mind.

When the arrow has left the bowstring, it no longer belongs to the archer, and when the word has left the lips, it is no longer controlled by the speaker.

—Heinrich Heine, *A Winter's Tale*, Preface

ROB ESHMAN: EDITOR OF "THE TRIBE"

The *Los Angeles Jewish Journal* has launched an offshoot of its publication program called *Tribe,* a monthly magazine dealing with the life and activities of the Jewish population in the Conejo Valley, west of Los Angeles proper.

When I first saw the title of the publication, something within me felt uneasy. And so I went to the Webster Collegiate Dictionary to find the definition of the words "tribe" and "tribal." This is what I found on page 126:

tribe: a social group comprising numerous families, clans or generations together with dependents or adopted strangers.

tribalism: tribal consciousness and loyalty; *especially exaltation of the tribe above other groups,* strong in-group loyalty.

The creators of the new magazine would, no doubt, assert that the connotation of tribe/tribalism as defined by Webster's, as the "exaltation of the tribe above other groups," is not at all what they had in mind when putting the publication together. Nonetheless, the words mean what they mean as per the dictionary and in the popular mind.

Would it then appear legitimate to ask if this was an appropriate title for a magazine that chronicles the life and times of the Jewish group in our community?

Spinning words, we are much like the spider spinning its web out of its own body. We, however, unlike the spider, may be enmeshed in our own web.

—Isaac Goldberg, *The Wonder of Words,* p. 298

ROBERT GORDIS: "YIDDISHE KUP" AND DISTINCITIVENESS

The Chautauqua Institution in upstate New York is a unique institution. During the summer, its program features presentations in music, dance, drama, opera, as well as study opportunities and major lecturers on contemporary religious and general topics. Sunday religious services (Protestant) take place in a huge amphitheater attended by over two thousand earnest Christians. This all takes place in an old Victorian, village-like setting astride a sparkling lake, the population overwhelmingly Christian both in number and spirit.

Most of the lectures in the institution's storied Hall of Philosophy are on non-Jewish religious topics. Yet there is usually a spot featuring a scholar of Judaica. On one such occasion when Leah and I were present, Rabbi Robert Gordis, the distinguished and brilliant Jewish scholar, delivered a series of lectures on the basic perspectives of Judaism.

Some four hundred persons packed the hall. Seated in the back row, Leah and I beheld a sea of white-haired, older ladies intently listening to the lecture. It was a scintillating performance, indeed. At its conclusion I tapped one of the old white-haired, petite Protestant-like ladies on the shoulder and asked her what she thought of the lecture. She turned to me and pointed a finger to her head and said, "Yiddishe kup," i.e., a "Jewish head," indicating the sharpness of a Jewish mind. Clearly, the entire audience was not Christian.

Mr. Goldstein is returning by train from New York City to Glens Falls, a small town in upstate New York. Seated next to him on the train is a young man he doesn't know. As the ride is long, Goldstein starts a conversation with the young man. His name is Alan Levine, and he is also heading for Glens Falls.

"Are you going there on business?" Goldstein asks.

"No. It's a social visit."

"Do you have relatives there?"

"No."

"Are you married?"

"No, I'm not."

Goldstein thinks to himself: "He's going to Glen Falls, he's not married, it's not business, and he has no relatives there. So why is he going? Obviously to meet a girl or, more likely, her family. Perhaps to confirm their engagement? But with whom? There are only three Jewish families apart from mine in Glens Falls—the Resnicks, the Feldsteins, and the Cohens.

"It couldn't be the Resnicks. Resnick only has sons. The Feldsteins have two girls, but one is married and the other is studying in Europe for the year. It must be the Cohens. They have three daughters: Marsha, Sheila, and Rachel. Marsha is already married. Sheila is too plump an unattractive for this handsome young man. So it must be Rachel. Yes, Rachel! A wonderful girl."

With this, Goldstein breaks the silence and smiles at the stranger. "Well, congratulations on your forthcoming marriage to Rachel Cohen."

The young man stutters, "We haven't told anybody. How did you know?"

"Why, it's obvious," answers Goldstein.

A "Jewish head" at work!

HENRY AND EDITH EVERETT:
PROUD JEWISH PHILANTHROPISTS

The Chautauqua Institution is a major religious, cultural and artistic institution in upstate New York. Leah and I have spent considerable time there during vacations. It is predominantly Protestant-Christian, with each of the denominations having its own "house" — separate headquarters that fosters its own particular religious practices and perspectives, yet unites in the common larger program facets offered by the institution. Thus there are Methodist, Presbyterian, Lutheran, and Baptist "houses" as well as a Catholic one. However, there has never been a Jewish "house" — until Henry and Edith Everett came along.

Some within the Jewish population at the institution met only for Shabbat services and for select occasions in an accommodating church. They were otherwise fully involved in the general life of the place. Jews as individuals were quite prominent at Chautauqua. At one time or another, the orchestra conductor was Jewish; the opera impresario was Jewish; the dance troupe manager was Jewish; the orchestra's first cellist was Jewish; some major financial contributors to the institution's annual fund were Jewish. These people functioned not as Jews but as non-Christian Chautauquans.

A Recent Development

The institution's huge amphitheater presents classical orchestral music some three times a week. An observation that seized my attention: after the concerts a bevy of people would regularly gather together for small talk. The give-and-take was usually animated. They would be talking about the quality or lack of quality of the performance and other matters of common concern. One could tell that they had a kind of natural comfort with each other. The group consisted of fellow Jews — a distinctive unit within the larger Chautauqua community. Their conversations echoed, their opinions emphatic, their gatherings lengthy and regular throughout the season; an "in-group" element seemed at play; a Jewish "tribe" was present, separate from the rest.

Henry and Edith Everett believed the time had come to openly and proudly establish a distinctive Jewish identity and presence at Chautauqua even as the other religious groups did. Their belief and logic were obviously compelling and the famously liberal leadership of Chautauqua was responsive to their proposal: the Everetts would provide $1.5 million to establish a Jewish "house" at the institution. This would serve not only as a place of Jewish worship but as a center of Jewish and religious activities, creatively programmed, widely varied, embracing of all Jews of whatever perspective, welcoming the participation of non-Jews—and more. And so, *The Everett Jewish Life Center* is now an established Jewish entity at the Chautauqua Institution.

I can see the flashes of righteous indignation on the faces of fellow Jews who are steeped in pride about their identity should questions be raised about the implications of a Jewish house at Chautauqua. Surely the institution should have a distinct Jewish presence along with fellow non-Jewish religionists!

So what is the problem? It is Jewish history and experience through the ages, especially in the areas of learning and culture in the context of the larger societies in which Jews have lived—when those societies were embracing. Emma Lazarus back in 1882 wrote that "Jews are the intensive form of any nationality whose language and customs they adopt." (My father regularly described the Jews as "the salt of the earth.")

Indeed, because the characteristic Jewish drive and talent and resources, honed by years of being actually or psychologically "outsiders," there was often the tendency to stand out as a distinct group, even to come to dominate in the realms of learning and culture, leadership and finance. Such condition, in turn, provoked unease and resentment on the part of the larger society, and included measures of containment.

While Jews represent but two percent of the general American population, they now constitute some twenty-five percent of

Chautauquans. This condition of prominence could conceivably come to pervade the entire Chautauqua Institution. Already, in fact, there are murmurings about a Jewish "ghetto" emerging at the institution. Such a condition could then witness the long hand of history reaching into Chautauqua in the years ahead and temporize such pervasiveness.

Now, I'm quite aware that the reader of this will probably bristle at the oversensitivity depicted. After all, our society affirms distinctiveness within its overall structure. I respect that kind of critique and try to back away due to its vehemence and emphatic assertions of Jewish pride, self-respect and the rest. After all, I, too, share that affirmative attitude. Yet my ambivalence persists…

In any case, The Everett Jewish Life Center adds significantly to the already heavy participation of the Jewish cohort in the general life and program of the Chautauqua Institution. The center is now in full operation, its varied and enriching, creative and ambitious activities emanating from a state-of-the-art, spacious and highly attractive physical facility, are as inevitable as the sun rising and setting each day. And, if history is to repeat itself, as it has so often in the past, so, too, the reaction?

———————————————

The Jewish love affair with education has continued in America. A New York Times *article on the training of real estate brokers notes the guidelines given for selling to different groups: "If they're rich, tell them about the country club, and the high quality of people they'll meet there. If they're a young couple buying their first home, emphasize the low property taxes. If they're Jews, tell them how good the school system is."*

PEOPLE IN THE U.S. ARMY

Upon graduation from the seminary, I entered the United States Army as a chaplain with the rank of first lieutenant (a prestigious rank as far as I was concerned!). Since this was in the still sensitive aftermath of the Korean War, the various seminaries had entered into an agreement with the military that they would provide the needed chaplains. Thus my seminary (JTS) required each of its incoming students to agree as a condition of admission into the rabbinical school to enter a branch of the Armed Forces for at least a two-year stint upon ordination.

And so, following a summer-long training period in Fort Slocum, a military base off the shore of Mount Vernon, New York, I was shipped off, along with my bride of two months, Leah, to Fort Chaffee, Arkansas, a faraway, unfamiliar locale deep in the American South. We lived off base in a small house in Fort Smith, a little ramshackle town. Coincidentally, the second president of the Jewish Theological Seminary, Cyrus Adler, was born in the neighboring town of Van Buren.

At Chaffee, I shared the chapel building with a Catholic priest and a Protestant minister in friendly and respectful personal and professional fashion. An interesting feature of the chapel ark was that it revolved: on Friday evening and Shabbat day, the ark housed the sefer Torah in its section, and for Sunday church services it was turned around to show the cross in its section. I always found that ark a powerful symbol of positive co-existence between Christian and Jew.

The Personalities

Chaplain (Lieutenant Colonel) Harry W. Webster

My supervisor was Chaplain Harry Webster, a kindly, devout Christian of the Christian and Missionary Alliance denomination. He managed his chaplains with warmth and tolerance and decidedly unmilitary (i.e., non-authoritarian) fashion. Once in discussing our religious beliefs, Webster indicated that he personally experienced Jesus in his life, whereupon I, with a bit of too much emphasis, challenged the notion of a human being believed to be divine. His reaction was mild, simply saying that this was his experience. I remember feeling that I'd gone a bit too far in challenging someone else's strong beliefs, and that more tolerance of other people's faith was called for on my part. I was twenty-six years old.

Chaplain (Major) J. Wilkinson Alsworth

A rare but memorable anti-Semitic encounter occurred at Chaffee with Chaplain (Major) J. Wilkinson Alsworth, a fundamentalist preacher from his hometown of Hattiesburg, Mississippi. When Chaplain Webster was away, Alsworth took charge. One day, armed with his new authority, he bounded into our chapel with a retinue, demanded that I salute him and that "this chapel needs cleaning up; you Jews need some straightening out." Startled, I did salute him, as army protocol required, but objected to his peremptory and condescending manner. "This is no way to talk to a fellow clergy colleague; besides, the chapel looks okay to me." Whereupon with disdainful anger he exited the chapel while indicating that he would report me to Chaplain Webster for "insubordination."

Alsworth indeed reported me to Webster, who called me into his office and, instead of a reprimand, simply said with his characteristic mild manner that one needs to understand where Alsworth was coming from but not to worry. The matter was dropped. This incident taught me three things: vestiges of anti-Semitism do exist in some American quarters; you do need to show respect for your "superiors" in the military; and it was clear that the military mindset did not square with mine.

Chaplain Billy Cox

I struck up a warm friendship with Chaplain Billy Cox, a Baptist preacher from the hardscrabble Arkansas countryside. Once he invited Leah and me to visit with him and his family overnight at his farm home. We slept in an ice-cold room, warmed ourselves in the morning by a wood-burning stove in the kitchen, toured the farm observing the cackling chickens, grunting pigs and lowing cows, and were taken by the fresh outdoor smells and the energy of the family members who worked the farm. When introducing his mother to us, Cox related that his "mama" rarely left the farm and once when she came with him to Little Rock and saw an elevator, she was startled; you see, she had never been in an elevator in her life!

Cox took us to his local Baptist church—an old-time fundamentalist one in which he had been reared. It was the Wednesday night worship gathering. Lasting some two and one-half hours, the preacher shouted out the gospel with unrestrained passion to the equally impassioned clapping response on the part of the worshippers. A feature of the proceedings was that a number of the congregants got down on their hands and knees, loudly "speaking in tongues" and vigorously pounding the church floor—this all to exorcise the evil spirit from their souls. Cox had briefed us about this and, with his typical wry humor, told us that he personally had departed from this practice—but that tradition is tradition.

A Catholic Priest

Another chaplain I became friendly with, a Catholic priest (alas, I forgot his name; I've been writing this chapter from memory after some fifty years after the experiences described). He was a mild and lonely man. He had been sent to a remote village in the hills of Colorado to pastor a flock of a mere fifty souls. "You will go where your bishop tells you to go," he told me. Then, fortunately, he was sent to Chaffee to serve the Catholic soldiers. There were times when he would disappear from his duties; I was told that whenever this occurs, one should go looking for him at the nearest bar in town and it's likely that he'd be found there.

My priest friend once invited me to accompany him on a hunting trip; he was looking for wild rabbits. I remember quite vividly the fierce look on his face as he held the rifle on his shoulder with his finger on the trigger, aimed at a scampering rabbit. I turned away as he shot the rabbit. When he picked it up, I asked what he was going to do with it. He said he would dump it somewhere. You see, it was the excitement of the hunt itself that was the purpose of the expedition. I learned another vital lesson from this experience and ever after invoked it when talking about the Jewish kashrut regimen with its proscription of hunting.

A Jewish Army Dentist

This man was assigned to oversee my chapel fund, which was used for various special needs for my work with the Jewish soldier constituency. He and especially his wife were extremely sensitive about Leah and me being too open and demonstrative about our Jewishness. On the various social occasions, "Mrs. Dentist" (I have forgotten her name) prodded Leah on the subject, asking, for example, "When a non-Jew asks you about what you do as a Jew, what do you say? I hope you're careful."

There were lessons I learned from the army experience: first, that some American Jews still "look over their shoulders" about their Jewishness in the larger America society, that the "galut mentality" often renders some overly sensitive about what gentiles think of Jews. Shemaryahu Levin, the Hebrew writer and Zionist leader, once said that "it is easier to take the Jew out of exile than to take exile out of the Jew."

Secondly, and on the other hand, I learned that Jews can sometimes be overly assertive, that the chutzpah which prompts some to wear their specialness on their sleeves can be grating and unproductive. I have always believed that a delicate balance between these two attitudes — self-affirmation and over-emphatic self-assertion is called for by Jews living in a predominantly non-Jewish society.

A NON-JEWISH ELDERHOSTEL COORDINATOR FOR NORTHERN CALIFORNIA

I was in San Francisco for a meeting of leaders of the regional Elderhostel program. This was a venture the University of Judaism was about to launch at its Los Angeles Mulholland campus conference grounds in Ojai. Many thousands of persons in their later years traveled all over the country to college and universities that offered programs of study in a wide variety of subject matter. A huge percentage of the participants were Jewish, as one would expect in a people who value education out of proportion to their numbers. Our administration felt that a distinctive Jewish program within the Elderhostel network was called for; we would offer a wide selection of courses in Bible, Jewish history, Jewish thought, Jewish arts, etc.

During the San Francisco conference I detailed our plans to the Elderhostel coordinators for our region, who had been conducting a wide variety of programs in northern California. Instead of expressing some concern about possible competition for participants, she was unusually positive about what I told her. "What a good idea," she said effusively. "I'm glad that you'll have Jewish students."

When I asked her why she was so positive, she said the Jewish participants were very demanding; they were constantly complaining about the accommodations, about the food, about the quality of the instructors, about the substance of the classes. On the whole they were a difficult group to please. As I listened to the coordinator's edgy words I began to understand that since the University of Judaism's program would have a goodly number of Jewish participants, we had better go the extra mile in providing solid learning substance as well as physical amenity.

A Jewish "tribe."

A RABBINIC BLESSING ON
NEW ORLEANS' ANTIQUE ROW

We Jews are understandably sensitive when encountering incidents of anti-Semitism. However, more often than not, we take for granted incidents of philosemitism, when non-Jews express strongly positive sentiments about Jews, Judaism and Israel. In America, especially, we need to appreciate more keenly the enormous measure of goodwill non-Jews harbor toward us. A personal story informs this observation.

I was in attendance at a national continuing education conference in New Orleans, Louisiana. During a break in the proceedings, I sought out (as is my habit while traveling) the antique district in New Orleans in search of old, often discarded items I might convert into Judaica. I entered a fascinating-looking antique shop, searched around, asked the proprietor some questions, and chose an antiquated oval-shaped silver butter dish with an eye to converting it into a spice box for use at the *havdalah* ceremony.

Apparently having detected something about me from my questions, the ruddy Italian proprietor, with dark flashing eyes, asked me, "Are you Jewish?" I replied that I was. He then proceeded with a passionate comment: every time I hear people talking negatively about Israel, I become furious…the Jew went through so much…he's entitled to a land of his own…let him live in peace…we Christians owe the Jews…the world owes them so much…let the Jew have his due…and on and on. I smiled and thanked him for his warm and affirming comments, finalized my butter dish purchase, gave him a bear hug and said goodbye.

I had proceeded out of the antique shop onto the old New Orleans sidewalk bustling with people, whereupon the shop proprietor hurriedly appeared, stopped me in my tracks and asked: "By the way, are you a rabbi?"

A bit taken aback, I replied, "Yes, I am."

"Rabbi," he urged, "please give me a blessing."

Deciding to make the most of the situation, I asked him to bow his head. I then mustered the full and dignified gravity in my rabbinic arsenal, raised my arms, placed my hands on his bowed head, and proclaimed the priestly blessing contained in Numbers 6:24-26, in Hebrew and then in English:

> May the Lord bless you and keep you; may the Lord cause His countenance to shine upon you and be gracious to you; may the Lord lift His face unto you and grant you peace. Amen.

After lifting my hands off his gray, hoary head, there was a moment of silence.

And then, with tears in his eyes and a glow on his face, the man looked at me earnestly and said, "Thank you, thank you, Rabbi—you and your people are a blessing."

He then turned, went back into his antique shop, and I proceeded back to my conference with my old butter dish/ potential Jewish spice box.

The Jew has friends in America.

PART TWO

– Chapter Nine –

EARLY INFLUENTIALS

We well know how determinative early experiences in one's life can be. They help mold one's mindset, one's sense of self, one's personal and professional choices, all of which can be long-lasting. And when these early experiences are recollected they appear brand new and do, indeed, shed light on the life of the recollector who muses about the past in later years. This section portrays some of these experiences of mine through the prism of a set of people I call "influentials."

RAV FRANKEL: A FIFTH-GRADE HEBREW TEACHER

The classroom was filled with some twenty-five ten-year-olds. The youngsters were in school six days a week, each day from 9:00 a.m. to 6:00 p.m. (Judaic studies were from 9 a.m. to 3 p.m., with secular studied from 3 to 6 p.m.) Sunday was a full day and Friday ended at 1:00 p.m. since it was *Erev Shabbos*, the period before the onset of the day of rest. The only respite from study was a 20-minute recess in mid-morning and a forty-five-minute lunch period.

Thankfully, during the summer we were off from school. It was a rough educational regimen for the kids, but they knew of no alternatives so they accepted the situation with minimal grumbling. Such was the condition at Yeshiva Rabbi Chaim Berlin in the Brownsville section of Brooklyn, New York.

I was one of those ten-year-olds—but also one of them who grumbled at times in the Judaic studies classes. I preferred the intense twenty-minute recess of punch ball on the then relatively safe roadway.

I liked to allow my mind to wander during the endless repetition of the same Talumudic text. Most of the time I caught on, but not frequently enough for my teacher of Jewish studies—Rav Frankel. He often admonished me in exasperation. Yiddish was the only language we used in class, so this is how it came out:

דו האָסט אַ גוט'ן קאָפ יענק'ל, ס'אין אַ שאָט אז דו ניצט דאָס נישט

You have a good head, Yankel, it's a pity you don't use it.

For an acerbic yet benign teacher to tell a ten-year-old that he has a "good head" has consequences. Throughout the years, whenever I had doubts about my "good head," Rav Frankel's admonition restored my confidence and spurred me on to use what the teacher thought was "good."

אָמַר רַ׳ סִימוֹן: אֵין לְךָ
כָּל עֵשֶׂב וְעֵשֶׂב שֶׁאֵין לוֹ מַזָּל בָּרָקִיעַ שֶׁמַּכֶּה אוֹתוֹ וְאוֹמֵר לוֹ: גְּדָל!

There is not a single blade of grass that has not its own star in heaven that strikes it and says: "grow."

—Genesis Rabbah 10:16

B.J. COOPER:
AN EIGHTH-GRADE GENERAL STUDIES TEACHER

You are thirteen years old and you are at home marking the test papers of your classmates. They are exams in spelling. Your teacher gave you these test papers to grade because he knew you could spell and because he trusted you not to alter anything as a favor to a particular classmate.

How do you think that experience made the eighth grader feel? How do you think the thirteen-year-old felt about that teacher?

I was that eighth grader/thirteen-year-old at Yeshiva Chaim Berlin (my parochial elementary school) in Brooklyn, New York; and that teacher was B.J. Cooper, our instructor in secular studies. The test paper experience was an affirmation of me as a person, a confidence builder as a student which has stayed with me throughout the years. That teacher evoked reverent feelings in me for him personally and respect for an educator who influenced my professional life in significant ways.

B.J. Cooper was a career teacher of English in a neighborhood high school; he taught there mornings and early afternoons, and then came to us from 3:00 to 6:00 p.m. He was in his fifties, stern in demeanor, erect in posture, articulate, master of his subject, and a disciplinarian. Above all, he taught with clarity and precision—with a method that was graphic and comprehensible. A student had to be mighty slow, or unfocused or so resistant to B.J. Cooper's ways as to not catch on.

He taught us how to read and write and spell and the basics of grammar. He taught sentence structure in the form of diagrams; from these diagrams I learned what a noun, pronoun, verb, adverb, and adjective were, and how to use them in writing—knowledge ever after in my possession.

Over the years, this discipline helped in the writing of articles for my synagogue publications, scholarly essays, educational

pieces and course descriptions for continuing education cata-
logues. I know there are other ways to effectively teach sentence
structure and grammar, but this was our way back then with its
results deeply embedded in my reading and writing arsenal.

For our eighth-grade class, B.J. Cooper instituted another unusual practice. For a pause in our studies, he had the entire class
stand up at our seats, the classroom door opened (the windows,
too, when not too cold outside) and proceeded to lead us in a
stretching exercise. "Both arms up, rise on your toes, breathe
deeply"—this all to a rhythmic chant.

Something in me resonated to this exercise and I took to it as
I did to our teacher's English lessons. Noting my attitude, he
asked me to lead the exercise for the entire class. (Others, on a
rotating basis, were asked to lead it as well.) While this might
seem a trivial matter now, it was then of enormous value in bol-
stering my sense of self.

Once during a snow-filled winter day at recess time, I spotted
B.J. Cooper, bundled in his heavy coat, fur hat, scarf around his
neck, walking in his usual confident stride across the street. As
usual, we youngsters were scampering around and throwing
snowballs in all directions.

Then some of my classmates began throwing snowballs at B.J.
Cooper—my teacher who I (surreptitiously) admired and respected. Spontaneously I cringed as I watched this disrespectful
scene. I did not join my classmates in hurling those snowballs at
our teacher; but neither did I intervene and demand that they
stop doing that terrible thing. After all, I didn't want to appear
like a "teacher's pet" and endure the derision of my classmates.

To this day—well over a half-century later—and throughout
the years, I consider holding back from speaking out on that cold
winter day one of the shortcomings of my life. In fact, without fail,
every time I think about B.J. Cooper and all he meant to me, and
then about that snowball incident, I am seized by a feeling of remorse and regret. But—I learned from that mistake. It is to speak
up in dissent when legitimate authority figures are degraded.

B.J. Cooper: thanks for evoking in me deep respect for teachers. Thanks for getting me in the habit of encouraging others to acquire and revere mentors. Thanks for demonstrating how a teacher can hone a student's skills which can last a lifetime. Thanks for building confidence in me and many others. Thanks for everything.

Few have yet fully realized the wealth of talent and potential, the hidden capacity to think clearly and discern critically, to sympathize with others hidden in the mind and soul of the young.

The task of the true educator is to unlock that treasure, to stimulate the youngster's impulses and call forth his/her best and ablest—and noblest—tendencies.

—Emma Goldman, *Living My Life*

SAM LEE AND HARRY COHEN: A WORK ETHIC

On the street level of our apartment house on Howard Avenue in Brooklyn, New York, two establishments were located—one was a Chinese hand laundry, and the second a candy store. Sam Lee, who was proprietor of his place, laundered men's shirts and stood at his ironing board for a minimum of twelve hours a day, ironing the shirts one by one.

This was the only thing he did each day besides packaging the shirts and collecting his fees. He did this same thing six and one-half days each week year after year after year. I remember him disappearing form his shop on Sunday afternoons, the only time he took off from work, and telling me once that he went to Chinatown in Manhattan to be with his fellow Chinese.

Harry Cohen ran the candy store, a staple establishment at the time that dispensed all manner of sweets, small cakes, seltzer with or without syrup, gum and various other items the people of Brooklyn consumed between regular meals.

Harry's store was open some fifteen hours a day, seven days a week. With partial relief from his wife, who attended to their household and children located in an apartment in back of the store, Harry was ever-present running his establishment. Dealing with the demanding adult customers and often rambunctious juvenile customers, dispensing, collecting, ordering and accounting, he was a visibly tired man practically all the time.

I remember the weary look on his face, the reddish hands with their broken nails, and his lumbered gait as he walked back and forth behind the narrow aisle in back of the fountain counter that divided him from his customers. Indeed, he was always on his feet. This was Harry Cohen's scenario year after year after year.

The scenes described above were observed by me from ages eight to eighteen. I write this vignette a half-century later. Throughout the years I've never ceased being astonished at, and instructed by, the work ethic of Sam Lee and Harry Cohen—and full of admiration for their patience and persistence in grappling with their endless toil and travail.

Sometimes nothing is harder in life than just to endure. There are two types of strength. There is the strength of the wind that sways the mighty oak, and there is the strength of the oak that withstands the power of the wind. There is the strength of the locomotive that pulls the heavy train across the bridge, and there is the strength of the bridge that holds up the weight of the train. One is active strength, the other is passive strength. One is the power to keep going, the other is the power to keep still. One is the strength by which we overcome, the other is the strength by which we endure.

—Harold Phillips

SADIE GOLDSTEIN AND HOW PEOPLE USED TO BE CALLED TO THE PHONE

In the Brownsville section of Brooklyn, New York, where I lived in the 1940s, very few people had their own phones. The only place on our street that had a telephone was the candy store located at the street level of our apartment house on Howard Avenue. How, then, were people to reach others via a telephone?

This is how it worked:

The phone would ring in the candy store. The caller would ask to speak to Sadie Goldstein, who lived in apartment 3D, on the third floor of 530 Howard Avenue. Please call her to the telephone, urged the caller.

If I or another youngster was in the store at the time, Harry Cohen, the proprietor who answered the phone, would ask the youngster to go to Mrs. Goldstein's place and tell her that Mabel Shwartz was on the phone and wanted to talk to her.

This little errand fell into my hands frequently. I would proceed down Howard Avenue, four apartment houses from the candy store, climb up three floors and knock on Sadie Goldstein's door. "Who is it?" she'd ask. When I told her of my mission, she'd respond, "I'm getting my coat on and I'll be down in a few minutes." I then would proceed back to the candy store.

Some ten minutes later, Sadie Goldstein would come huffing and puffing to the store, take hold of the phone receiver and speak for some ten minutes to Mabel Shwartz. When Sadie emerged from the phone booth, she rummaged through her *pockabook* (i.e., purse), fished out three cents and handed them to me for my effort.

This entire phone experience lasted some fifteen minutes to arrange the connection, another ten minutes for actual talk, throw in another five minutes for unavoidable delays and you get a good idea about phone usage in the 1940s.

Today, with the touch of a button on a handheld cell phone, taken out of one's pocket in the midst of a grassy park, one can speak to a relative or friend or business associate located anywhere in the world.

MY FATHER: LOUIS SHECHTER
FROM SBOROV, POLAND, TO AMERICA

For the first six months of the year 1954, Dad kept a diary contained in four small booklets. With his old-fashioned fountain pen filled with dark blue ink, he recorded in great detail the trials and tribulations of his illness while confined to a room in the Veterans Administration Hospital in Brooklyn, New York (Dad had served as a corporal in the U.S. Army during World War I). His script was slanted to the left, dignified and stylized, and appeared like Old English. It was extraordinary to behold, as was the clarity and color of his writing.

In one section of the diary, he writes about his life as a young boy in the village of Sborov, Poland in the early 1900s. He never had much. His parents were poor. His father managed to scrape together a "ranish" (the equivalent of a dollar) a day, which he gave to his mother. With this, he writes, "there was enough to cook a soup with a piece of meat, and for two 'greatzers' (pennies) *kashe* (groats) with lima beans—that was the main dish—with black bread along with a large onion chopped with *shmaltz* (goose fat). And for dessert a couple of cooked prunes. That was about it every day for one person, a growing boy of ten.

Then Dad asserts, "I observed all that with a burning desire that as soon as I grew I would learn a trade and get out of this decrepit town of Sborov and make my own living." He continues that his studies were not as up to par with the other boys as he would have liked. He didn't feel like sitting on a hard bench and studying, having to eat the end of a piece of bread with garlic rubbed in it for dessert. He wanted very much to study, but the house was too poor.

And so Dad left Sborov at the age of seventeen for America. He learned the printing trade, married my mother, opened a printing shop in what was then "rural" Englewood, New Jersey, and fathered three children, Evelyn, Harriet and me.*

The diary records that as a young man full of life and energy and ambition, Dad would have nothing stand in his way to make a good living. He remembers buying his "first brand new Ford open-roof car, getting ready to go for the Fourth of July to the mountains in the Catskills." At first he bought a modest house and later a more upscale one directly across from a park.

Dad was a typical young immigrant Jew at the time. He was eager to become "Americanized" as quickly and fully as possible. His strikingly handsome appearance and stylish mode of dress, his regular reading of the *New York Times,* his preoccupation with socialist politics, his admiration for America as the proverbial "goldene medina," were unabashedly integral to his persona.

He had somewhat unconventional ways; he once dug a deep hole in our backyard and set a large bathtub into it and proceeded to populate it with some half-dozen good-sized fish. On another occasion he built a sukkah behind our garage and arranged for him and me at age seven to sleep in it overnight. I doubt there were many sukkot at the time (the 1930s) in the state of New Jersey, let alone father and son sleeping in one. He was a determined, strong-willed, hot-tempered and decisive man— indeed.

Though he parted from some of the religious ways of the old country, he was inevitably Jewish at his core. His synthesis of the traditional and the modern manifested itself in an interesting way: he wanted me to become a *Conservative* rabbi. Why? Because you'll talk of contemporary issues and deliver your sermons in English; you'll wear a gown while conducting services; you'll adopt a dignified bearing; your *temple* (*not shul*) will be physically impressive and be characterized by order and

* At age eight I moved with the family from Englewood, New Jersey, to Brooklyn, New York, due to Dad's illness. That story is told elsewhere in my book *Journey of a Rabbi.*

decorum, neatness and cleanliness, and the congregants will be quiet and reverential. This is the way things are done in America.

Fast Forward…The Sanctuary of Congregation B'nai Israel in Pittsburgh Where I Served as a *Conservative* Rabbi for a Decade

The synagogue structure was designed by the prominent architect Henry Hornbostel in the mid-1920s, a period of bold and imaginative fashioning of religious structures. There was only one other synagogue in the Pittsburgh region designed by Hornbostel, the striking Reform Rodeph Shalom Temple on Fifth Avenue and Morewood in Oakland.

B'nai Israel is housed in a unique building. Set atop a grassy slope along residential Negley Avenue, the structure has a massive stone rotunda and tall arched stained-glass windows. The main building, a three-tiered drum form with Roman arches, features an entry porch with a vaulted ceiling constructed of Guastivino tiles; the tiles frame a stone-etched double tablet containing the first initial letters of the Ten Commandments. The main space is a wood truss rotunda with a span of one hundred twenty feet.

When Leah and I came to the congregation for an interview for the job as rabbi. I was only thirty-five years old and Leah thirty-one. After being duly impressed with the building's exterior, we entered the sanctuary; it was for us an awesome experience, and we remember saying to each other that our interview would give us an enjoyable experience, but that there could be no way we would occupy this pulpit.

I also recall thinking how my father would have reacted had he seen the place and the possibility that his son, Jackie, might actually preside as rabbi in such a sanctuary: feelings of pride mixed with astonishment would have overwhelmed him. I mused that as an immigrant from an impoverished shtetl (small town) in Poland, a large and staid American Conservative synagogue such as this was his ideal of integrating into America as a religious Jew—and his son being part of its realization no less!

The sanctuary seated one thousand fifty people. It had a massive, tall dome "clothed" with dark blue material delicately decorated in a gold-leaf Persian motif. A huge chandelier hung down into the space from the center of the ceiling. The wide pulpit had seats for the laity and what can only be described as a "throne-like" chair for the rabbi. Alas, the cantor's chair was less impressive which caused me some difficulty. The *bimah* also contained a matching set of two huge candelabras that graced its corners. The Holy Ark doors were fashioned from carved wood revealing a variety of intricate designs. A choir loft was built into the right upper wall; in the sanctuary back framing the stained-glass windows hung nine decorative lamps. A giant support beam jutted from the ceiling, anchoring the entire circular space. A band around the upper ceiling facing the back of the sanctuary contained the following Hebrew dictum from the book of Micah 6:8:

הִגִּיד לְךָ אָדָם מַה טּוֹב וּמָה ה' דוֹרֵשׁ מִמְּךָ כִּי אִם עֲשׂוֹת מִשְׁפָּט וְאַהֲבַת חֶסֶד וְהַצְנֵעַ לֶכֶת עִם אֱלֹהֶיךָ

The corresponding band around the ceiling facing the front of the sanctuary contained the translation:

He has told thee, O man, what is good and what the Lord requires of thee: Only to do justice, and to love mercy, and to walk humbly with thy God.

I sat on the bimah of that Congregation B'nai Israel's sanctuary in Pittsburgh for ten years embracing the riveting scene surrounding me which characterized a modern Conservative synagogue; I have always wished my father had lived long enough to witness that scene with his own eyes.

BEA BLEIFELD: AN AFFIRMING AUNT

It was graduation time from the elementary school of Yeshiva Rabbi Chaim Berlin in Brooklyn, New York. I was thirteen years old. My parents, sisters, aunts and uncles and grandparents were all present. For my family this was an important milestone. My aunt Bea (Beatrice Bleifeld, my mother's sister) was present.

Now, Aunt Bea was a special persona. She was physically attractive; she had a flashing smile, expressive eyes and a confident gait. Most characteristic about her was her articulate speech, sparkling conversation and ready wit. She and her husband, Dick, were especially popular in the family; we were all drawn to them and they were always welcoming and embracing of the young members of the family. Words from Aunt Bea were always welcome and valued.

The scene at the elementary school graduation: I was walking down the steps of the school at the ceremony's conclusion when Aunt Bea seized my hand, looked directly at me with those riveting eyes of hers and, with a look of love and pride radiating from her whole presence, said to me, "Jackie, you're a good and smart boy."

Lives can be positively affected with a single look radiating from the face of another. Someone once wrote that "there is power in the direct glance of a sincere and loving human soul." Aunt Bea's look at me at the milestone of a young boy's life, accompanied with her comment, "Jackie, you're a good and smart boy," have stayed with me throughout my days. For, you see, even if it was not really true, I believed it.

Much of our face-to-face time with people is spent looking at their faces. The signals they send out with their eyes play a vital part in revealing their thoughts and attitudes. In fact, of all our body language signals, the eyes reveal our thoughts and emotions most accurately. They're placed in the strongest focal position on the body, and because the pupils respond uncon-sciously to stimuli they can't be artificially manipulated or controlled. Your eyes are the gateway to the soul and reveal what's going on inside of you.

Communication through our eyes is a two-way street. In our complex society, we are dependent on one another. Eye contact helps regulate conversation. Some people instinctively know how to use their eyes to garner sympathy or to deliver a message. We look at the role that eyes play in communicating your feelings and intentions. Over the course of your life you discover how to use your eyes to command attention, display interest, show disapproval, create feelings.

—Westside Toastmasters, Santa Monica, CA,
The Eyes Have It, Chapter Eight

SIDOR BELARSKY: JEWISH FOLK SINGER

I was reared in a traditional Jewish environment from age eight on after our family moved from Englewood, New Jersey, to Brooklyn, New York due to my father's illness. Thus throughout late elementary and high school I attended the Orthodox Yeshiva in Brooklyn's Brownsville section. With unfailing regularity, Shabbat and holiday meals were taken at the table of pious grandparents (my mother's parents). Religious ritual was meticulously practiced. Indeed, traditional Jewishness was the dominant force.

During the last two years of high school, this Jewish way began to erode. When college time came, I opted out and into the secular world of City College of New York, intending to minimize the ties with my traditional upbringing. I wanted fresh air, the experience of the larger world, the opportunity to pursue my natural interests in music, art and English literature.

At the end of my freshman year at college, I took a summer job at a hotel in Seagate—a resort area on the Atlantic coast. It was a job which yielded some needed monies, as well as exposure to an exciting, free-wheeling secular world.

One night a Yiddish folk singer, Sidor Belarsky, appeared on the hotel stage. With great skill and passion he rendered a set of Hebrew and Yiddish ballads about love and family, tradition and learning, suffering and hope, and pride. At that very place and hour something clicked inside my heart and head with startling clarity: I felt connected with the content and spirit of Belarsky's songs and the feeling with which he sang.

I felt warm inside. I felt that this was who I really am as a person and as a Jew. The Jewish words and music which poured forth from that hotel stage corresponded to my true feelings and interests. I did not identify with the sensuous vulgarity which dominated the Seagate resort. I didn't belong in that world.

The next morning, I called my uncle, Rabbi Herschel Schacter, a prominent Yeshiva University alumnus, and asked him to facilitate my enrollment in Yeshiva University, where I knew I belonged.

A moment of personal discovery.

ALTER LANDESMAN: POINTING THE WAY

Throughout my high school and college years, I attended the religious services of the Orthodox Young Israel, which was housed in the community center known as the Hebrew Educational Society (HES) in the Brownsville section of Brooklyn, New York. The director of the HES was a Conservative rabbi, Alter Landesman.

Rabbi Landesman, a long-time alumnus and passionate supporter of the Jewish Theological Seminary and the Conservative Movement, embraced the Orthodox Young Israel as part of HES's all-inclusive mission, even though he often dissented from some of the group's religious views and practices.

During my college years, when religious services concluded and we young people were on the way out of the building, Rabbi Landesman, who did not attend the services, would stand outside his office and greet those who would be willing to shake his hand and accept a "Shabbat Shalom." I was among those who did. Something within me prompted interest in the man and what he was about. He was short and bald with a rasping voice, yet always immaculately dressed, dignified in manner, highly intelligent, affirming and embracing. To this day I remember the soft warmth of his handshake.

He detected my interest and so regularly invited me into his well-appointed office to chat. He showed me his extensive Judaic library, talked about Israel and general Jewish affairs of the day. Included in our chats were comments about the people and concerns of the Jewish Theological Seminary about which at the time I was dimly aware.

On three different occasions, he excitedly swept off his desk a book recently published. Look, he said, Abraham Joshua Heschel's *The Earth is the Lord's*. On another occasion it was Heschel's *The Sabbath,* and yet again it was Heschel's *Man is Not Alone.* "Look what seminary professors are producing," he would enthusiastically say. "Look at the profundity of these books. Look how lyrical yet truly relevant for our time these are.

Read them, you'll like them," he urged. And I did.

These experiences with Rabbi Landesman were among the factors that pointed me to the path enroute to the Jewish Theological Seminary and the Conservative Movement.

Director of the HES for four decades, Rabbi Landesman was a major leader of the life in Brownsville, which at its height was the center of some four hundred thousand people, seventy-five percent of them Jewish. He authored a marvelous volume about the place, *Brownsville: The Birth, Development and Passing of a Jewish Community in New York.*

This was a locus of my youth and early maturity where I was privileged to encounter Rabbi Landesman at a crucial juncture in a young man's life. Indeed, I entered the Jewish Theological Seminary and was ordained a rabbi in 1957—an item recorded in the Brownsville book. My copy contains the following inscription:

To: Rabbi Jack Shechter, in esteem and affection

Alter F. Landesman

Over the years, Rabbi Landesman would tell me how proud he was of one of his "Young Israel boys." My recollection of him personally, along with his *Brownsville* book, encases appreciative memory of him, and his book stands tall on a shelf in my library.

The nobleman has taken us by the hand, and its scent lingers.

Talmud, Z'vachim 96b

SHLOMO SCHULZINGER, BILHA SHUDOWSKY
AND TWO SEMINARY PROFESSORS:
LEARNING VIA "TERROR"

During college years I attended Camp Massad, a Hebrew-speaking, Zionist-oriented summer camp located near Tannersville, PA. The first summer I worked as a waiter serving some thirty youngsters three meals a day. Special programs in Jewish current events and ideologies as well as socializing were made available to the waiter staff of which I took advantage.

Shlomo Shulzinger, a native of Israel, was director of the camp. His flowing white hair, sparkling eyes and commanding demeanor were matched with a fervent love for the homeland and absolute commitment to the use of the Hebrew language in all camp activities. He had peremptory ways and when he shouted out his orders, it was often with a temper that pierced right through the system of his auditors. The staff was disciplined, the camp bunks and grounds well kept, and the program extremely effective. A Massad summer was an experience never to be forgotten.

Shlomo apparently recognized something in me. One day late in May I received a phone call at home: it was Shlomo Shulzinger. I immediately got the jitters because talking to him on the phone, let alone when in his physical presence, was a happening. He said to me in his clipped Israeli Hebrew:

יַעֲקֹב, אֲנִי רוֹצֶה שֶׁתִּהְיֶה רֹאשׁ הַמֶּלְצָרִים הַקַּיִץ

Yakov, I want you to be head of the waiters this summer.

He said I needed to organize the waiter's assignments, their work schedule, eat with them, make sure they participated in the after-work cultural activities, assure their tent bunks were clean and orderly, etc. All this was to be conducted only and consistently and uncompromisingly in *Ivrit*—in Hebrew. His stipend was relatively generous.

I listened to Shlomo's rapid-fire Hebrew in stunned silence, and finally blurted out in hesitant Hebrew:

אֲנִי חוֹשֵׁב שָׁאוּכַל לְמַלֵּא אֶת הַתַּפְקִיד שֶׁתֵּאַרְתָּ אֲבָל לְדַבֵּר
עִבְרִית כָּל הַזְמַן קָשֶׁה לִי

I think that I would be able to do the job you described, but to speak Hebrew all the time is difficult for me.

It's true, I continued, I had a Yeshiva education, but it was textual Hebrew, not spoken Hebrew. To this Shlomo responded that I had a month to study up on my Hebrew and get ready for the job. Remember, יַעֲקֹב, רַק עִבְרִית (Yakov, only Hebrew). Whereupon Shlomo didn't even wait for my assent to the job. He assumed I agreed and hung up the phone. I did agree; after all, Shlomo Shulzinger himself was giving me the job.

I panicked. I got hold of the Massad dictionary, which contained everyday Hebrew vocabulary for food, sports, clothing, etc., and practically memorized that dictionary containing hundreds of Hebrew words. I found a booklet containing common phrases and idioms for everyday use and swallowed them. Then I got tables of conjugations of basic words, which got me up to par on the Hebrew tenses: present, past, future, imperative and reflexive. Throughout the month of June prior to camp opening I studied and practiced all of the above. How else could I face Shlomo Shulzinger when the time came?

Who says terror cannot motivate learning a spoken language!

Fast Forward: It is Eighteen Years later; I'm Now a Rabbi in Pittsburgh; I Have Three Sons, Reuven, Age Twelve, David, Age Ten, and Judah, Age Eight

Camp Massad summers in the 1950s had been highly influential experiences during my college years with the emphasis on Hebrew, Zionism, Jewish culture and religious practice. Now in the 1970s, I wanted my boys to imbibe something of the positive experience I had had at Massad.

And so, I got on the phone and called Shlomo Shluzinger. "Do you remember me, Shlomo?", I asked. "*Betach*" (of course) was the enthusiastic response, and in his signature rapid-fire Hebrew, proceeds to say how good it was to have had me at Massad in those early years. I realized I had to speak Hebrew with Shlomo, so I told him in my rusty spoken version that I had three sons and wanted them to go to Massad, though, it would be a bit difficult financially. "Yaakov," said Shlomo, "send me your three boys and pay whatever you can. I could use more Shechters in my camp."

And so it was: The boys spent full eight-week summers at Camp Massad in Tannersville, PA—Reuven, five times, in 1971, 1972, 1973, 1974 and 1975...David, four times, in 1971, 1973, 1974 and 1975...Judah, three times, in 1973, 1974 and 1975.

Every July I would fly our three sons from Pittsburgh, PA to Tannersville, PA for the Massad experience. I remember the first time I introduced Judah, age 10, to Rivka Shulzinger (Shlomo's wife) upon arrival at camp. Rivka bombarded the poor lad with her quick, clipped Hebrew greeting along with a wave of instructions. Judah just stood there listening, befuddled. I thought for sure that Judah would urge me to take him back home with me to Pittsburgh. He didn't; in fact, he imbibed the spirit of the place, including the Hebrew, over the years as did Reuven and David.

Now back to motivation for learning.

Bilha Shudowsky was Shlomo Shulzinger's sister. She was in charge of the food service and kitchen staff at Massad. She was my "boss" when I served as head waiter. She was a vigorous woman, very demanding, with a booming voice that was often heard over the רָם קוֹל, the loudspeaker, throughout the campgrounds: יַעֲקֹב, בֹּא לְחֲדַר הָאֹכֶל, "Yakov, come to the dining room." She did have a benign streak in her which she revealed to me now and then. She was charged with enforcing Shlomo's dictum about the consistent use of Hebrew. Most of all, Bilha's piercing voice, meticulous standards for order, promptness and diligence, and demanding manner provoked me to organize and implement quite well my work as head of the waiters. Indeed, it was at Camp Massad that I discovered an affinity for organization and administration that has characterized my life's work as rabbi and educator.

Who says that (benign) terror cannot motivate learning to be an administrator!

Professors Lieberman and Ginzberg

During my student days at the Jewish Theological Seminary, I once undertook to read the Torah portion of *Yitro* in the traditional manner: directly from the scroll, without the Hebrew vowels, and with the standard *trop*—cantillation. This took place in the seminary synagogue, attended by many members of the institution's distinguished faculty.

The standard practice was for Dr. Saul Lieberman, one of the world's great Talmudic scholars, to stand on one side of the lectern, and Dr. H. L. Ginsberg, a renowned Bible expert, on the other side. I stood between them. They both listened intently as I chanted, looking for the slightest error in pronunciation or chant.

It was the vision of those two demanding professors that pushed me to prepare with special focus the Torah reading of the Sidra *Yitro*. I made not one mistake when the time came. And more: that biblical portion, its pronunciation and cantillation, has been embedded in my mind and psyche ever since.

Who says that terror cannot motivate mastery of a Torah reading?

Modern educators stress that "positive reinforcement," warm and patient prodding and as the Vilna Gaon put it, "conveying information easily and agreeably" are the most effective teaching methodologies; indeed, these are, it is claimed, the factors that motivate a student to learn.

Question: in light of the above vignettes, is that all there is to it?

– Chapter Ten –

ZAYDEH:
A CONSEQUENTIAL GRANDFATHER

In one of his books, Robert Fulghum tells about the things in life he doesn't have that he really wants. He says he'd like to be able to see the world through someone else's mind and eyes for just one day. There's a morning in the summer of 1984 he'd like to live over just as it was. He'd like to speak ten languages well enough to understand the humor of another culture. He'd like to talk to Socrates and watch Michelangelo sculpt David.

Most of all, Fulghum says, he'd like to have a living grandfather. He never knew his; both were lost to him in the vicissitudes
of life. In the fairy tale factory of his mind, he imagines that if he
had a grandfather, he'd be old and wise and truly grand.

Fulghum had no such grandfather, but I did, in real life, and
he was, indeed, old and wise and truly grand. His name was
Pinchas Schechter. I called him Zaydeh, in the Yiddish. I harbor,
vivid, energizing memories of him to this day still—over a half
century since his passing.

Unlike Fulghum, who conjured up in his imagination all
manner of wise deeds by his grandfather on his behalf, I insist,
as I proceed in this memoir, that nothing I say is the product of
the imagination, of nostalgia or exaggeration. It was Grandfather
as he really was and as he affected me. Honest.

The full story of what brought us together and our numerous
encounters throughout my youth into college years is told in my
book, *Journey of a Rabbi*. Here I focus on but a few items which
are, for me, special.

AN IMMIGRANT IN MANCHESTER, NEW HAMPSHIRE

Zaydeh arrived with Miriam and the children in America in 1903. When they embarked at Ellis Island, Zaydeh was told by the leaders of New York Jewry that the town of Manchester, New Hampshire, needed a *schochet*. And so, he moved the family there.

Once Zaydeh started an account of this early experience in Yiddish and then suddenly launched into English, I was startled. He spoke without the usual immigrant's guttural sound but with the English "r." It was good English! He looked and sounded like Abraham Lincoln what with his beard and stately demeanor. He said he had to learn English to "get along" in America. He soon lapsed back into Yiddish and it was but once in a while thereafter that I heard his English again.

I learned later about Zaydeh's Manchester sojourn. As director of the New England region the United Synagogue, headquartered in Boston, I had occasion to visit our Manchester congregation. At one of our meetings, an officer of the congregation asked me if I was related to a Pinchas Schechter, who had been a *schochet* in the city years ago and whom his grandfather had known.

I told him that I was Pinchas Schechter's grandson. Hearing this, he bounded out of our meeting, went to his home and came back with a picture. Lo and behold, here was Zaydeh with his then dark brown beard, high hat, starched shirt collar under his black coat, sitting, of all places, in an open-air coach drawn by a horse!

Yes, indeed, Zaydeh and Bubbeh and family resided in Manchester, New Hampshire, in the early days upon coming to America from Sborov in Poland at the turn of the twentieth century. And it was there in New England where he learned to speak English—almost like a native. I asked the man if he would give me the picture of Zaydeh in that horse-drawn coach; he gave it to me and it is now secure in my archives.

How did Zaydeh become a schochet?

My uncle Herschel Schacter (Zaydeh's son, my mother's brother) once told me how it came to be: while yet in Europe, Zaydeh had married Miriam, the daughter of Mr. Shimmelman. The couple had two children. Zaydeh has been living off the largess of his father-in-law. Mr. Shimmelman felt the time had come for his son-in-law to make his own living and support his family. He suggested that Pinchas become a schochet. *The young man recoiled. "I'm afraid; it's such a big responsibility; if I made a mistake the whole town would be eating* traif *(non-kosher food)."*

Mr. Shimmelman suggested they go see the Stretiner Rebbe, their spiritual leader, for guidance. They presented their cases. The rebbe looked at Pinchas and said:

ווער דען זאָל זיין אַ שׁוֹחֵט - דער וואָס האָט נישט קיין מוֹרָא

"Who then should be a schochet, someone who is not afraid?" You need to be "afraid" in this task, explained the rebbe; this will make you careful, meticulous, and "fearful" of making mistakes as you perform your task. And so, Zaydeh became a schochet.

OUR "SHUL"/SYNAGOGUE

Our place of worship and study was called a *shtibel*, Yiddish for "room." It was actually the converted bottom floor of a house containing the prayer and study areas. The upstairs was for the women worshippers. The shul's name was *Reyim Ahuvim* ("Beloved Friends").

Its ritual and atmosphere were in the Hasidic tradition. I remember Zaydeh telling me of his and Bubbeh Miriam's trip back to Europe in 1935. Accompanied by a family entourage to the dock, they boarded a ship for a visit to the *shtetl* (small village) in Poland—*Sborov* was its name—which was located several miles from Lemberg (now Lvov in Russia). This was the area in Galicia from which they had emigrated around the turn of the century. The folk in that *shtetl*, Zaydeh told me, knew all about *Reyim Ahuvim* in America—about the piety and learning of its members, its adherence to the traditional ways on the part of the Jews who had migrated.

In this religious setting I learned a good deal about the spiritual way. Among much else, I learned the *nusach* (melodic form) of the prayers. I witnessed prayer with *kavanah* (focus, sincerity). I saw genuine piety in a Mr. Groner, a Habad follower, whose talit-covered head and outstretched hands made me think that his heart beckoned heaven itself to respond to his earnest pleas. He no doubt was aware of the passage in the Talmud (*Taanit* 8a) which emphasizes that "prayer is heard only if the soul is offered with it." Elizabeth Barrett Browning has described this type of person: "Earth is crammed with heaven and every common bush afire with God. And only he who sees takes off his shoes, the rest sit around it and pluck blackberries."

I experienced the congregants sitting with bated breath as they waited to find out who was going to lead the service on that Shabbat or Festival evening or day. And woe betide the leader who did not accurately coordinate the Hebrew prayer text with the melody he had chosen for a given element of the service!

Through all this, I sat with Zaydeh at the *mizrach vant*, the eastern wall of the synagogue, a special location. I watched him and he watched me.

Developed in the exile as a substitute for the Temple, the synagogue soon eclipsed it as a religious force and a rallying point for the whole people, appealing through the prayers and scriptural lessons to the congregation as a whole. This institution was limited to no one locality, like the Temple, but raised its banner wherever Jews settled throughout the globe. It was thus able to spearhead the truths of Judaism to the remotest parts of the earth, and to invest the Sabbath and Festivals with deeper meaning by utilizing them for the instruction and elevation of the people. The soul of Judaism has lived indestructively in the House of Prayer and Learning.

—Kaufman Kohler, *Jewish Theology*

CARING FOR FAMILY I: THE CHILDREN

The dictum with regard to family that Zaydeh taught me and followed personally, along with Bubby Miriam, was manifest especially with regard to their ten children. This is a tale of endurance, care, compassion and resourcefulness. It is, indeed, a phenomenal story of parents/grandparents vis-à-vis their progeny...

Of endurance: The loss of five children under the age of thirty, the demise of a son-in-law at the age of thirty-two, of another at the age of fifty-two, and the condition of another son-in-law who suffered illness at age fifty-five which lingered to his demise at sixty-two.

Of care and compassion: Four grown children each with their families occupied separate units in the apartment houses of their parents at little or no fiscal cost to them.

Of parental resourcefulness: Fashioning the wherewithal with which to do all that they did. You see, Miriam and Pinchas managed to purchase their two buildings in the 1920s; Miriam managed them in distinctly frugal fashion and Pinchas was always gainfully employed as a *shochet*.

Family is always building up. It puts some line of beauty on every life it touches. It gives new hope to discouraged ones, new strength to those who are weak, new joys to those who are sorrowing. It makes life seem more worthwhile to everyone into whose eyes it looks.

—Lewis Mumford

CARING FOR FAMILY II: A NEPHEW AND HIS FAMILY BROUGHT TO AMERICA FROM MILAN, ITALY

I remember a number of study sessions with Zaydeh when he focused on the obligation to take care of one's family and others in need. He pointed to the dictum in Leviticus 19:18, וְאָהַבְתָּ לְרֵעֲךָ כָּמוֹךָ, and you shall love your neighbor as yourself. He told me that according to the sage, Rabbi Akiba, this was the greatest principle in the Torah (Sifra on Lev. 19:18); the "yourself" of the verse, he said, means that your family is just like yourself, so you have to watch out for them. And as for "your neighbor," even though he's a non-family person, one is obliged to treat him/her as you yourself would want to be treated.

I knew early on that Zaydeh practiced what the Torah preached. My grandparents did, indeed, take care of their family. At one time or another no less than four of their children and their families were housed in the apartment houses they owned—at adjusted rent or rent-free.

One of Zaydeh's nephews, Shulka (son of Zayde's brother, Uri), his wife and four children were stranded in Milan, Italy after World War II. Zaydeh sent me to the Hebrew Immigrant Aid Society (HIAS) headquartered in lower Manhattan to bring him the required documents so he could arrange to bring the family to America. So it was. The transportation from Italy, wholly financed by Zaydeh and Bubbeh, was arranged, and the family of six was set up in one of the apartments in the building in which my grandparents themselves lived. All of the family's needs were provided for and each of its members launched into the life of America.

Incidentally, when I asked Zaydeh how I was supposed to get to the HIAS headquarters, he replied with a favorite dictum of his, יענקל, אױף דעם שפּיץ צונג ליגט די גאַנצע װעלט, *Yankel, on the tip of the tongue lays the whole world*, i.e., just ask.

Where there is room in the heart there is always room in the house.
                                                    —Thomas Moore

CHICKENS FOR SHABBOS

I found out later of another instance which showed that Zaydeh practiced what the Torah preached. I was at a convention of the Rabbinical Assembly at the Grossinger hotel in New York's Catskill Mountains. While sitting in the coffee shop, a prominent colleague took a seat next to me. He said he was eager for some time to share something with me.

He proceeded to tell me that during the heart of the depression in the 1930s his father was out of work and his family which lived on the same block as my grandparents, was in dire straits. Every Friday afternoon for an extended period of time one of Zaydeh's daughters (Gracie—he still remembered her name after over thirty years) appeared at his family's door with a package of chickens for Shabbos. It was sent by Zaydeh, brought from the slaughterhouse where he worked as a *schochet*.

With palpable emotion, my colleague told me how this *mitzvah* on my grandfather's part helped sustain his family throughout a very difficult time, and that Gracie was like "an angel of mercy" as she appeared weekly at his doorstep.

And he added that a number of other families in the neighborhood similarly received Zaydeh's Friday afternoon packages of chickens from Gracie's hands. My colleague wanted me to know the kind of grandfather I had.

Neighbor is not only a geographic term. It is also a moral concept.

—Rabbi Joachim Prinz

LERNEN…LEARNING…STUDY

Study of sacred texts was ever at the top of Zaydeh's agenda for me. He made regular, unannounced visits to the Yeshiva (Chaim Berlin in Brooklyn, New York, my elementary school) to find out how I was doing. I used to grimace every time he actually walked into my classroom. He would engage in Torah conversation with Rav Pam, our teacher, and then listen intently as we eighth graders recited the Talmudic passages being studied. After all, grandfather paid the school *skhar limud* (tuition), so he had the right to know how I was doing.

On Friday evenings following Shabbos dinner, I had to go back to the synagogue with Zaydeh for some serious Talmud study. This session was designed to demonstrate to him what I had learned at school that week. I did my best through his intense probing. He was benign about the exercise but insistent. All week long I knew I'd have to face this ordeal so I was a bit more alert and focused on my studies.

Shabbos afternoons: another required session. After the usual full lunch meal and Zaydeh's nap (a religious tradition) for which I helped prepare by removing his high-laced shoes, I appeared for more study. This time it was *Chumash* (Pentateuch) and Rashi (the classic commentator). Zaydeh knew the entire Pentateuch literally by heart since he was the synagogue Torah reader for decades, and he otherwise studied it ceaselessly. And so he'd say to me: "Yankel, *zug Rashi*" (start with the Rashi). "But, Zaydeh, we need to start with the *Chumash* text first, no?" To which he'd say: "You know that already, start with Rashi." I, of course, did not necessarily know the *Chumash* text already, but Zaydeh was the teacher and the authority, so I went along. And on and on we'd go.

Zaydeh's emphasis on *lernen*, on study, which was so pronounced during my youth with him, was manifest in additional ways to those depicted above. Once during a summer day, Zaydeh stealthily followed me as I made my way to the Sutter

Theatre to see a movie. He approached me at the ticket window and gently said to me, "Yankel, this is *bitul torah*" (time taken away from Torah study). Come with me to the *Bais Medrish* (the House of Study) and we'll learn together." I acceded. I must have been twelve years old at the time.

Zaydeh retired as a *schochet* at the age of sixty-five. For the next twenty years he spent literally all of his days in the *Beit Midrash* of our shul studying Talmud. This kept his mind alert to the very end of his life. It energized his spirit, stoked his piety, deepened his focus on religious observance, and gave him the drive (and time) to pass on this commitment to learning to his grandson.

Listen, my child, you must study diligently. You are fortunate that you are studying under your grandfather. It is written that when grandfather and grandchild study Torah together, the study of the Divine Law will never forsake the family but will be handed down from generation to generation.

—Moses Hess, *Rome and Jerusalem, Sixth Letter*

Note: The statement of Hess' mother is an allusion to Isaiah 59:21 which reads as follows: "The words I have placed in your mouth shall not be absent from your mouth nor from the mouth of your children nor from the mouths of your children's children, *said the Lord, from now on, for all time."*

ON COMING TO THE SYNAGOGUE EARLY

As a youngster, from age eight to thirteen, I accompanied my grandfather to the mikveh (ritual bath) every Friday afternoon in preparation for the Shabbat. After the ritual cleansing we proceeded together to the synagogue. It was late afternoon and we were the only ones there. Grandfather always made it a point that we be the first present. We partook of some tea and warmed *arbes* (chickpeas), studied some *Chumash* (Pentateuch), and chanted the *Shir Hashirim* (Song of Songs) as the worshippers gradually entered the synagogue.

Grandfather had a favorite saying which he regularly invoked in expecting me to come early for Shabbat morning services: מְמַהֲרִים לָבוֹא וּמְאַחֲרִים לָצֵאת, one is obliged to *come hastily (i.e., early) to the synagogue and delay (i.e., late) in leaving*. While we both did indeed get to the synagogue well before services began, there was a certain "regular" known for his pronounced piety who was always there first, alone in the place; he was waiting for others to arrive so that he could pronounce "Amen" after the morning blessings recited by those he was able to corral for the purpose—me included.

As a youngster, I vaguely understood Grandfather's insistence on getting to a synagogue early. It was only much later that I got a fuller grasp of what probably motivated Grandfather in this regard. It was a passage I came across in the *Zohar*, the chief source of medieval Jewish mysticism that had come to infuse the religious life of Hasidic Jewry in which Grandfather was immersed. The passage captured for me the piety of the man.

Let's look at the passage excerpted from Daniel Matt's translation on pages 128-129 in his *Zohar: The Book of Enlightenment*, published by Paulist Press:

> Happy is the holy people! Their Master searches for them, calls to them to bring them close to Him. So the holy people must join together and enter the synagogue. *Whoever arrives earliest* joins himself to the *Shekhinah* in a

single bond. Come and see: *the first one present in the synagogue,* happy is his portion. He stands on the level of the *Tzaddik* together with the *Shekhinah.* This is the meaning of 'Those who seek me early will find me' (Proverbs 8:17). This one ascends very high.

After reading this *Zohar* passage, I came to understand the meaning of coming early to the synagogue. My grandfather taught me many things when I was young; bringing me to the synagogue before almost anyone else was present was one of them.

"Come early, leave late."

During a visit to Petach Tikvah in Israel, Mordecai Oshinky, Leah's cousin, hurried me to Shabbat afternoon Mincha services. When I asked him what was the rush, he said that it was a mitzvah to make possible the required quorum of ten. We would be observing the mitzvah because those who came later, no matter how many, would not be necessary to constitute the minyan.

THE MIKVEH

Every late Friday afternoon I had to appear at the neighborhood *Mikveh* (ritual bath) and immerse myself along with the adults in preparation for Shabbos (this was how we called Shabbat in those days). Zaydeh was there to meet me and to supervise the proceedings. He made sure I recited the proper blessing and immersed myself in the water in appropriate ritual fashion. I did this with him for some five years every Friday, with some exceptions during the summer months. How vivid is my recollection of his person as we left the Mikveh together en route to our nearby synagogue: his clean face with damp beard glowed. He had been "cleansed" and was now enabled to proceed "unblemished," as it were, and now ready for another great day of rest.

We proceeded to the synagogue, sat together to chant the weekly Torah portion (once in Hebrew, twice in Aramaic) and the *Shir Hashirim* (Song of Songs) which segued into *Kabbolos Shabbos* (Friday evening service). And then we left to his and Bubbeh's home for Shabbos dinner.

Immersion in water brings a regeneration because dissolution of a person immersed is followed by a new birth when the person emerges.

—Mircae Eliade, *The Sacred and the Profane*

When experiencing the waters over one's head, a person enters an environment in which he/she cannot breathe and cannot live more than moments. It is the "begone" of that which has gone before. As one emerges from the gagging waters into the clear air, one begins to breathe anew—and live anew.

—Maurice Lamm, *Becoming a Jew*

TZITZIS INSPECTION: THE SMALL TALIS

The Shabbat and holiday services with Zaydeh at our synagogue featured, among much else, "tzitzis inspection." This little drama required me, a preteen, to prove that I was wearing under my shirt the required four-fringed garment (*talis katan,* "small talis") to be kissed at the designated passages in the prayer service—a sign of one's loyalty to and affection for the good God. And so, I unbuttoned my shirt, drew the tzitzis out, showed them to Zaydeh, he nodded in approval, I rebuttoned the shirt. I passed the test.

Ever since, whenever I touch and kiss the fringes of my adult talis, I am transported to a grandfather's "tzitzis inspection."

The Talmud in tractate Berakhot 60b:

כִּי מְעַטַּף בְּצִיצִית לֵימָא: "בָּרוּךְ אֲשֶׁר
קִדְּשָׁנוּ בְּמִצְוֹתָיו וְצִוָּנוּ לְהִתְעַטֵּף
בְּצִיצִית."

Upon wrapping oneself in the ritual fringes (tzitzit) *one should recite: "Blessed...who has made us holy through His commandments and has commanded us to wrap ourselves (in a garment) with ritual fringes."*

Thus when a youngster wraps his very body under his shirt with the ritual fringes, he is reminded that his whole self is to be rendered holy via a life of religious action.

MY BAR MITZVAH SPEECH:
WHY THE SUBJECT OF TEFILLIN?

My Zaydeh's decision to choose the issue of tefillin as the subject
of my bar mitzvah talk had a crafty purpose. You see, while an
early (and late) teenager, I had a substantial pile of hair on my
head and no one could convince me to shorten it. Zaydeh de-
vised a halakhic strategy: he chose an authoritative Talmudic
text to, at last, persuade me to shorten the "*tchup*," the hair mass,
especially, he thought, because this was bar mitzvah time and he
wanted his grandson to model good religious/traditional appearance as required by the *halakhah* itself.

Hence the *halakhah* of tefillin which required that nothing was
allowed to be present between the head tefillin box and the head
itself. The Talmud (tractate *Arakhin 3b*) was clear about this:
Scripture (Leviticus 6:3) speaks of the sacred clothing of a priest
in biblical times which needed to rest directly on the priest's
body; thus too the tefillin were like the sacred clothing, Zayde
inferred.

דִּכְתִיב (ויקרא ו, ג) יִלְבַּשׁ עַל בְּשָׂרוֹ שֶׁלֹּא יְהֵא
דָבָר חוֹצֵץ בֵּינוֹ וּבֵין בְּשָׂרוֹ

> As it is written (with regard to the priestly vestments):
> "He shall put them upon his flesh" (Leviticus 6:3) which
> teaches that nothing may interpose between the priestly
> vestments and his (the priest's) flesh.

Now, even though the latter section of this Talmudic text did
not directly include hair on the head as barring usage of the head
tefillin, Zaydeh decided to include hair as integral to the prohibition and thus, with a triumphant tone, said to me: "Yankel, the
text of your bar mitzvah speech is clear about your "*tchup*; take
it off, it will interfere with your tefillin; the *halakhah* says so."

This was a demand I managed to evade—rare what with
Zaydeh's established authority. The speech was delivered in
Yiddish and I doubt if most of the people present had the

foggiest notion of its content. But no matter, the speech was integral to the rite of passage intended to show that if I could do what adults did, that's what counted. Zaydeh succeeded on this score but, may he forgive me as he now lies at rest, not on the hair-tefillin matter.

A wily Talmudic argument that did not convince! The rabbis often did accept as authoritative minority opinions. For example, see the Ramban (Nakhmanides) who argued that whenever the minority opinion appears superior to the majority opinion, the position is as if those opinions are divided equally and either may be followed.

THE SHABBOS TABLE

All Shabbos and holiday meals were taken at Zaydeh and Bubbeh's table from the age of eight to sixteen at which time, alas, Bubbeh passed away. Using the classic Jacob Emden siddur, each Friday evening meal began with *Shalom Aleichem*, followed by *Ribon Kol Ho-olamim* (a lengthy persónal/family prayer thanking God for Shabbat contentment) followed by the *Eisheschayil* (Woman of Valor) poem from *Proverbs 31*), followed by the Aramaic *Askinu Seudasa* from the Zohar (the "Bible" of Jewish mysticism), which introduces the sacred song composed by the kabbalist Rabbi Yitzchak Luria extolling the virtues of the Sabbath, followed by *Kiddush*, followed by the ritual handwashing and its blessing, followed by the *motzi* blessing over the bread. I am not exaggerating!

All this Friday eve chanting took a good ten minutes to complete. Shabbat noon had its chanting as well. It started with *Askinu Seudasa*, followed by *Mizmor L'Dovid* (Psalm 23), followed by *Im Tashuv* (Isaiah 58:13-14), followed by *V'shamru* (Exodus 31:16-17), followed by *Zachor* (Exodus 20:8-11), followed by the wine blessing, followed by the hand-washing and blessing, followed by the *Motzi*. This took "only" about five minutes to complete!

Finally came the traditional Shabbos/holiday foods whose aroma I can still smell fifty years later. A feature of these meals: before each course, we all had to pause and say, *l'kovod shabbos*, that is: "I'm eating this food in honor of the Sabbath." This before the fish course, before the soup, before the chicken, before the dessert. I can produce witnesses to testify to the reality of that ritual.

The *Zmiros* (table songs), including the Friday evening *Kol Mekadesh Shevii* and the Saturday noon *Baruch Hashem Yom Yom*, and all the rest were chanted with unfailing regularity in their traditional melodic form which I once calculated to be at least one hundred and fifty years old. Once when we visited the son of his Hasidic rebbe from the old country (of the Stretiner dynasty), Zaydeh insisted that all assembled listen to his grandson chant the entire Shabbos day table song by heart. I did well. He was so proud.

"I am eating this food in honor of the Sabbath."

The Proverb (3:6) points us to a basic imperative, בְּכָל־דְּרָכֶיךָ דָעֵהוּ, *"Know God in all your ways." One must express awareness of The Lord via the specifics of each person's ways of life. Indeed, no area of life is excluded from reaching for this goal. Moreover, "all your ways" refers to the full resources a person possesses, including consumption of food.*

KIDDUSH CUP AND A BESOMIM (SPICE) BOX

As a bar mitzvah, Zaydeh presented me with a Kiddush cup which I've used for over fifty years at my own Shabbat and Holiday table. From a larger Kiddush cup which I inherited from him after he passed away, I pour the wine into this smaller cup and drink. And so, my grandfather has been with me and my family in this way every Shabbat and holiday throughout the years.

Another ritual object I managed to "inherit" from Zaydeh was his *besomim* (spice) box. Actually, I had become so attached to it that I spirited it away from his house following his passing (I do hope that God understood and has forgiven me for that "spirited" act!). That spice box has been used at my family's *havdalah* ceremony over the years. I subsequently gave it to my son, Reuven (Pinchas), who was named after my Zaydeh.

Once when my cousin Lenny Model (Aunt Gracie's son) on a visit at our home in Los Angeles saw Zaydeh's spice box on display, he was riveted. It transported him back to his youth decades ago when he, too, had experienced some of Zaydeh's ways including the one with that spice box at *havdalah* time.

———————————————

I often think that Zaydeh's spice box influenced a serious hobby of mine through the years: fashioning spice boxes and havda-lah *sets out of various old or used materials in accordance with the dictum of Rabbi Isaac Kook,* לְחַדֵּשׁ אֶת הַיָּשָׁן וּלְקַדֵּשׁ אֶת הֶחָדָשׁ, *to renew the old and sanctify the new.*

ZAYDEH TOWARD THE END

The Passover Sedarim were, of course, always at our grandparent's home. The Schechter/Shechter/Schacter clan was there. I used to look at Zaydeh in awe as he sat in his white *kittel* (loose-fitting gown) and tall white skullcap at the head of the table. The Patriarch was presiding. Doggedly but patiently he led the often inattentive family through the Haggadah; the meaning of the text often got lost but not the spirit of the occasion.

As the years passed, Zaydeh grew weaker and weaker. His voice began to fade. He couldn't lead the Seder as usual. By then I was in my mid-teens; and so, spontaneously, I picked up the slack and led the chanting with the vigor of youth and with the method I had long since imbibed. It was "a coming of age" time for me as Zaydeh benignly and proudly allowed me to take over.

Toward the end of his years, Zaydeh enlisted my Uncle Herschel in a special project. Herschel had emerged as a distinguished Orthodox rabbi, no doubt in large measure because of the same religious regimen I had experienced. His was of course more intense than mine since Zaydeh was younger and more vigorous during his son's youth and because the boy lived at home, directly under his father's umbrella.

Herschel was doing much for me during these college years at Yeshiva University, as he later did for my son, Reuven, at Yeshiva U. this all in the spirit of his father's tutelage of him—and me.

The project: a gift for me from Zaydeh. Herschel helped him locate the volumes. They consisted of two all-Hebrew classical Judaic collections: a set of *Mikraot Gedolot*—the entire Bible (Pentateuch—Prophets—Writings) with the major traditional commentaries, and a set of *Shas* (the Babylonian Talmud with its basic commentaries). In each of the twenty-five volumes he inscribed the following:

תש י״ג

ב״ה ר״ח

זֶה הַמִ״ג מִנְחַת זִכָּרוֹן הִיא שְׁלוּחָה לְנֶכְדִי הַתּוֹרָנִי הַיָּקָר

מַר יַעֲקֹב שעכטער שליט״א

פִּנְחָס שעכטער שו״ב

Baruch Hashem   Rosh Chodesh   Tashyag

Zeh Hamikro-os Gedolos minhas zikaron hee shluha l'nehdi hatorani hayakar mar Yaakov Shechter Shlita.

—Pinchas Schechter, Shub

Blessed be God   Rosh Chodesh   5713 (1952)

This *Mikroot Gedolot* is a gift of remembrance presented to my dear scholarly grandson, Mister Ya-akov Shechter. May he live a long and good life.

Pinchas Schachter, *Schochet & Bodaik*

(For the Talmud set the acronym used was ש״ס— "Shas"—meaning six *Sedarim* [tractates]).

I have used these Hebrew volumes throughout the past half-century as my basic reference works in the Jewish classics. Every time I open one of these volumes, I think of Zaydeh and his many gifts to me.

Once I did complain a bit about all the time I had to spend in synagogue, about the studying, the religious observances and all the rest, Zaydeh said to me:

יענק׳ל, ווען איך וועל שוֹין לאַנג אויף די וועלט נישט זיין וועסט

דו מיר דאַנקן

"Yankel, when I will long since be gone from this world, you will thank me."

Zaydeh, I do, indeed, thank you. I thank you for grounding me in the Jewish way. I thank you for teaching me the enormous value of learning and for steering me toward the role of teacher of the content and spirit of Judaism. I thank you for reminding me to try to pray with sincerity. I thank you for modeling how to rear my own children. I thank you for showing me how to be a Zaydeh/grandfather myself.

I thank you, too, for prompting me to meet the obligation of *hakarot hatov*, to recognize the good bestowed, and to keep alive the memory of the good-giver. This I've sought to do by always including you and Bubbeh Miriam at Yizkor time, a practice of the past half-century, by carrying on your name via the person of my son, Reuven, whose Hebrew name is *Pinchas*—and via this memoir.

Note: Pinchas Schechter died on 9 Heshvan 5713 (October 28, 1952)—just five weeks after he inscribed and gifted the Bible and Talmud sets to me at Rosh Hashanah time, September 1952.

I wrote this memoir fifty years later, just after Rosh Hashanah 5763 (October 2002) to mark Pinchas Schechter's Yahrzeit, and as a way to articulate a grandson's profound appreciation.

זֵכֶר צַדִּיק לִבְרָכָה

May the memory of this righteous man be a blessing.

It is. It continues to be.

Because the writer of this essay has so been heavily influenced by his grandfather in terms of learning, religious observance and a quest for piety, throughout the years, at his Yahrzeit and Yizkor time, I unfailingly recite the kaddish in his memory. At these times, I again gaze at the picture of Zaydeh that graces the wall of my home study and have this dialogue:

"Zaydeh, how am I doing?"

"Gut, but Yankel, did you study some Torah today?"

"Not really Zaydeh, I'm so busy with my administrative work."

"Yankel, no good. You must study every day some."

"Yes, Zaydeh, I'll try. I promise."

The next conversation would go like this:

"Zaydeh, I studied a good amount of Chumash (Pentateuch) today in preparation for my class."

"Gut Yankel, and did you daven (pray) today?"

"Yes, but hurriedly."

"You should daven with kavanah (sincerity)."

"I try, Zaydeh, it's not easy with so many things on my mind."

"Yankel, the Ribono Shel Olam (Master of the Universe) expects all His creatures to thank Him for all the good things in life we have. Daven every day and mean it."

"Yes, Zaydeh, I'll keep trying."

– Chapter Eleven –

HERSCHEL SCHACTER:
A SPECIAL UNCLE

There is an important concept in Jewish teaching encapsulated in the words, *hakorat hatov* (recognition of the good) which means that one must openly and positively recognize and thank the person who has bestowed benevolence on you. I do so here by expressing my profound thanks to Uncle Herschel for the good—the very good—he has showered upon me and my son Reuven, the good which has benefitted our lives in seminal ways.

THE RABBI OF BUCHENWALD

Herschel Schacter was my mother Pauline's brother (Pauline married Louis Shechter, a cousin). Herschel was always a special presence in the life of the Shechter family. One Sunday afternoon the entire family gathered in the home of our grandparents. The time was immediately following the end of World War II in 1945. The occasion was to hear from Herschel who had been a chaplain in the U.S. Army and to hear about his searing experiences in the war's aftermath which left millions of Jews gone into the ashes of the war's conflagration. Herschel detailed his experiences. We were all painfully mesmerized by his graphic remarks.

In the biography about Herschel's life and career written by Raphel Medoff, Professor Deborah Lipstadt of Emory University wrote this:

> *The life of Rabbi Herschel Schacter constitutes a roadmap through American Jewish history during the last seven decades of the 20th century: the Holocaust, Soviet Jewry, Israel, and Orthodoxy in America. There is much about his life that is both fascinating and revealing.*
>
> *Nothing can compare, however, to the day, when he, a 27-year-old recently minted rabbi, walked into a barracks at Buchenwald and announced to the inmates, who looked more like cadavers than humans,* Yidden, ihr zent frei! *Jews, you are free! For that moment alone and all that he accomplished to help bring those survivors back to life, his story would be worthy of a biography. But that was just the beginning of his multitude of accomplishments.*

The biography did, indeed, come to be its title, *The Rabbi of Buchenwald: The Life and Times of Herschel Schacter*, tells the full story, including his prominent leadership in the Orthodox Movement and as a loyal alumnus of Yeshiva University.

On a personal level, the following three vignettes depict postwar personal encounters in which my distinguished uncle was involved. His family was very important to him indeed.

MY ENTRY INTO YESHIVA UNIVERSITY

During the last year of high school, the Jewish way began to erode for me. When college time came, I opted out and into the secular world of city College of New York. I wanted fresh air, the experience of the larger world, the opportunity to pursue my natural interests in music, art and English literature.

At the end of my senior year at the Mesivta Chaim Berlin in Brownsville, I took a summer job at a hotel in Seagate, a resort area on the Atlantic coast. It was a job which yielded some needed monies, as well as exposure to an exciting, free-wheeling secular world.

One night a Yiddish folk singer, Sidor Belarsky, appeared on the hotel stage. With great skill and passion, he rendered a set of Hebrew and Yiddish ballads about love and family, tradition and learning, suffering and hope, and pride.

At that very place and hour something clicked inside my heart and head with startling clarity: I felt connected with the content and spirit of Belarsky's songs and the feeling with which he sang. I felt warm inside. I felt that this was who I really am as a person and as a Jew. The Jewish words and music which poured forth from that hotel stage corresponded to my true feelings and interests. I did not identify with the sensuous vulgarity which dominated the Seagate resort. I didn't belong in that world.

The next morning, I called my uncle and asked him to facilitate my enrollment in Yeshiva University, where I knew I belonged. Without hesitation and because of his influence with the institution, he proceeded to arrange it. My parents were unable to finance the venture, and so Herschel arranged for the four years of studies in both the secular YU college and the required full-time studies in its Teachers Institute, a full tuition-free scholarship, plus no-cost dormitory, plus a food plan at no cost, all of which covered each of the four years at the school.

MY SON REUVEN AT YESHIVA UNIVERSITY

A generation later, my son Reuven was in the same position as I was after graduation from high school and in his case, following a year of study and a stint in the Israeli army as a tank driver. He wanted to enter YU.

I called Herschel. Even though, in Reuven's case, I was able to assume some of the financial burden, Herschel supplemented our support with what almost amounted to a good share of the support he had arranged for me decades earlier. This covered a five-year period of study which culminated with Reuven's ordination as an Orthodox rabbi. Herschel felt compensated somewhat by this for my having responded to his benevolence in my time by becoming a *Conservative* rabbi!

Read on…

MY ENTRY INTO THE JEWISH
THEOLOGICAL SEMINARY:
ANOTHER TRANSITION PERIOD—AND DECISION

Toward the conclusion of my studies at Yeshiva University's college and Teachers' Institute, I was determined to find a balance in the religious life. I wanted to remain observant of Jewish traditional practice, yet also occupied with the more open critical studious ways of the Jewish scholarly world. Yet more, I felt the need to be more accepting of the developing understanding of the thought and ways of the contemporary Jew. This led to the compelling decision to carry on my religious journey at the conservative Jewish Theological seminary.

Trouble. My uncle Herschel Schacter was perturbed as was the authorities of the Yeshiva. Rabbi Sar, one of YU's key executives, knew me well as a student and via my influential uncle Herschel. And so, he summoned me to his office and with anguished tone asked, "Yaakov Shechter, I hear you are thinking of entering the seminary, could this be true?" To which I responded coyly, "Me, a Shechter, how can you think of such a thing?" He calmed down, though he knew better because at the time, many students were departing YU for the "liberal" seminary. I thought I might be in the clear.

But then my uncle came into the picture. He knew of my plans and began to try to talk me out of them. To no avail. Whereupon he got his prominent colleague, Rabbi Joseph Lookstein of the modern Orthodox Kehilat Yeshurun Synagogue, to join him in a last-ditch effort. They were good colleagues and of the same mindset.

The two more moderate Orthodox rabbis were very well known and highly respected at the time, extremely eloquent and articulate; they took me for a long walk along Riverside Drive— me in the middle of the two "powerhouse" rabbis, committed leaders of the Orthodox Movement and of Yeshiva University.

"We are just as modern as the seminary. Our rabbis are quite familiar with modern Jewish thought, very aware of the needs of the modern Jews"—and on and on for some two hours. These were two preeminent figures, who corralled many a skeptic in their day. Everything I said drew a sophisticated rebuttal. Their persistence got from me weary promise, "Okay, let me think about his some more."

I decided to enter the Jewish Theological Seminary in the fall of 1953 and ordained in June 1957 with the title, "Rabbi, Preacher and Teacher in Israel."

To be honest, an additional reason for choosing the seminary included the prospect of having my own two-room dormitory "suite" taken care of daily by an attendant, plus advantages such as quiet, order, cleanliness, appropriate dress, etc.; these came with the theology.

– Chapter Twelve –

MENTORS

וּבְדִיל רַבָּה אָכִיל תַּלְמִידָא

By the merit of his master the pupil is nourished.

—Talmud, Yoma 75b

Fortunate, indeed, is the one who encounters mentors who profoundly influence one's rabbinic journey. I have had that good
fortune. This chapter seeks to depict these mentors, in all cases
with but one exception (Franz Rosenzweig), through the prism
of personal experiences with them.

ABRAHAM JOSHUA HESCHEL:
HERALD OF JEWISH SPIRITUALITY

Abraham Joshua Heschel was one of the great thinkers and personalities of our time. He was reared in a Hasidic environment in Poland and then entered the world of secular life and learning in Berlin. Arriving in the United States in flight form the brutalities of Nazi Germany, he taught first at the Hebrew Union College in Cincinnati and then for many years as the Professor of Jewish Ethics and Mysticism at the Jewish Theological Seminary in New York. A revered mentor whose pen poured fourth arresting poetic prose, he emerged, as Reinhold Neibuhr, the great Protestant theologian put it,"the most authentic prophet of religious life in our culture."

Over the years as student and practicing rabbi, I was attached to Abraham Heschel. What follows are a number of personal experiences with him.

• He taught me the meaning of spiritual "enjoyment." I had remarked during one of those ubiquitous seminary elevator rides that I had enjoyed the Tisha B'av services at Camp Ramah in the summer just ended and felt uneasy about feeling good during commemoration of Jewish tragedy. "Mr. Shechter," he quietly reacted, "you mean you appreciated the services and resonated to them with compassion for your people; you grasped their depth and meaning; it's right and good to appreciate that kind of experience."

• Having been reared in a Hasidic milieu, I had learned the traditional *nusach* (prayer chant) characteristic of that milieu. Often I would lead Shabbat services in the seminary synagogue during the four-year student period. Dr. Heschel recognized my/his *nusach*, and at the conclusion of the services would embrace me. As I write this, I feel the affirming warmth of those embraces yet again.

• During the weekend of graduation from the seminary, my soon-to-be bride Leah and I were invited to Dr. Heschel's home on Riverside Drive for afternoon "tea" —a transition "rite" from student status to rabbi. With his usual personal warmth, Dr. Heschel said to Leah, "You know, you and I have something in common." "What is that?," Leah asked. He responded, "We have a mutual admiration for Jack." Leah and I have recalled that comment throughout the years.

• After graduation from the seminary, during my tenure in a rabbinical post in Pittsburgh, I had organized a popular public lecture series and, among others, invited some of the seminary luminaries at the time to lecture: Dr. Louis Finkelstein, Dr. Simon Greenberg, Dr. Robert Gordis and, of course, Dr. Heschel.

I arrived at the airport to pick Dr. Heschel up. We embraced as he deplaned. We walked to my car. I had a cigarette in my mouth as I opened the door of the car to let him in. He stopped short and glared at me, "You're smoking. This is not good." "Yes, I know." "You must stop." "Yes, Professor." "Jack, I will not enter this car until you promise to give up smoking." "Yes, I'll try, Professor. It's not easy."

"I refuse to get into this car. You are transgressing the law about taking care of your body. Don't you realize that the body is a sacred vessel, that through it you are able to do God's will? Don't you remember my book, *God in Search of Man*? God wants you for His service and you must respond. You cannot, you must not, smoke. As a rabbi, you are a teacher of so many people. You must teach them reverence for life, awareness of God's presence in the world. I will not get into this car until you promise to stop smoking." "Yes, Professor, I'll try." "No, that's not good enough. Promise and mean it." "I promise, I promise." I said so several times in order to finally get the good professor into my car. All this at an airport parking lot!

I learned much from my experiences with Dr. Heschel. What Jews—all people—need are not more textbooks, but, as Franz Rosenweig put it, more "text people," people like Abraham Heschel who, through personal encounter, teach. Teach what? The inner feel and purpose of religious ritual. The loving embrace of others. Deep respect for learning about the life of the spirit. Appreciation of authentic prayer. Reverence for life. These are the things I imbibed from personal encounter with Dr. Heschel and, of course, from his extraordinary body of spiritual writing.

Give thanks, O heart, for the high souls

That point to the deathless goals

Brave souls that took the perilous trail

And felt the vision could not fail.

—Edward Markham

MORDECAI KAPLAN: A MENTOR FOR COMMUNITY

Mordecai Kaplan was one of the seminal Jewish thinkers and leaders of the twentieth century, and one of its most stimulating, controversial and courageous personalities. His voluminous writing, evocative classroom teaching, and popular lecturing in the spheres of Jewish culture, religion and community spanned seven decades.

He served as Professor of Homiletics and the Philosophies of Religion at the Jewish Theological Seminary where he also had served as Dean of its Teachers Institute. He was the founding rabbi of the Reconstructionist movement's "mother" synagogue in New York—the Society for the Advancement of Judaism. From those berths he exerted enormous influence on generations of rabbis, educators, professional and lay communal leaders. His profound and provocative activity formed the basis of creative and effective approaches to Jewish life.

As a rabbinical student at the seminary in the late 1950s, I attended classes in Midrash and the Philosophies of Religion taught by Mordecai Kaplan. I was mesmerized as well as unsettled by the power, passion and courage of the professor as he articulated his notion of "Judaism as a Civilization," as well as his decidedly non-traditional conception of the God idea. Like so many others in those days (and today, as well), I took to the civilization aspect of his teaching but resisted his ideas about God.

A Personal Encounter

In January 1957, I went to Dr. Kaplan's Manhattan apartment to talk to him personally about my ambivalence concerning his notion of God as a "process" rather than a Being to whom one can pray. *I learned four decades later that he recorded our conversation and his opinions about it (and me) in his extraordinary diary.* My cousin, Rabbi Jacob Schacter, told me this; he had read through all of the six-decades-long diary in preparation for his and Jeffrey Gurock's volume on *Kaplan: A Modern Heretic and a Traditional*

Community. I subsequently went to the seminary archive room and copied by hand Dr. Kaplan's handwritten entry about my visit with him. (For a full account of our conversation, see *Journey of a Rabbi,* Volume One, p. 62-67)

Dr. Kaplan wrote up a lot of things about a lot of people in his voluminous diary, some flattering and some not so flattering, about people he had encountered in his personal and professional life. The entry about me reveals aspects of my struggles and searching as a young, twenty-five-year-old, soon-to-be-ordained rabbi. "The listening and arguing with Schechter for a full hour and a half" that Dr. Kaplan referred to included my resistance to his notion about God.

Knowing this and making little convincing headway on that score, Dr. Kaplan proceeded to lecture me about the importance of Jewish peoplehood and why Judaism as a civilization was so vital for the health and welfare of the Jewish people.

He stressed how crucially important it is for Jews to creatively encounter the larger world and assimilate its best features into a revitalized Jewish context in the present. And, most especially, the significance of the notion of "Judaism as a Civilization" in that Jewish life encompasses not only prayer, religious observance, and abstract theological affirmation, but also full experiences of everyday life in all its manifestations including the arts, music and drama, dance, painting and sculpture and the rest. This approach, Kaplan emphasized, must characterize the work of the synagogue, the Jewish community and all of Jewish life.

It was an extraordinarily illuminating discussion. Then and there the years of study with Dr. Kaplan came into focus for me. I got a firm grasp on the utility of the Jewish civilization notion, that it had a concreteness to it, that it dealt with the real world and conditions of the present. I could see specific strategies, programs and projects for education and study with young and old, including the areas of music, dance, drama, painting, etc. These were specific means towards the end of vitalizing Jewish life.

This perspective resonated within me. I understood it and it corresponded to my natural inclinations.

I left Dr. Kaplan's Manhattan apartment that night with a handle for my rabbinate: the synagogue was to be a "Synagogue Center" with Judaism as a civilization its modus-operandi. This was how I would function as a rabbi in Israel—combined, I hasten to add, with a strong commitment to the traditional notion of God and religious ritual impressed on me by my other seminary teacher, Abraham Heschel.

When I got home to my dormitory room that night, I recorded this in my Kaplan notebook: *"Without question, I am the better for having come into contact with Dr. Kaplan. I have a chance in the rabbinate because of him."*

Education is not to teach students facts, theories or laws, not to reform or amuse them or make them expert technicians. It is to unsettle their minds, widen their horizons, inflame their intellect, teach them to think straight, if possible, but to think nevertheless.

—Robert Maynard Hutchins

WOLFE KELMAN: LEADER OF RABBIS

As part of a course in "Practical Theology" for the senior class in the Rabbinical School at the Jewish Theological Seminary, arrangement were made to hear from the executives of the various arms of the Conservative Movement, the Women's League, Federation of Men's Clubs, the United Synagogue, the Ramah Camps Association, and others. Rabbi Wolfe Kelman, the executive vice president of the Rabbinical Assembly, was one of them.

I write this some fifty years since Wolfe Kelman's entry into that seminary classroom and quite vividly remember his talk. With verve and clarity, with resonant voice and his signature authority, he portrayed a strong, vibrant and caring rabbinical association; it consisted of the Movement's spiritual leaders in the field who guide and direct an often indifferent laity, yet with courage and imagination help translate indifference into Jewish and religious commitment—this in hundreds of congregations throughout the land.

That session helped plant in me a special interest in rabbinic and synagogue work both in the pulpit and the larger Jewish communal arena—and secured in my mind Wolfe Kelman as a prime mentor.

Rabbi Kelman's "Annual Executive Vice President Report" was always a feature at our annual Rabbinical Assembly conventions. They not only contained astute analyses of the state of the Conservative rabbinate and larger Jewish communal concerns, but also embodied a kind of weight and authority that bred confidence in his colleagues. Most especially, they contained deep concern for the health and welfare of the individual rabbi as he toiled in the demanding arena of the synagogue.

I remember an early convention I attended as an army chaplain. Kelman's eyes were riveted on me; he wanted to know about my work and life at Fort Chaffee, Arkansas, about my future plans in rabbinic work and the rest. He truly cared about his rabbinic constituents. However, a fuller and frank picture will

show that his often acerbic evaluations of some colleagues did
not endear him to all; he was somewhat selective on whom he
bestowed his attention and favor. I was fortunate to be one of his
"favorites." He knew I considered him my mentor.

A "Torah Corps"

Following a two-year stint in the army chaplaincy and another
two years in a pulpit in Warren, Ohio, I was appointed director
of the New England Region of the United Synagogue of America
at the tender age of thirty. I was sitting in the Boston Airport ter-
minal reading the *Boston Globe* and came upon the story of the
creation of a "Peace Corps" by President Kennedy. The idea was
to gather together the talents and expertise of Americans and deploy them around the world in efforts to improve the lot of the
people in underdeveloped countries.

Then and there an initiative to be launched by the United Synagogue seized my mind and would not let go. Why not organize
the talent, expertise and experience of our synagogue constituency and deploy these in the various areas of New England.
There was a dire need for this in order to strengthen the health
and welfare of our cause. Thus the idea of a "Torah Corps" venture was born. (For details of this venture, see *Journey of Rabbi*,
Volume One, p. 136-146)

Meetings were then held with the various New England arms
of the Conservative Movement, including the rabbis, cantors, ad-
ministrators, educators and laity. Rabbi Kelman was present at
the Rabbinical Assembly regional meeting in Boston when I proposed the program and solicitated participation which was
warmly agreed to by the some three dozen rabbis present. Wolfe
soon after wrote me a letter saying how deeply "impressed and
moved" he was by what he witnessed at that session. He elabo-
rated his enthusiasm and support for the venture in ways of encouragement with which a young rabbi could not help but forge
ahead. That letter has always been one of my prized possessions.
It reflected incorporation in the program the spirit and passion
for service to the rabbinic and synagogue life imbibed by Wolfe.

"You Can't Eat the Chicken, But You Can Pluck Its Feathers"

While later serving in a pulpit in Pittsburgh, interactions with Wolfe were constant—at conventions, regional meetings, via phone and meetings in his office which encounters were, for me, always memorable. To cite one instance of "following the leader!"

During a talk by Rabbi Ralph Simon of Chicago, Ralph described an Orthodox *meshulach* (emissary) for a yeshiva who requested a substantial donation. When Ralph asked the man why he was in contact with a Conservative rabbi for whom he had no use as a religious figure, the *meshulach* responded bluntly in Yiddish, "*Der hune toor min nisht essen, uber fliken im meg min* (We are not allowed to eat the chicken but plucking its feathers is permitted)."

When Wolfe heard this exchange, he was furious. "Why should we support Orthodox causes so freely while they have such disdain for us?" he thundered, and then proceeded to enumerate the numerous causes and needs within Conservative synagogues and the larger movement that needed the support from the numerous *Rabbi Discretionary Funds* which habitually dole out their resources to the Orthodox.

When I heard this from Wolfe's agitated voice, I asked him to send me his list of Conservative causes needing support. For years thereafter, I distributed the monies from my discretionary fund from Wolfe's and my own Conservative Movement's list of needy causes.

The disciple followed his mentor.

A Special Convention

Wolfe had something to do with my chairing the seventy-fifth anniversary convention of the Rabbinical Assembly scheduled in May 1975 at the Grossinger Hotel in upstate New York. This

was a high honor. It entailed a massive amount of planning.
Once during a walk outside the seminary talking about the convention, I was adamant about putting together a complicated
consultation feature for the program; Wolfe demurred, I insisted;
he consented. The mentor allowed his charge to chart his own
course.

Once when in Wolfe's office, I saw a picture of him and Professor Abraham Joshua Heschel in conversation in the seminary
outdoor rotunda as commencement ceremonies were being
readied. I liked the picture. Without a moment's hesitation,
Wolfe took the picture off his wall and gave it to me. That picture
has hung on my study wall for the last fifty years.

———————————————

*The rabbis attached much significance to discipleship. In the
opening section of* Ethics of Fathers, *the chain of tradition
from Moses to Joshua and down to the "Men of the Great Synagogue: is recorded and is then followed by the requirement*
הַעֲמִדוּ תַּלְמִידִים הַרְבֵּה, *"Raise many disciples."*

 *The Talmud contains numerous admonitions to teachers
to impart their knowledge to their disciples and that they pay
respect for their mentors. The disciple was urged to serve
teachers by observing closely their ways as guides for the disciple's own ways.*

SIMON GREENBERG: MODEL RABBI

Simon Greenberg had what I would call "rabbinic gravitas." His erect posture, resonant voice and lucid speech were arresting. His knowledge of Jewish scholarly sources and simultaneous strong embrace of American idealism was a healthy synthesis. This all plus a combination of traditional religious observance with an openness to those with more relaxed observance positioned him for me, as for many other nascent and practicing rabbis, as a model for the Conservative rabbinate.

Rabbi Greenberg had served a major congregation in Philadelphia for some fifteen years during the '20s and '30s. His massive accomplishments there led to his becoming vice-chancellor of the Jewish Theological Seminary and professor of education and homiletics. His essential portfolio included serving as guide, mentor and advocate for the congregations in the field and their rabbis.

As a last-year rabbinical student when Leah and I were engaged to be married and embark on rabbinic work, we came to Rabbi Greenberg for a premarital interview. Among other personal helpful suggestions, he told us this: the most effective sermons, Jack, you will ever give will reflect the kind of life you and Leah fashion together—a thought that stayed with us throughout the years.

A Letter to Arkansas

I served as chaplain at Fort Chaffee, Arkansas, following seminary ordination. Leah and I had been invited for dinner at the home of one of the civilian leaders in neighboring Fort Smith, a person who organized hospitality as a JWB volunteer for the stationed soldiers. It was not a kosher home. Leah and I did not know how to handle the situation. Leah wrote to Dr. Greenberg. He responded immediately with a long and detailed letter. Yes, you always need to be meticulous about kashrut observance. However, there are times when an overriding principle and objective is involved—bringing Jews closer to the Jewish way. Yes, you should accept the invitation and tactfully make suggestions about the food. Bring these people close to you and your cause.

This four-page letter laden with numerous specific examples of a sensitive and nuanced approach to this matter exemplified for me and Leah that of a master mentor. It reflected the adjustments that had to be made by Conservative rabbis who seek to maintain tradition as much as possible in face of the demanding changing religious ways of its constituency.

The basic approach unfolded in this letter has helped guide Leah and me (and so many others) throughout our rabbinic career.

At the University of Judaism

I had been brought to the University of Judaism to work as dean of continuing education with the role of serving the larger Jewish community with educational fare in addition to program and administrative help for the congregations of our Conservative Movement. Rabbi Greenberg had been president of the university after he and Dr. Mordecai Kaplan founded the school in the mid-1940s.

Rabbi Greenberg remained deeply caring for the institution from his perch in New York and during regular periodic visits to Los Angeles.

During one of these visits in Los Angeles, I had expressed concern about the complexity of the work, the personal and political difficulties, and whether I had become involved in something more than I should have. To which Rabbi Greenberg responded with two Hebrew words: לְכָּךְ נוֹצַרְתְּ, "For this you were created." And then: you have the capacity, Jack, this work is the kind you were destined to undertake. Forge ahead, do what's necessary to succeed, you will.

By having someone who knows more than yourself share advice, offer guidance and be a sounding board for your thoughts, you stand to benefit from experiences beyond your own. Whether in your career or persona life, having a mentor is crucial for continued growth and development.

—Matthew Reeves

ISRAEL LEVINTHAL:
MASTER PREACHER AND SYNAGOGUE LEADER

During his long tenure as the rabbi of the Brooklyn Jewish Center in New York, Israel Levinthal developed a national reputation as an outstanding preacher and orator. His sermons were known to have been repeated by his colleagues time and again, from many pulpits. Numerous Conservative rabbis regarded Levinthal as their mentor in preaching and his sermons their model for the ideal Conservative sermon.

Furthermore, many lay people, seminary students and young Orthodox and Conservative rabbis, such as the late Professor Moshe Davis, recall walking great distances on Friday evenings, in rain and snow, to hear him speak. These sermons attracted hundreds of people on a weekly basis for more than a half century. His publications, as well, were avidly embraced by the country's leading Jewish professionals.

The congregation Levinthal led was one of the most influential in the country. It was among the first to develop the "Synagogue-Center" from a concrete model stemming from the creative mind and practical action of Mordecai Kaplan. Thus the synagogue was not only to be a place of worship, but the home of the Jewish experience and many of the functions of a Jewish community center.

He also served as professor of homiletics at the Jewish Theological Seminary and as president of the Conservative Movement's Rabbinical Assembly. He was a leading force in the Zionist movement as was his brother Louis, who served at one time as president to the Zionist Organization of America (ZOA).

My encounters with Rabbi Levinthal have had significant influence on my life as a teenager, rabbinical student and practicing rabbi.

A Student Sermon

Who would have thought that as a rabbinical student I would have the opportunity to sit at the feet of Rabbi Israel Levinthal, the renowned leader of that great institution! Yet more, and that I would occupy this rabbi's very pulpit to deliver a student sermon!

During the 1955-1956 academic year Rabbi Levinthal conducted a comprehensive course of study in the art of sermonizing and general speech-making as well as the methodology for the rabbi-to-be in the conduct and development of synagogue/center life. It was an extraordinary experience.

I was in the habit of taking copious notes of these sessions and wound up with more than fifty pages of fascinating material on the subject. I have these notes before me as I write this vignette a good sixty years later!

One entry dated December 22, 1955, recorded the content of a student sermon I delivered in class. The text was from I Kings 6:4, "וַיַּעַשׂ לַבַּיִת חַלּוֹנֵי שְׁקֻפִים אֲטֻמִים" Solomon was to fashion in the Temple he was constructing "windows wide on the outside and narrow on the inside." Why? Because the outside windows which narrowed to the inside of the building would minimize the light and heat from the sun. Whereas the opening of the wide outside windows would shower much light into the outside world. The message: the temple would project much religious light on the world; this was its task.

This was the sermon I was scheduled to deliver at the Brooklyn Jewish Center. My notes recorded this:

Jan. 12, 1955

Dr. Levinthal just told me that I probably will preach at the Brooklyn Jewish Center on Friday eve, Feb. 18, 1956, as my outside sermon. How do you like that!?

Incidentally, some fifty years later, Rabbi Harold Kushner who, unbeknownst to me, was present at that sermon time, told me that he remembered the full content of that sermon. You see, the center was Harold's synagogue. He was a fellow rabbinical student whose father was once president of the Brooklyn Jewish Center.

Encounter at Camp Ramah

During rabbinical student days at Camp Ramah as supervisor of the waiter staff when Rabbi Levinthal and his wife spent their vacation time at the camp together with a set of rabbinic colleagues and their families. He spent his time preparing sermons and lectures. I had obtained a month-long job in Mexico City spanning the High Holy Days and Sukkot designed to nurture a newly developing Conservative community in the city.

I told Rabbi Levinthal about this. I know that my Orthodox uncle Herschel Schacter as a teenage preaching "prodigy" was a fan of Levinthal and usually borrowed some of the master's sermons, memorized and proceeded to deliver them. And so I wrote the following Hebrew letter sent to Herschel (usage of Hebrew was strongly encouraged at Ramah in those days):

On Camp Ramah Stationary

Dated July 10, 1955 • 20 Tammuz 5715

זאת היא הפעם הראשונא שאני כותב מכתב עברי'
עם סכונת בח'בה, הסבונגא הזאת עומדת בספריה חסיד
והתחילה לדרוש פמני להשמאם בה,הצתארבה? רק כם' שהיא
לכתוב אלי| וִהתרתי בכם, תםלחן לי בזה שאני לוסר
איך לספרם על התמגון שלבם, אתם הקרובגוה.

קבלתי משרה כשביל ימים הנוראים בםקסיקו סיט'
ואתא םם בערך חודש ימים, עד אחרי סוכוה, יש בם?
יהודים אמריק'ים צעירים שהשתקעו שם והם רוצ!ם
לבנוה קהילה קנסרבטיבית הדשה, פון לספי'גרים בשביל
עזרה זהםם'גר'ם בחר בי ללבחשששם להשתדל לעשוח סאם!אה,
בסונבג,זאה היא משרה חשובה וזה ה'| צריכ'ם לבזור
בפ'שהוא י'זר מבוגר וזמ|ם,מסוום, אבל ה'וה זהם א'נם םם-?ו
ם'ם,הרבה כסף בחו| בסוז|נם, ואנ' הסטודנם.

דר. לו*נטל שאמרבו היהודי בברוקלן, כן, חלו*נטל
הספורדפם, סבלה באן בל ימי הספגרה שלן יחד עם אשתו,
הוא סכין את געוים*ו בשביל השנה הבאה, מפ:בן היהה
לי הזדמנות סצויינת להתיפץ אתן על אודות כל הענין
הזה ולא הזנחתי אותה, רק לפני בסה תחשים*ס שב מחיו.ו
של הקה*ללות השונות בארצות הבריה ורבש הסון רעיונוה
על ט*בם, התפחהותם וכו*.

לבן בשהגדתי לו על אזדוה

הסשרה במקסי*קו סיטי התלהב סאד והיה בע*ן בסעי*ו
הסהגבר", נהן לי הסון רעי*ונוה על סם לספוה וזאת
לעשוה את העבודה, גם בן, *שב אסי* שעוה ונהן לי
הרבה סחשבוה בשביל הנעוסי*ם שלי עד בלי.בך שאני*
בכראסם יהיה התזנון של געוסי* בשביל ראש השנה. וכלוי*
בל נדרי, יום ב*פור וסוכבוה, בסיב אצהיד לפפה אוהם
בעצסי. ואפי*לו בזה עזר לי הרבה, בסי*להו י*ש לי סזל.

Translation:

This is the first time that I'm writing a Hebrew letter on a typewriter. This machine has been standing in the library constantly and has started to request of me to use it. I only needed someone to whom to write with it, and I chose you. Forgive me that I'm learning how to type at your expense. You are the "sacrifices."

I got a job for the High Holy Days in Mexico City and will be there for approximately a month until after Sukkot. There are a number of young American Jews who have settled there, and they want to build a new Conservative community. They approached the seminary for help, and the seminary chose me to go there and try to accomplish something. Of course, this is an important task, and they should have chosen someone more mature and experienced. However, because they are not spending much money, they chose a student, and I am the student.

Dr. Levinthal of the Brooklyn Jewish Center—yes, the famous Rabbi Levinthal—spends his entire vacation here at Camp Ramah together with his wife, and is preparing his sermons for the coming year. Naturally, this is for me an excellent opportunity to consult with him about this (Mexican) matter and I did not neglect it. Only a few months ago, he returned from a tour of various communities in America, and accumulated a huge amount of ideas about their character, development, etc.

And so, when I told him about my job in Mexico City, he

became very enthused and became a kind of "overflowing well." He gave me a huge number of ideas about what to do and how to execute the job.

He also sat with me for hours giving me many ideas for my sermons to the point that I already know what will be the content of my sermons for Rosh Hashana, Yizkor, Kol Nidre, Yom Kippur and Sukkot. Of course, I will have to develop them myself, but even with this he helped me a great deal. In a word: I am lucky.

The Brooklyn Jewish Center as a Physical Structure

While growing up as a pre-teen and into my teens, I always prayed in a small *shtibel*, a converted single-story house that was fashioned into a place of worship and study. We sat at tables; the spaced was quite small, the accoutrements worn. The prayer was passionate; the setting was, indeed, physically modest.

And then as a teenager I ventured out onto the expensive, tree-lined boulevard of Eastern Parkway: I would keep going until reaching the majestic edifice of the Brooklyn Jewish Center. I remember being awed by the impressive steps framed by the tall stone columns leading up to the elaborately carved entrance doors. At first, I would simply gaze at the exterior since this was a *conservative* institution and orthodox teens could not be seen entering the building. Eventually, however, I did not enter the building.

It was an impressive sight indeed: the high ark fronted by elaborately carved tablets with marble pillars on its sides, the sparkling stained-glass windows, the soft-cushioned pews, the balcony surrounding the sanctuary, the large brass menorah on the pulpit, the huge stars of David strategically placed. As I looked at all this, I remember being palpably moved, and felt like an outsider peering at such an arresting sight. Eventually, I mustered the courage to enter the place unbeknown to anyone else.

The Sanctuary at B'nai Israel in Pittsburgh

Who would have thought that later as an ordained rabbi I would occupy the pulpit of a synagogue comparable to the Brooklyn Jewish Center! Here is a description of the Pittsburgh building:

The synagogue structure was designed by the prominent architect Henry Hornbostel in the mid-1920s, a period of bold and imaginative fashioning of religious structures. There was only one other synagogue in the Pittsburgh region designed by Hornbostel, the striking Reform Rodeph Shalom Temple.

B'nai Israel is housed in a unique building. Set atop a grassy slope along residential Negley Avenue the structure has a massive stone rotunda and tall arched stained-glass windows. The main building, a three-tiered drum form with Roman arches, features an entry porch with a vaulted ceiling constructed of Gaustivino tiles; the tiles frame a stone-etched double tablet containing the first initial letters of the Ten Commandments. The main roof is a wood truss rotunda with a span of one hundred and twenty feet.

The sanctuary seated one thousand and fifty people. It had a massive, tall dome "clothed" with dark blue material delicately decorated in a gold-leafed Persian motif. A huge chandelier hug down into the space from the center of the ceiling. The wide pulpit had seats for the laity and what can only be described as a "throne-like" chair for the rabbi. Alas, the cantor's chair was less impressive, which caused me some difficulty.

The *bimah* also contained a matching set of two candelabras that graced its corners. The holy ark doors were fashioned from carved wood revealing a variety of intricate designs. A choir loft was built into the right upper wall. In the sanctuary back framing the stained-glass windows hung nine decorative lamps. A giant support beam jutted from the ceiling, anchoring the entire circular space. A band around the upper ceiling facing the back of the sanctuary contained the following Hebrew dictum from the book of Micah 6:8:

הַגִּיד לְךָ אָדָם מַה טּוֹב וּמַה ה' דּוֹרֵשׁ מִמְּךָ כִּי אִם עֲשׂוֹת מִשְׁפָּט וְאַהֲבַת
חֶסֶד וְהַצְנֵעַ לֶכֶת עִם אלֹהֶיךָ

The corresponding band around the ceiling facing the front of the sanctuary contained the translation:

> *He has told thee, O man, what is good, and what the Lord re-quires of thee; Only to do justice, and to love mercy, and to walk humbly with thy God.*

As I sat on the *bimah* of that synagogue for ten years, one can imagine my musings as I contemplated the early years as a youth in the small *shtibel* I was raised in, and the synagogue site I later experienced!

The Brooklyn Jewish Center and Pittsburgh's B'nai Israel: As Community Centers

The Brooklyn Jewish Center structure contained more than an impressive sanctuary. It had vast facilities for its Hebrew school, for informal activities, for its youth, a gym, a pool and much more in order to fulfill its role as a center for the social and recreational life of its community.

Fast forward: the building of the Congregation B'nai Israel in Pittsburgh was similarly equipped and contained a huge program including its basic religious school as well as a gym, youth league and other facilities for its nursing school and informal activities for its youngsters and teens and adults for socializing and more.

I learned about this approach to synagogue life not only from Mordecai Kaplan, but in concrete form from Israel Levinthal as well.

Who would have thought!

As in my Hebrew letter to Uncle Herschel:

יֵשׁ לִי מַזָּל

Yesh hi Mazal

I was a lucky student and have been a fortunate rabbi.

NAHUM SARNA: A PRIZED TEACHER

There is a rabbinic dictum called *hakarat hatov*, "the recognition of the good," that is, the obligation to express gratitude about a person who bestows beneficence upon another. In this connection I repeat here what I wrote about such a person in the preface of a previous book of mine, *The Land of Israel: Its Theological Dimensions*:

There is a person to whom I owe thanks for the seminal influence he had on me in the area of biblical studies. He is the late Dr. Nahum Sarna, who served for many years as Professor of Biblical Studies at Brandeis University outside of Boston. At the time I was Director of the New England Region of the United Synagogue of America headquartered in Brookline, Mass.

For five consecutive years we sat together as congregants in the pews of Congregation Kehillath Israel in Brookline. This was every Shabbat and holiday service, the consistency about which we both complained yet from which we rarely absented ourselves. Nahum was a warm, friendly and embracing persona and most especially a profoundly informed and creative biblical scholar.

I had arranged a wide-ranging seminar program for rabbis and educators in Boston featuring Dr. Sarna and his path-breaking approach to Bible study. His approach successfully reconciled biblical tradition with the new literary, historical and archaeological findings that have emerged from the studies of scholars of the ancient Near Eastern milieu. This helped cement a bond between us.

At each of the Shabbat and holiday services before, during and after the Torah reading (yes, we were a bit out of line on this score), Nahum would share with me his interpretations, replete with documented data, insights, bon mots that illumined for me fascinating traditional and modern approaches to the world of the Bible. The utter consistency and substantive content of these encounters constituted an education (tuition-free) in Scripture of the first order.

Gifts

Before leaving Boston for Pittsburgh to take up my post as a pulpit rabbi, Nahum gifted me with a fourteenth-century illuminated manuscript reproduced from the original. It was a prayer in an Ashkenazic Yom Kippur prayerbook. Framed by an *Aron Kodesh* (Holy Ark), towers, birds and figures in various praying postures was the text:

> *Barukkh Ata Adonay Elohaynu Melekh Ha-olom*
> *Hapotayakh Lanu Sha-ar.*

> Blessed are You O God, King of the universe,
> who opens for us the gates.

Nahum reminded me that this, of course, meant the gates to heaven asking for forgiveness; but also, he said, it meant the "gates to learning" as I proceed to my new task.

He also took me with him to the Andover Theological Seminary library in Newton to study the collection of biblical books and made sure that I had the latest comprehensive publications containing the standard resources for intensive Bible study.

I've long since been persuaded that the five-year encounter with Nahum Sarna laid the groundwork for the kind of work on Bible I was engaged in. Yet more: When I applied for admission to the doctoral program in biblical studies at the University of Pittsburgh/Pittsburgh Theological Seminary, Nahum wrote a recommendation for me which helped in no small measure. Nahum has since passed away. The memory of him is, indeed, a blessing.

———————————

The core ideational idea which was Nahum Sarna's special gift to me (and so many others including my wife, Leah) was the need to integrate traditional biblical ideas and institutions with the doctrines and practices of the ancient Near East. This approach was at the time a new one and resulted in massive new and constructive religious thinking on the part of the traditional modernist.

JEWISH STUDY IN THE MODERN AGE:
FRANZ ROSENZWEIG

I did not encounter Franz Rosenzweig personally as I did with all the other persons vignetted in this book. I make this single exception because, even though at a distance in time, I have always considered Rosenzweig a presence in my personal and professional life. Indeed, he has been a consequential mentor.

Communities seek to preserve and transmit their fundamental values through education, thereby ensuring their own continuity. This has been true for the Jewish community throughout its history.

In modern society, the traditional system broke down under the impact of Emancipation. Many Jews embrace secular society in which the texture of consciousness, the modes of experience, perspectives on the world, and basic values differ significantly from those of traditional Jewish society. At the same time, Jews, for the most part, seek to preserve their distinctive ethos, character and way of life. This struggle—to simultaneously retain Jewish distinctiveness while integrating with the larger world—is at the core of the character of the Jewish community today and constitutes its greatest educational challenge.

In response to this fundamental challenge there entered onto the Jewish scene a person of great vision. Indeed, the creative spirit and religious genius of Franz Rosenzweig have revolutionized adult Jewish education in the modern world. His thought and practical work encased a groundbreaking methodology. It was a way for the Jew who is positively immersed in the contemporary secular world to simultaneously and meaningfully embrace his Jewish roots—an integration that he needs and for which he yearns. What follows seeks to articulate the essence of this approach and to do so through the prism of the life and work of the man, Rosenzweig.

A New Approach

Soon after Franz Rosenzweig saw his way clear to remain a Jew and to dedicate his life to the cause of Judaism, he realized the need for a radical reorganization of Jewish instruction on all levels. While serving as a German soldier on the Balkan front in March 1917, Rosenzweig wrote down, on army postal cards, a kind of manifesto under the ringing title, *It Is Time! (Zeit ist!)*

In this epistle on Jewish learning, the "Jewish philosopher of the trenches" proposed that a synthesis of general and Jewish scholarship and its effective dissemination would provide a way for European Jewry to end its stagnation. Moreover, it would counteract the problem of assimilation and form the basis for a renaissance of Jewish life.

Three years later, early in 1920, he pressed forward his ideas on the revitalization of Jewish learning in an essay entitled *Bildung und Kein Ende*, which can be freely translated as Education without Graduation. In this appeal for German Jewry to establish schools for never-ending Jewish learning, he laments the fact that "Jewish study and teaching, Jewish learning and education are dying out among us," and hails the beginnings of the Jewish adult education movement "...as the latest and perhaps most important movement among contemporary German Jews."

What Rosenzweig articulated in lucid, striking and convincing fashion was that a new learning was called for, this in order to bring the Jew from the periphery of Jewish life which he inhabits back into the core of Judaism for which he yearns either wholly or glancingly.

The modern Jew needs to start the process of learning from where he stands in life—the known, the familiar, the larger world in which he functions and which envelops him. If this start is accomplished creatively with full awareness of the contemporary mindset, the learner then moves from that "outside" into the "center" of Jewish ideas, sources, and subject matter. Indeed, Jewish learning must be appropriate to the ways of Jewish existence in the modern world if the Jewish community is to endure.

Learning is still at the center, but it is a learning of new modes, through new methods, and channeling via new sources of truth.

This approach has been encapsulated in the phrase "From the periphery to the core." Thus, for example, comparative religion and literature, general history, political science, the sociological, psychological and other disciplines and perspectives are employed in studying the bible. Such is the case, as well, for Jewish history and community, Jewish custom, practice and thought, and Jewish literature, rabbinic literature and law studied through the prisms of general culture and Zeitgeist. This approach has stimulated much creativity and has been wide-ranging and embracing in terms of subject matter and teaching resources.

Rosenzweig's extremely insightful methodology heavily influenced my two decades long work in the field of adult education in connection with my deanship in this area at the University of Judaism. The approach has stimulated a good deal of creativity, and was responsible for the institution's adult learning program to be wide-ranging in subject matter and teaching resources, serving thousands of learners in Los Angeles and the West Coast. Indeed, the University, through the Whizen Center for Continuing Education (previously called *The Department of Continuing Education*) continues to contribute significantly toward a renaissance of Jewish life in America.

The old learning had its starting point in the Torah and was designed to lead into life. The new learning will lead from wherever we stand in life back to the Torah. This new learning will be a process from the periphery, where we stand in life, back to Judaism, which we still feel to be the center despite our alienation.

—Franz Rosenzweig: His Life and Thought
"The New Thinking"

– Chapter Thirteen –

NON-JEWISH GUIDES

As this chapter will soon seek to show, professors Von Waldow, Barth and Knierim shared a lifetime preoccupation: a commitment to rapprochement between Christian, Muslim and Jew. They were personally sensitive to the traumatic aftershocks of the Holocaust, the condition of the contemporary Jew and the situation of the state of Israel today and its relation to the Arab world. As faithful religionists, they sought guidance from Scripture for the vexing religious and political issues of the day.

I do think that this preoccupation had much to do with their embrace of me as a Jew and rabbi and of my role as a student of theirs. As to Professor Paul Lapp, a different factor was involved. Lapp was less sympathetic about the relationship of Israeli Jews and Palestinians in the present. Yet with me as a Jew and rabbi he had somebody to "dialogue" with about the problem in scholarly terms. And so, he welcomed me as his student and did so with much cordiality.

בֶּן־זוֹמָא אוֹמֵר   אֵיזֶהוּ חָכָם הַלּוֹמֵד מִכָּל־אָדָם
שֶׁנֶּאֱמַר מִכָּל־מְלַמְּדַי הִשְׂכַּלְתִּי

Ben Zoma said, "Who is wise? He who learns from every person. As it is said (in Psalm 119:99), 'From all my teachers I get enlightenment.'"

—Ethics of the Fathers 4:1

The long and bleak history of the treatment of Jews in the world is painfully familiar. But we should nevertheless be aware of how much Jews have absorbed from the non-Jewish world. Aristotle, for example, influenced the philosophy of Maimonides.

Without the Arab bards of medieval Spain, we would not have the poetry of Judah Halevi and Solomon Ibn Gabirol.

In every age, Jews have not only contributed to the world but have also sought knowledge outside their own heritage. No people is so wise that it can figure out this baffling world alone.

One of the greatest gifts to have come from the Jewish people is the Ten Commandments. Yet the Torah portion that contains the commandments is named after a non-Jew—Yitro (Exodus 20). Yitro was Moses' father-in-law. He was wise, helping Moses set up a judicial system that enables him to ease some of his burdens. Here Moses teaches a great lesson: Torah can be enriched by wisdom, whatever its source.

Many great scholars of the Bible, past and present, have not been Jewish. For example:

- *William Foxwell Albright, the prominent archaeologist whose work has illumined many practices in Scripture based on his studies of the ancient Near East.*

- *John Bright, whose "A History of Israel" has anchored the period of the patriarchs in concrete history.*

- *Gerhard von Rad, whose theological studies have shed much new light on the book of Deuteronomy.*

Even some notable scholars of rabbinic literature, of the Talmud and Midrash, have been non-Jews.

- *R. Travers Herford's commentary on Pirke Avot is very informative.*

- *George Foot Moore's "History of Judaism" during the classical rabbinic period is a work of vital information and insight.*

- *Herman Strack's "Introduction to the Talmud and Midrash" has been extremely valuable to the students of rabbinics.*

H. EBERHARD VON WALDOW

While serving as rabbi in Pittsburgh, I knew I had to continue to study. The Pittsburgh Theological Seminary, a prominent liberal Protestant institution, was nearby. I enrolled in its doctoral program which was conducted in conjunction with the graduate school of the University of Pittsburgh. At the seminary I met Dr. Eberhard von Waldow, professor of Old Testament.

Reared in the German city of Jenna, east of Weimar, von Waldow was a scion of German nobility dating back a full thousand years. His family tradition included its progeny choosing either a career in the military, the Christian ministry or in an area of religious scholarship. Interestingly, during von Waldow's own lifetime, he embraced all three occupations, one in the German army ("my unsuccessful career in the German army contributed to the loss of the war in 1945"), another as a young Lutheran pastor, and another as a teacher and researcher of Scripture with a Ph.D. in Bible from the University of Bonn, at a protestant seminary in Berlin, and eventually at the Pittsburgh Seminary.

A tall, erect, confident and proud-bearing persona, von Waldow had been a member of the Nazi youth organization which, he told me, evoked in him intense remorse. He sadly observed that that exposure as a young man to its raging hostility of the Jews had a role in his prolonged and intense preoccupation with Jewish-Christian relations, the modern state of Israel and the tense involvement of Israel with the Palestinians and the Arab world.

von Waldow's special interests included the prophet Jeremiah, the book of Deuteronomy, form criticism and biblical theology. He was also a vigorous and demanding teacher with a unique interest in the mental acuity of his students often honing their minds with cutting-edge comments. Many of his students are unlikely to forget being singled out by his officer's baton for failure to respond, or by a withering remark concerning a late arrival. Some were intimidated by his manner, only to discover the depth of his compassion, combined with personal warmth which revealed the sensitive spirit that was his.

A fortuitous development: Professor von Waldow found a rabbi in a Jewish synagogue interested in studying at the Pittsburgh Theological Seminary, physically but blocks away! And so, since he was deeply immersed in the subject of the land of Israel as a "holy" land, he welcomed me into his orbit and persuaded me to undertake for my Ph.D. dissertation the subject "The Theology of the Land of Israel in Deuteronomy." He became my guide, mentor and friend throughout the years of doctoral studies, and did so with discernment, patience and good will.

A humorous aside: during my frequent meetings with Dr. von Waldow, we regularly shared his favorite cup of wine, Johannisberg Riesling. Fast forward: I flew from Los Angeles to Pittsburgh for the comprehensive examinations leading up to writing the dissertation and brought with me an attractive bottle of Johannisberg Riesling as a way of expressing thanks. The question: should I present the bottle to him before or after the examination?

Conscience is that which witnesses and binds, incites and accuses, stings and rebukes.

—Thomas Aquinas

MARKUS BARTH

At the Pittsburgh seminary, I met another special man: Dr. Markus Barth, then Professor of New Testament and later in that position at the University of Basel in Switzerland. The son of the renowned theologian Karl Barth, Professor Barth was particularly interested in the biblical perspectives on the land and their pertinence to the contemporary situation. His personal passion for this subject, combined with a penetrating intelligence and incredibly luminous persona, stimulated me in no small measure to pursue this subject.

A prolific scholar, Dr. Barth was best known for his contributions to the Anchor Bible Series with a new translation and commentary to the New Testament's Colossians, Letter of Philoman and Ephesions. He also authored "Jesus the Jew," "Israel and the Church" and a number of articles on Jewish-Christian relations.

Ours was a long and friendly and, at times, intense "dialogue" association in Pittsburgh. Once I invited Barth to speak in my congregation's public lecture series. He presented his views about what Israeli and Arab leaders needed to do via mutual compromise in order to bring about peace between Israelis and Palestinians, and some tranquility into the roiling condition of the Middle East. He made his case with eloquence, careful reasoning and passion.

It was clear that our Jewish audience demurred from his views, and that Dr. Barth and I could not agree on aspects of my land studies as they applied to the contemporary Arab-Israeli-Jewish relations. This was later reinforced when the professor asked me to provide a written endorsement of his Pittsburgh address which was about to be published in a new book of his. I had to decline, but our personal friendship endured.

After Dr. Barth left Pittsburgh to assume a professorship at the University of Basel. Leah and I were hosted in his home in Basel under the attentive care of his wife, Rose, and met his elegant and articulate pipe-smoking sister! We toured his impressive university and attended a local Sunday morning church service; we visited with Rabbi Adler, Basel's Jewish religious leader and attended a Shabbat morning service in his synagogue where I received an *aliya* standing at the very same bimah on which Theodore Herzl stood for his *aliya* during the First Zionist Congress in 1897. We also visited the learned sister of Rabbi Leo Jung of Manhattan's Jewish Center following a weekday morning minyan, we also discussed Barth's problem son, Lukas, who was bent on converting to Judaism; and we discussed Barth's work on his father's literary archive.

Markus was everywhere with us during this memorable visit. This, along with the memory of him before and since, had been an enriching one indeed.

Some years later, in order to reconnect with Dr. Barth, I phoned his number in his Basel suburb home. His brother answered and told me that Markus had passed away and that the family home was now his and his nephew Lukas'.

He then proceeded to tell me about Lukas' "hounding" of Rabbi Adler urging the rabbi to study Judaism with him and then convert him to the Jewish faith. The rabbi deemed Lukas psychologically unbalanced and resisted his "annoying persistence." Such was the destiny of Markus Barth's son, and of the great Protestant theologian Karl Barth's grandson.

PAUL LAPP

When I began at the Pittsburgh Seminary I also came under the tutelage of Dr. Paul Lapp, who had just come to the seminary as Professor of Old Testament and Archaeology after eight years as director of the American Schools of Oriental Research in Jerusalem. Born in Sacramento, California, Lapp was a vigorous and deeply informed scholar who received his Ph.D. in Semitic studies at the University of California and his Ph.D. from Harvard.

During Lapp's eight years in Jerusalem and environs he directed numerous archaeological excavations, among them the caves of the Wadi Daliya, the necropolis and cemetery of Babedra, the tells of Rumath and Taanach. His activist approach to work, adaptability to the environment, and his inquisitive and retentive mind produced in the years 1960 to 1968 a treasure trove of field archaeology which uncovered much about life in biblical times.

Moreover, his book "Biblical Archaeology and History" (which I fully absorbed during my own studies about the "holy land") was noted for the links Lapp sought to forge between his findings and the scriptural accounts of early biblical times.

Lapp's work was conducted and written about in Jordanian Jerusalem. The six-day war which resulted in the reunification of the city meant, in his view, "occupation by a conquering power with fear that a knock on the door at night be followed by an arrest and indefinite incarceration." Nonetheless, since that conflict, it was made possible for Lapp to observe the archaeological work in Israel, and relations with Israeli colleagues were cordial in sharing materials and ideas. However, Lapp's political and ideological views about the land never left him.

Dr. Lapp's deep interest in the land of Palestine/Israel as a religious entity was pervasive. And so, in numerous personal discussions at the seminary and, more often, in the cordial ambiance of his home, he "provoked" me to pursue research on the subject. His was a combative and controversial approach to the

matter laced with command of the details. He did, indeed, succeed in stimulating me to delve with real focus on my studies.

Alas: Lapp's adventurous nature led to an exploration of ancient life off the shore of Cyprus. He had been in the midst of an
archaeological expedition on the island. During an off-duty
swim while underwater, a strong current flushed him out of the
water onto the shore—dead. It was a significant loss to many in
the field of archaeological and biblical scholarship. He had been
in the midst of updating a definitive survey of the field of biblical
archaeology launched by William Foxwell Albright, the leading
scholar in the field.

I remember sitting sadly at Dr. Paul Lapp's funeral service
conducted at the Pittsburgh Seminary chapel.

---

*Perhaps the discoveries of Jerusalem are even more important
that those of Cape Kennedy. The discoveries at Cape Kennedy
are concerned with the expansion of man's world. The discoveries in Jerusalem concern man himself. Perhaps historians
have more to contribute to our society than cosmic theoreti-
cians. Perhaps archaeological discoveries in Palestine will en-
lighten men more than finds from an excavation on the moon.*

*Perhaps it is more important for man to understand him-
self than to expand his world. Perhaps men need more desper-
ately to understand each other than to discover new creatures
out in space. If such should be your conviction, ancient and
biblical history and archaeology offer stimulating opportunities to expand your horizons.*

—Paul Lapp, final paragraph
of *Biblical Archaeology and History*

ROLF KNIERIM

Upon leaving Pittsburgh for Los Angeles, with my dissertation yet to be completed, Dr. von Waldow enlisted his colleague, Dr. Rolf Knierim, to take me on as his student, and guide me in my land studies. Knierim was professor of Old Testament at the Claremont School of Theology in California.

Knierim was a founding director of Claremont Graduate University's Institute for Antiquity and Christianity. It was there, as a recognized expert in the field, where he initiated and led the Form-Critical Project which produced the institute's long-running and prolific publication series, *The Forms of Old Testament Literature (FOTL) Series.*

Knierim was born in the city of Pirmasens in the Rhineland—Paletine region of Germany near the French border. In December 1943 the studies of the teenager at the city's gymnasium were interrupted when, during World War II, he was forcibly conscripted with his class into the German military and assigned to an air defense unit.

In his essay "On the Subject of War in Old Testament and Biblical Theory," Knierim describes the experience of his conscription into the army alongside the parallel experience of his friend and Bible scholar Hans Eberhard von Waldow, stating that, "these experiences followed by the impact of the Holocaust, or *Shoah*, profoundly influenced the direction of our lives, including our commitment to Old Testament studies." Indeed, Knierim's and von Waldow's experience in what was then known as the Nazi Youth Organization induced in them intense feelings of guilt and remorse. Their conscience haunted them. Their careers sought ways to ease the pain.

Following the war Knierim studied for the church ministry at a Methodist seminary in Frankfurt en-Main, and then at the University of Heidelberg for the doctorate in biblical studies under the tutelage of the famed Gerhard von Rad. The Ph.D. was awarded in 1955. He subsequently was called to Claremont,

California, as professor of Old Testament at its School of Theology and the university's graduate school. Here is where we met.

In Dr. Knierim I encountered scholarship in depth, methodological meticulousness and high standards of study. (Incidentally, Leah also studied with the good professor). He helped me develop the plan and methodology to be employed in my dissertation about the land. His consistent encouragement and support—and rigorous demands—had a major role in navigating the work to its conclusion.

A sad ending: at age ninety, Rolf and his wife were enroute back to Claremont from a vacation in Arizona when their car veered off the highway and crashed, leaving them both on their way to the great beyond.

Conscience is that court within the soul which concerns itself with the distinction between what is good and bad.

—Martin Buber

– Chapter Fourteen –

EMPOWERING OTHERS

One of the highlights of my life and career has been an effort to help others realize their full human potential. So many of us do not fathom their innate capacity for personal growth, for development of skills as individuals, as people in the workplace, and generally, for the business of life.

I remember well the story Dr. Louis Finkelstein the Chancellor of the Jewish Theological Seminary told us students when he was dean of students at the seminary and professor of theology. He found that some students in the classroom were somewhat meek and slow; however, when they were in his office where they sought help on personal matters, they waxed eloquent, focused and quite attentive. The contrast: in personal matters of real concern, much more of themselves was involved; more of their innate capacity came to the fore.

What follows are a few examples of what can happen when one is helped along.

MICHAEL MELNICK: A BAR MITZVAH BLESSING

Michael Melnick's family belonged to Congregation B'nai Israel in Pittsburgh at the time I served as its rabbi. Michael had undertaken to write a history of the congregation in the year 2018 in the prefaces of which he thanked a number of people. This is what he wrote about his Bar Mitzvah which had taken place decades ago…

> I would like to acknowledge Rabbi Jack Shechter, who was my family rabbi at the time of my Bar Mitzvah on July 1, 1972.
>
> "As a person walks through a dark, blackened hall with no light at all in it and not knowing where he's going, he walks in fear and confusion. His steps falter. But when one walks through even a dark hall and sees at the end light, he knows where he is going, and therefore, the way in which he goes through that hall is firm and comforting."
>
> These words were spoken at my Bar Mitzvah on July 1, 1972, by Rabbi Jack Shechter when he and Hazzan Mordecai Heiser, together with the B'nai Israel Choir, blessed me with the Priestly Benediction. That blessing from the rabbi has reverberated in my mind all these years and has really kept me going.

בָּרוּךְ אַתָּה ה' אֱלֹהֵינוּ מֶלֶךְ הָעוֹלָם אֲשֶׁר הֵכִין מִצְעֲדֵי גָבֶר

Blessed are You, Lord our God, King of the Universe, who makes firm the steps of a person.

Thank You, God, for planting within me the capacity to choose my goals in life, to set these goals today and then be able to muster the conscious purpose to go forward and reach them on the morrow. How confident can one be in one's choices when one's goals are clearly set. Thank you, again, for this. Amen.

—JS

SHELLEY BLUMENFELD: ARTIST

During my Pittsburgh tenure, the congregation harbored a talented artist in the person of Shelley Blumenfeld. Her beautiful impressionist paintings expressed profound sensitivity about the world about her. Her canvas contained colorful and highly skilled brush strokes which riveted the eye of the beholder. And so, I pressed Shelly into Judaica artistry when a decision was made to produce a booklet titled *Shabbat Shalom: The Song and Ceremony for Shabbat Observance.*

I served as compiler and Shelley Blumenfeld produced three paintings—one picturing Shabbat evening via a kiddush cup, wine decanter, challah, flower vase; a second suggesting Shabbat noon via an impressionistic canvas suggesting the light of day; and a third for the transition period from Shabbat to weekday via an *havdalah* set containing a spice box, kiddush cup and three-braided candlestick, this all with twisting rays in the background. Each painting was reproduced in the booklet containing the various table songs and prayers. Her paintings bathed the whole publication with luminous yet soft light; they evoked the Shabbat mood of tranquility and aesthetic celebration.

Shelley then enlisted her father, Larry Resnick, for our project. Larry had an artistic bent of his own, from whom, no doubt, Shelley inherited hers. He was an active member of our congregation who produced all manner of handsome signs and posters promoting the synagogue's various programs. Larry provided the striking calligraphy for the booklet. Shelley also helped design the work as a whole. Her participation in the project was the key to the booklet's emerging from a pedestrian effort to a work of Jewish art.

Indeed, I have long since been persuaded that Shelley's artistry which was channeled into Judaic form, has been a key factor in the widespread adoption of the booklet, not only in Pittsburgh's B'nai Israel, but in numerous homes elsewhere.

Planting a Seed

Note this letter received from Shelley Blumenfeld 25 years after we collaborated on the artistic features of our Shabbat guide:

> Dear Leah and Rabbi:
>
> I think of both of you often. I thought you might be interested in how our collaboration on the *Shabbat Shalom* has evolved.
>
> Many years have passed and I suddenly wanted to do a Judaica series for my grandchildren about the holidays and Shabbat. I did a series of paintings on canvas for them as a diary of our shared celebrations. These included ones on Passover, Shavuot, Sukkot, Chanukah, Purim and Rosh Hashanah. It turned out that others were interested and I produced a limited edition of the lithographs which I am marketing.
>
> *Our* candlesticks will be used by Hallmark when they use my Shabbat painting as a cover card in their tree of life line coming out in 1999. Next Rosh Hashana they will produce my Rosh Hashana painting in their fine arts Judaica series.
>
> The Pittsburgh Theological Seminary had a show of my paintings which was quite a happening in the Christian world. A church in the North Hills will now show them for six weeks in November. It is my hope of getting the lithographs into Day Schools and Sunday Schools. Thank you so much for drawing me into the special artistic realm.
>
> I wish you and yours a happy, healthy New Year.
>
> Love, Shelley

On the back of the Hallmark card containing Shelley's painting is this note:

> The artwork on the cover of this card is a lithograph by

Rochelle Blumenfeld, entitled 'Shabbat.' Blumenfeld combines her experience as a Jewish woman with her expertise as an artist to create her beautiful holiday paintings. Her artwork reflects her life, using personal Judaica that have been handed down through the generations. Blumenfeld is an award-winning artist whose paintings are found in many private and public collections, including the Carnegie Museum of Art, Pittsburgh, Pennsylvania. She has also had numerous exhibitions throughout the United States and Europe.

Yet More...

For many years Shelley's *havdalah* lithograph, attractively framed, has hung on the living room wall of our home. Framed smaller versions of her other works—Passover, Shavuot, Sukkot, Chanukah, Shabbat, Purim, and Rosh Hashana—grace a wall of my study. The lithographs also grace the homes of our sons.

Yet more: these stellar works of Judaica now enhance the walls of the chapel of Temple Etz Chaim in Thousand Oaks, California. They were donated by Leah and me honoring the Bar and Bat Mitzvah occasions of our grandchildren.

Planting a seed which could well produce fruit and even flower into more fruit on the morrow is an act of no small consequence.

—JS

BARUCH GOLDSTEIN: THE SAGA

I have been moved by the story of Rabbi Baruch Goldstein, a survivor of the Holocaust who rose from the ashes of the catastrophe phoenix-life to live a productive life. I will let his own words
tell about one key turning point in his life.

In chapter sixteen of Baruch's book, *For Decades I was Silent*,
titled, "I Find My Calling," he writes this:

> The year 1964 marked the beginning of more big changes
> in my life. In the spring of that year, Rabbi Jack Shechter,
> executive director of the United Synagogue of New Eng-
> land, suggested that I apply for the rabbinic position at
> Temple Emmanuel in Wakefield, Massachusetts.
>
> Rabbi Shechter and I had met a number of times at
> conferences and conventions, including at conventions
> of United Synagogue Youth, and he had befriended me.
> At first I declined even to consider applying, for I was
> not really interested in seeking the pulpit. I had received
> such offers before but had always declined. I was content
> to continue in my position with the Beth Israel Syna-
> gogue in Worcester. Again, I felt that my qualifications
> were not good enough to assume the position of spiritual
> leader.
>
> Rabbi Shechter was persistent. After several phone
> calls, I agreed to meet with the board of directors of Tem-
> ple Emmanuel in Wakefield to be interviewed for the po-
> sition of rabbi and education director of the congregation
> and its religious school. I was hoping that I would not be
> acceptable for the position.
>
> Again Rabbi Shechter contacted me and asked me to
> meet with him in his office in Boston. He wanted to know
> my reason for not accepting an offer to negotiate a con-
> tract with the Wakefield congregation. Trying to come
> up with an argument that would end the discussion, I

told him I objected to the idea of playing an organ at Sabbath services. I was sure that this would be enough of a reason for the congregation to withdraw their offer and that therefore the subject would be closed.

Rabbi Shechter tried to persuade me that the organ was acceptable in many Conservative synagogues in the country and used during Sabbath services. This was true, but I convinced him that I was not going to change my mind on that issue.

He shared this information with the congregation's president. A few days later, Mr. Rubenstein informed me that the temple board had agreed to discontinue using the organ on the Sabbath if I accepted the offer. I then felt bound to agree to begin serving the congregation as rabbi and education director. Following my resignation from the Beth Israel congregation, Riva and I moved to Wakefield, and I began serving the congregation of Temple Emmanuel of Wakefield effective August 1, 1964.

During the following High Holidays that September, when all members of the congregation usually attend worship services, I was welcomed by all very warmly. Soon after the holy days, I reorganized the Jewish youth of the community and affiliated them with the national and regional organizations of United Synagogue Youth. By the end of the first school year, I had upgraded the curriculum of the religious school. I increased the number of days and hours of instruction to three days, six hours per week, for six years to qualify for bar and Bat Mitzvah and graduation celebrations. These were all standards projected by the United Synagogue.

Rabbi Goldstein continues to tell that over time he introduced adult education programs and established contacts with the non-Jewish community and clergy, that he was blessed with the support of the congregation and loved the pleasant association with his congregants, and that his wife, Riva, took much pride in her husband's accomplishments. These warm friendships, he said, lasted throughout the seven years of his tenure with the congregation and that many of the friendships have continued into the present.

Prior to and Following Wakefield

Before coming to Wakefield, Baruch had served as principal of the religious school of the Conservative Beth Israel Congregation in Worcester, Mass. He had established strong ties in Worcester and so decided to leave Wakefield and accept the position of assistant rabbi at the much larger congregation. When the senior rabbi of Beth Israel retired, Baruch assumed the senior rabbi position and for over a decade served the congregation with his singular skill and passion and palpable distinction.

———————————

My Dear Friend, Rabbi Jack,

I take the liberty to send you my recently published book with the hope that you will find it of interest. I was moved to write it, not only to tell the experiences and losses I suffered during the Shoah, but also to convey a message for the future.

I shall never forget your friendship and the inspiration you gave me in finding my calling. I can look back to the years past with a sense of satisfaction for not having wasted my time which God granted me to live.

With my best wishes to you and your beloved family,

Baruch

NEIL WEINBERG AND THE INTRODUCTION TO JUDAISM/CONVERSION PROGRAM

For many years the University of Judaism conducted an Elderhostel program designed for seniors at the UJ building and its conference grounds in Ojai, California. The late Shabbat afternoon program featured a discussion with a set of converts to Judaism. I often asked the fifty to one hundred persons assembled from all over the country to raise their hands if their families had experienced an intermarriage. Invariably and over a period of fifteen years, approximately ninety percent of the hands were raised!

This is a microcosm of the extraordinary degree of intermarriage between Jews and non-Jews that prevails in our time.

When I arrived at the university as dean of continuing education, I was assigned the task of directing the Introduction to Judaism/Conversion Program designed to meet the challenges of the region's intermarriage problem; this was to lead the non-Jew to Judaism and its way of life. I tried hard given the few resources available.

Then a major development. Facing ever-increasing demand on my time and overburdened by administering the program in light of expanding tasks as DCE dean, I had a chance meeting with an active UJ board member, Louis Miller, in the garage area of the Federation building after we had attended a meeting. I unburdened myself about my problems and mused about how good it would be and what could happen if only we had a full-time rabbi responsible for the program, a full-time secretary, other specialized staff, and the means for publicizing our venture.

Mr. Miller asked me how much it would take to make that happen. I estimated $250,000. Right then and there, Lou responded, "Jack, you have it." Within two weeks a $250,000 check was deposited with the UJ—and it launched us into a new era of grappling constructively with the issue of intermarriage and conversion to Judaism.

I proceeded to engage Rabbi Neil Weinberg, who possessed special sensitivity for this genre of student, as director and instructor of the program. We also provided him with ample resources to proceed. He developed a full and comprehensive program of study and experience designed to impart knowledge and understanding of the Jewish historical saga and of the Jewish people today. He sought also to develop an appreciation of the basic tenets of the Jewish faith, of its fundamental values and characteristic practices.

The Hebrew language was introduced, leading to the ability to use the prayerbook in the synagogue, and to handle comfortably the corpus of Hebrew blessings, songs and prayers in the home. In addition to the "why's of Jewish law, custom and ceremony and the "how to" of these, the "spirit," the inner purposes of this religious action were stressed.

Over the years, Neil amplified the program by:

- Offering approximately fifteen to eighteen separate eighteen-week cycles throughout the year, rather than the five cycles as heretofore.

- Adding staff psychologists for individual counseling for the prospective converts who were dealing with significant emotional issues involved.

- Adding weekend/Shabbat retreats as an integral part of the program.

- Establishing support groups to discuss issues of concern for people who were choosing to become Jewish—this with others going through the same process.

- Continuing to refine the course content in light of our teaching experience.

- Clarifying and intensifying the requirements by the Rabbinical Assembly for conversion. This included requiring the Jewish partner to attend the classes; personal meetings with a local rabbi; attendance at synagogue services on a regular basis; acceptance of invitations to Jewish homes for Shabbat and Festival meals; examination by a *Bet Din* (Rabbinical Court) for knowledge of and commitment to Judaism and the Jewish way of life; full circumcision, or (if already circumcised) *hatafat dam brit* for male converts, immersion in the *mikvah* for both male and female proselyte; participating in a formal conversion ceremony marking completion of the study and conversion process.

- Participating in "Post Introduction to Judaism Program of Study."

- Offering separate eighteen-week cycles on five different days of the week—Monday through Thursday, plus separate cycles on Sunday—one in the morning and one in the afternoon. This was designed to accommodate the different time constraints and work schedules of potential students.

- Offering additional eighteen-session cycles in locales other than the UJ in Pasadena, Thousand Oaks, Agoura/West Valley, in Lakewood, Long Beach, Santa Monica, Corona, Westchester/Manhattan Beach.

This introduction to Judaism venture has served some one hundred students a year over the past thirty years. (This is not an exaggeration!) The vast majority of these students have been ushered into the Jewish fold. This program has shaped most of the career of Rabbi Neil Weinberg.

The following press release issued on June 5, 2020, captioned, "The Rabbinical Assembly (the national association of the Conservative Movement rabbinate), has partners with the Miller Introduction to Judaism Program."

The Rabbinical Assembly is pleased to announce official adoption of the Introduction to Judaism program of the American Jewish University (formerly the University of Judaism).

The program features a highly recommended curriculum and action venture for our congregations throughout the country as they offer prospective converts a home in the Jewish community. The Introduction to Judaism venture provides an exceptional, eighteen-unit foundational path designed to guide your students on a path to Jewish belonging. AJU has committed to create additional resources to help your teachers adapt to distance learning.

ARI VERNON: A STUDENT AND HIS TEACHERS

The following article was printed in the student newspaper of the University of Judaism. It was submitted by Ari Vernon, a student of mine in a Bible class I had been teaching. Ari went on to become a Conservative rabbi.

The name of our school presents a dichotomy, I was told recently. The students are interested in the university, and the founders are interested in the Judaism. Well, while many of the students did come here for the university, I am here for the Judaism. There are times when the Jewishness really shines through. Yes, it's wonderful to have Shabbat and Chanukah parties, but those pale in comparison to the evening my classmates and I spent at our teacher's home.

A Siyum Suggested

When Rabbi Jack Shechter suggested that we have a *siyum*, a ceremony marking completion of our semester of study, most of us leaned back in our seats, expecting some crazy fantastic idea. Rabbi Shechter is a teacher of the old yeshiva style, and after he explained it, we agreed to participate in what we thought was a quaint vestige of old-world Judaism. As the appointed evening approached, anticipation grew. Knowing there was more to Rabbi Shechter than meets the eye, we were excited to meet Mrs. Shechter and see their home.

The party started; Mrs. Shechter introduced herself, and we sat around the living room. As we began talking, Mrs. Shechter, who works for Stephen Wise Day School, asked if any of us were interested in teaching, so we started to talk about our interests. The Shechters also started telling stories of their lives. They wanted to share so much, and we were all ears. We got a tour of the house; not one inch of wall space is left uncovered. The study was a wall-to-wall reading room, complete with a comfy chair in the snuggle-up-with-a-book corner. On the wall of diplomas, I read the signatures on Rabbi Shechter's *smicha* (ordination). The names of Abraham Joshua Heschel and Mordecai Kaplan made me feel like I was in a holy place.

We washed before dinner in the traditional ritual fashion, made *motzi* and Rabbi Shechter told us that one of our responsibilities was to finish what Mrs. Shechter had prepared for dinner! I haven't had a more delicious meal since I came to L.A., and I'm sure that it was colored by the whole experience that evening. As we sat and talked, the Shechters played off each other, telling us about their congregation in Pittsburgh, their times at the seminary, and how they met.

I have never felt more surrounded by *yiddishkeit*. Rabbi Shechter likes to create Judaic art out of found objects. We found out that his artistic concentration is *"besomim boxes"* for *havdalah*. The dining room display had about twenty-five of them.

Divrei Torah Delivered

As the meal ended, we were asked to give the *Divrei Torah* we had prepared. Some of us shared what we learned in class; others expressed their understanding of the biblical narrative, tying a story or verse into something special about their lives. After each one, Rabbi Shechter and sometimes Mrs. Shechter would comment on something we said, enriching our words of Torah with theirs. When Rabbi Shechter asked his wife to give a *D'var Torah*, in declining for lack of preparation, she quoted verse upon verse of Torah in support of her declining.

After *Birkat Hamazon*, as the evening came to a close, we didn't really want to leave. The Shechters kept sharing stories, and we kept asking for more. As we got up to leave, we were still "drinking with thirst" the words of our teachers.

Ari concluded his article noting that the positive experience of Judaism that evening will remain. Such an encounter with his people, history and religion make it meaningful to be part of the Jewish experience, and the University of Judaism a special place. He then thanked Rabbi Jack and Leah Shechter for enriching the lives of those present that evening with the warmth and love shared and will continue to share with the UJ students.

Every student carries in his mind or heart or conscience a bit of the teacher. The teacher's example, ideas and values keep marching on—how far into the future and into what realms of our spacious universe the student may never know.

—Margaret E. Jenkins

AN EMAIL FROM HERBERT ROSENBLUM

It was a wonderful experience—receiving a copy of your latest book—*In Search of the Religiosity in Religion*. It confirmed my old feelings of affection and admiration for you as a friend and as a wonderful exemplar of what a modern rabbi should truly be.

It took me back to the old days when we worked so closely in a largely successful effort to upgrade the quality of Jewish life in the Boston area. You were a major part of my motivation to go on to work on my doctoral thesis at Brandeis on "The Founding of the United Synagogue of America in 1913. The other part of my motivation was my friendship with old Rabbi Herman Rubenovitz, who, in retirement, became an active member of my Temple Emunah congregation, and ended up giving me his entire correspondence as Solomon Schechter's appointee to the chairmanship of the Committee on Conservative Union.

I have already read half of your book, and it makes delightful reading. Your hand-written note to me was also very touching.

Meanwhile, love to Leah, who is undoubtedly very proud of her accomplished husband, and rightly so.

Hazzak, Hazzak,

Your old buddy, Herb

I had written an article intended for publication in the Boston Jewish Advocate. *It was highly critical of the organized Jewish community due to its perceived ignoring of the critical needs of the religious and educational elements of its synagogue constituency. As a persistent critic of the community's Federation as director of the United Synagogue in New England, I was fearful of yet another rebuke by my cautious superiors in the national New York office. And so, not to be fully deterred, I asked my colleague, Herb Rosenblum—a close collaborator of mine—to publish the article in the* Advocate *using his own name as an author. He did. I escaped yet more trouble.*

AFTER FIFTY-FIVE YEARS A WOMAN SAYS "THANK YOU"

Cast your bread on the waters, and after many days you will find it.

—Ecclesiastes 11:1

Among the various interpretations of the above saying in Scripture is this one: all too often when we bestow some good on another person, we do not receive gratitude on the part of that person. However, there are times when, after the lapse of years, the recipient does express words of gratitude.

Such is the case depicted in the correspondence reprinted below. Elouise Moody lived in the Shechter household during a hectic period when Leah and I were raising our three very young sons. Judah had just been born, David was age two, and Reuven was age four. I was a busy director of the New England Region of the United Synagogue of America, and Leah took care of the children and the household. She needed help. Elouise Moody was that help.

This was in 1963. On July 31, 2018—fifty-five years later!—we were astonished to receive a letter from Yolanda Kelly, Elouise's daughter, along with photos of her mother in 1963 juxtaposed with one as of 2018. As you will see, the letter was full of appreciation about her mother's stay with us, along with another letter from Elouise herself.

The Correspondence

Yolanda's letter…

July 31, 2018

Dear Rabbi Jack & Leah Shechter:

Once upon a time, in the year of 1963, a young girl named Elouise Moody from South Carolina came to work for you all when you all lived in Brookline, MA, and lived in your home, and babysat your three boys and did domestic work.

That girl is my mother.

My name is Yolanda. Throughout the years of my life, she often shared so much about you and your family, like how kind you all were to her and how you showed her so much caring and love!

For example, there was one time during her stay with you all, the rabbi took some time off of his work and took her to a black Baptist Church, and that you enjoyed the service yourself because of the enthusiastic worshippers.

It was a beautiful memory for her, just a simple act of kindness to a lonely girl, that she would never forget and would always treasure that act in her heart.

Also, she would share with us how when she went shopping for groceries, that there were certain things on the food labels that she needed to look out for in order to determine whether the item was kosher or not! I now sometimes find myself doing that, too!

So as a token of my appreciation, I just want to say thank you showing her how much you all cared about her!

Meanwhile, I also wanted to let you know that I have bought Volume One of your book, *Journey of a Rabbi*, and will be presenting it to my mom as a gift!

I'm sure that she will enjoy reading your journey of your past and your life experiences as a rabbi as well as seminary educator.

I myself have also enjoyed the book as I've learned more about Jewish traditions, cultural values and ceremonial practices, which may culminate with me taking a trip to Israel some day!

Lastly, I am pleased that you all were allowed to cross paths as I feel that our lives have been made all the more rich as a result!

All the best, Sincerely, Shalom.

Yolanda Kelly

Elouise's Letter

September 2018

Dear Rabbi and Mrs. Shechter:

I often thought about you all after leaving Brookline, MA, and wondered where you all were located. *Thank God for technology!* My daughter, Yolanda, looked you all up on the internet and found you all.

After leaving Brookline, I often wanted to tell you how much I enjoyed working for you and living in your home. At first, I really was afraid when I first came there of how you all were going to receive me. I remember when I arrived at the bus station I was nervous. I thought a rabbi with a black hat and flowing suit and long beard would meet me. Instead a clean-shaven and modern dress young rabbi was there. With enthusiastic voice and warm embrace you greeted me. How relieved I was and how good it felt!

You, Mrs. Shechter, accepted me and made me feel welcome and *trusted* me in *your home* and trusted me to take care of your sons. You taught me how to take care of your infant baby. He was just three months old when I came to work for you. By taking care of your infant baby and your family, I learned how to take care of my own family. It certainly was a learning experience. I wasn't just there for the money. I enjoyed what I was doing and it *truly* was a *joy* working for you. I learned many valuable things. The *food* was simply *delicious* too.

I learned a lot of things from and about Rabbi Shechter also. I learned about banking when you took me to a bank in Brookline and got me to open a bank account. You vouched for me. That was so kind and helpful.

I also remember that once you took me to the movies to see the *Sound of Music* and that you enjoyed it as much as I did. Ever since, I've loved musicals.

Yolanda mentioned the time when one Sunday you took me

to a Baptist Church for a bit of change from my work and for some spiritual uplift. I enjoyed it so. You told me how much you appreciated the service which was so full of joy and enthusiasm. "Those folks know to pray," you said.

I am so happy to hear that your sons are doing so well, and also to know that you both are also doing well and keeping active and that life has been good.

Elouise

Rabbi Jack's Letter

October 2018

Dear Elouise:

I usually am able to find the words to express myself. However, in this instance they elude me. This is because your letter and Yolanda's touched my heart and mind with strong impact.

First, of course, due to your sensitivity in expressing gratitude after so many years. Scripture tells us "Cast your bread on the waters, for after many days you will find it" (Ecclesiastes 11:1). Indeed, it is not often that one renders thanks for some good bestowed after fifty-five years! Your good heart did this and you have brought deep satisfaction to Leah and myself as a result. For this we thank you most heartily.

Yet more: the literacy of your letter, its accurate and neat handwriting, the progress you and your children have made in the world, the high quality of your spirit expressed so well, are elements of personality which are not only inherent but also products of a land of opportunity, no matter how flawed. For this, as a Jew whose people has been through so much difficulty, is a matter justly deserving of gratitude.

Leah's letter contains much of the rest about you and us which I share.

In the words of the priests in the Temples of old…as recorded in the Book of Numbers 6:24-27…

May the Lord bless you and keep you.

May the Lord cause His countenances to shine upon you and be gracious to you.

May the Lord turn His face to you, and grant you (that most precious of gifts) peace.

Amen.

Sincerely yours,

Rabbi Jack Shechter

_____

Yes, indeed, cast your bread on the waters, and after many years you will find it.

—Ecclesiastes 11:1

A "SHIDDUCH"

The young colleague of mine in his late twenties—tall, bright, physically attractive, well-educated—occupied a neighboring pulpit. In his busy life a wife eluded him. I felt for him.

It happened that I had an active United Synagogue youth program in my congregation which required skilled male and female advisors for the vigorous Jewish teens. A tall, highly attractive young lady was one of them. She was strongly committed Jewishly. She told me during one of the conclaves that she "had her eyes on" the attractive, "eligible" and unattached young rabbi in the city. I sprung into action.

I brought the two together to meet and probe the possibility. They met regularly. The young lady was eager, the young man hesitant. During several intense conversations with him, he agreed that the young lady had numerous good qualities: smart, attractive, talented, religiously oriented and more. But, *he was not sure that he was in love with her.*

I continued with my action plan at a personal meeting in my home on a Saturday afternoon with the young rabbi for an analysis of the subject of "love." Here I unleashed my "expertise" on the matter.

> Is love a purely emotional notion? Are there not numerous and important virtues that contribute to the notion of love? Compassion, intelligence, good education, talent, religiosity and more. Yet more: look more closely into this girl's expressive eyes; look at the way she looks at you with such yearning spirit; besides, you cannot survive these days in the rabbinic without a suitable partner...and I went on and on concluding: you've got to be crazy to let this young lady out of your gasp. If you do, she will surely marry another and you will regret it for the rest of your life! (Leah in clandestine had listened this "speech" of mine, and later told me she thought the

conversation might well "work."

The young rabbi listened and listened. Within a year, the two married, and over the years produced three lively children; he occupied his pulpit for over thirty years with marked success; and she as his wife at her husband's side was of enormous help in their personal and professional life. Boy, have they been "in love."

———————————————

Matchmaking is no small undertaking. I have always been proud of this achievement.

– Chapter Fifteen –

EXPERIENCES VIS-À-VIS YOUNG PEOPLE

כְּחִצִּים בְּיַד גִּבּוֹר כֵּן בְּנֵי הַנְּעוּרִים

As arrows in the hand of a warrior are the young.

—Psalm 127:4

LORI YOUNG: A YOUNG WOMAN
LEAVES HOME FOR AN IOWA FARM

The young woman's name was Lori Young, a distant cousin of mine. She grew up in a middle-class home. It was a typical Jewish home at the time—casually observant of religious ritual, Friday eve candle-lighting, the Passover Seder, High Holy Day services, partial kashrut observance, Sunday school.

Lori had a sensitive temperament and felt something lacking in her life and that of her family—the spiritual dimension. Something inside her yearned for the mystical, for personal meaning, for a connection with a force outside of herself. She felt that the sparse and mechanical ritual of her Jewish milieu did not speak to her heart.

Her search led her to Reverend John Davenport, leader of a religious commune located on a farm in Davenport, Iowa. (No connection between the Reverend's name and that of the town.) There Lori made "a decision for Christ," married a member of the commune (not Rev. Davenport) and had several children. She committed herself to a life of hard farm work combined with daily worship, meditation and religious discipline which "resonated in her soul," as she put it, which satisfied her yearning for the spiritual way. In the process, she abandoned her parents, her siblings, her Jewish home, her people.

Lori's parents were mortified. They came from New York to Pittsburgh, seeking counsel and how I might help in what they felt was a wrenching tragedy. I suggested they arrange for Lori and her mentor to come to Pittsburgh for a weekend and that the parents should join them. They would all stay with us. It was arranged.

I Had a Plan

I wanted Lori and Reverend Davenport to imbibe the spirit of a warm and happy Jewish home, starting with Thursday evening dinner with my wife and three animated sons. I wanted them to experience our Friday morning minyan at the synagogue with its singing service and contemporary prayer followed by our breakfast of good food and warm camaraderie. And then the Shabbat evening dinner with lit candles, ample festive meal, soulful kiddush chant and joyful table song. And then the Shabbat morning service in a beautiful synagogue sanctuary featuring majestic music by cantor and choir, followed by another Shabbat meal at noon at our home. And then Shabbat afternoon study and napping—this all to concluding with the moving Havdalah ceremony marking the transition from holy Sabbath to the ordinary weekday.

I thought this all would make a positive impression on Lori, and that along with conversation about the specialness of the Jewish way, we might make some headway with Lori.

It did not work out as I had planned.

A Consequential Coincidence

We had as our guest at the Thursday evening dinner Dr. Yosef Yerushalmi, a classmate of mine at the Jewish Theological Seminary, who was to serve as "Scholar-in-Residence" that weekend. A brilliant history professor at Columbia University, he was also an intense person with strong opinions. At the table Reverend Davenport was holding forth about the glories of Christianity and the spiritual power which Jesus had injected into the world.

Whereupon Dr. Yerushalmi literally exploded in anger, describing the pain and suffering Jews have endured through the centuries, inflicted by intolerant Christians in the name of a "loving" Jesus Christ. Startled as we already were by his words, the professor then rose from his seat and stormed out of the room.

I had planned a gentler approach with our visitors, but Dr. Yerushalmi was not to be managed.

"We Can't Stay Here Anymore"

The next morning, Lori, Rev. Davenport, myself, Lori's parents and our dozen and a half minyanaires sat at the breakfast table following the daily worship service. Suddenly Lori stood up, placed her hands confidently on the back of her chair and proceeded with calm self-assurance to speak. All eyes were riveted on her radiant face. "We can't stay here any longer," she said. "We've seen as much as we need to see. And it won't matter what you intend to show us tonight and tomorrow. I believe in the Lord Jesus Christ, who has enriched my life, my children, my new world. You Jews have nothing to offer me, nor do my parents. In the name of the Lord Jesus, Reverend Davenport and I bless you. Goodbye." They then walked out of the room.

Lori and her parents, along with the Reverend and me, came back to my home for the final encounter. With wrenching tears, Lori's parents pleaded that their daughter not abandon them, her religion and people. "We are your mother and father," they urged, to which Lori responded, "No you're not. Jesus is my father now." I continued to try to persuade her as did her parents. To no avail. Lori and the reverend proceeded to pack their sparse belongings and, Lori on the arm of Reverend Davenport, left the house, heading back to their Iowa farm.

Our planned weekend ended on Friday morning.

Five years later, Lori wrote to me and my wife, Leah, asking if we could recommend some children's books on Jewish religious subjects she could use for her children. She felt that Judaism was part of her children's heritage and wanted them to know something about it. We sent her a set of such books and asked Lori to stay in touch with us. She sent us a note of thanks. We have not heard from her since.

Lori's parents told us that Lori and her family have since left the commune. I've lost track of her whereabouts, but I do hope to hear from her again someday.

JASON NAROT...FORMERLY "NAROTSKY"

Following a two-year stint as an Army chaplain, my first pulpit was in the small Ohio town of Warren. I was a young, "green," twenty-eight-year-old rabbi.

I taught the confirmation class; it took place in my office with five teenagers. One was Jason Narot. I remember holding forth passionately about the "reprehensible" practice of some Jews altering their real last names in order to downplay their Jewishness, that this showed an absence of self pride, and on and on I went with what was, in my youthful and inexperienced years, a rabbi of deep conviction about the subject.

Suddenly, Jason got up from his chair and bounded out of the office. Startled, I followed him out onto the parking lot, where I saw tears in is eyes. "What is it?" I asked. He responded that his father altered his last name from "Narotsky" to "Narot" and they were good Jews and "you, rabbi, put us down. I'm in your confirmation class. Doesn't that tell you that we're okay Jews?" Seriously shaken up by Jason, I embraced him, apologized profusely and led him back into my office, and tried mightily to explain away my words to my five students.

What I learned from that jolting episode was the need for caution and sensitivity in a world where Jews strive to integrate into the larger society and yet retain their distinctiveness.

Avtalion said: חֲכָמִים הִזָּהֲרוּ בְּדִבְרֵיכֶם

"Ye sages, be heedful of your words."
— Pirke Avot 1:11

שִׁיתָה יְהוָה שָׁמְרָה לְפִי
נִצְּרָה עַל־דַּל שְׂפָתָי

"Set a guard, O Lord, over my mouth;
keep watch over the door of my lips."
— Psalm 141:3

VINCEY CAPARIZZO, JR. AND JUDAH'S YARMULKA

When we lived on Rippey Place in Pittsburgh during my pulpit days, we befriended the very Italian-Catholic Caparizzo family who also lived on Rippey Place. There was Vince Sr., his wife Marnie, daughter Ginny, son Vince Jr., and Marnie's sister Mary. It was a delightful, lively and friendly family.

Our three sons, Reuven, David and Judah ("Hooti" they called him) were pre-teens and constantly visited at the Caparizzos, playing theater games with talented Ginny and lively Vince Jr. (Vincey). Naturally, the three boys always had their yarmulkas on their heads, symbols of their strong Jewish religious ways.

"When we eat and pray and study—actually at all times—the *kipa* (skullcap, yarmulka) is always on their heads," Leah once explained.

Years later, in a letter to us in Los Angeles, Marnie reminisced about the good times with the Shechters. Here is an excerpt from her letter.

> One night (long ago, while still on Rippey place) I had made a nice supper with Vincy's favorite dishes. I called everyone in, they all sat down and Vincy started to cry. After much questioning, he finally sobbed that he could not eat supper because he didn't have on his yarmulka.
>
> I thought I'd die! I dashed into the living room— "Hootie" had left his yarmulka on the TV, I grabbed it, ran back to the kitchen and put it on Vincy's head. He was thrilled and started to eat. Much later I explained things to him, and all was okay! So many "cute" things happened like that—we love talking about them now.

In Talmudic times, covering the head was held to be a mark of piety. This is because "Heaven" is described as "up there." Consequently, the pious person covers his head in awe, creating a

*barrier between himself and "up there," so as not to become
overly familiar with the Divine. Thus covering the head is a sign
of respect for God. A folk etymology sees the object as an abbre-
viation of* yare malka, *"One who fears the King."*

A YOUNG MAN'S EYES RIVETED ON MINE

Personal identification with a rabbi takes many forms. Recently I had a striking experience of one such form. It was during a *shiva* call in a house of mourning. From the moment I walked through the door and throughout the evening's conversation, a young man's face was riveted on mine. We were talking about the purpose of various religious observances, such as Jewish mourning practices, the dietary laws, ritual in general. The young man was in his early twenties; his Jewish education and religious interests had been minimal; he was now married and living and working on a farm.

When I sought to explain the system of *kashrut* as designed to sensitize the Jew to the value of human life and to ennoble the simple act of eating, that consumption of meat was a "concession," as it were," to man's weakness, the young man reacted. He told me that he and his wife were vegetarians, speaking with quiet fervor and obvious conviction. With eyes sparkling, the young man with his earring dangling, urged me to try vegetarianism, that it was good for the spirit.

A Kindred Spirit

Then and there I sensed that I was in the presence of a kindred spirit, and I began to understand the focus on that young man's face.

The conversation moved on to the Passover seder. I made the point that the root purpose of the ritualized seder was to recall a particular ancient event that emphasized the notion of the Jewish people—and by extension all people—yearning for freedom. Whereupon our young man described the seder he, his wife and friends inaugurated recently in their home: they sat in a circle on the floor, sang freedom songs to guitar music, selectively recited some of the traditional text along with contemporary prose and poetry, used some of the seder symbols such as the matzah and horseradish, and followed the Haggadah in their own unconventional way.

All this was designed, the twenty-something said, to give expression to emotional impulses, to articulate the yearning for freedom, for liberation from the often oppressive shackles of modern society. And, yes, he and his friends recognized that some sort of form for the seder was necessary to effectively express these feelings. As the young man continued to talk with such clarity and passion, I realized increasingly that I was indeed in the presence of a kindred spirit. I now more fully understood the riveted intensity on his face as he listened and spoke to me.

I walked out of that *shiva* home that night uplifted—for reasons more than personal. I realized that this young man, until recently an estranged, indifferent Jew, was emotionally and psychically in sync with the inner rhythms of the religion of Israel—what I have called elsewhere, "the religiosity in religion."

Religion is the institutional, carefully structured, formal aspects of the faith community containing established doctrine and mandated action. Religiosity is the inner meaning, the irreducible spirit of the doctrines and practices of the faith community, that which constitutes one of the essential objectives of the institutional structure.

Thus, for example, in Martin Buber's landmark unpacking of the life and literature of Hasidism, he pointed out that what the spiritual leaders considered decisive in the observance of religious ritual was the intent and spirit, the aim of the action, the inner purpose of the panoply of practices the faithful were engaged in. Each person was obliged to unite action with its purpose and thus develop a truly religious personality. Indeed, Judaism at its most authentic can but be the fruit of the fusion of its religion with its religiosity. When this occurs, "there is the core of Judaism."

—From the back cover of Jack Shechter's
In Search of the Religiosity in Religion

ASHER MEIR: *YASHER KOAKH* ("WELL DONE")
AND HOW TO SHAKE HANDS

For some two decades I sat in the pews of Beth Jacob Congregation in Beverly Hills, California. Though I worked as dean of continuing education at the Conservative University of Judaism, Leah and I worshipped at this Orthodox congregation because the service was particularly satisfying, addressing as it did our traditional religious bent.

In the row just in front of me sat Rabbi Levi Meir and his son, Asher, every Shabbat and holiday. Levi was a warm and compassionate rabbi who served as the Jewish chaplain at Los Angeles' Cedars-Sinai Hospital. We became friends, and I became a friend of his son.

The friendship with Asher began when he was three years old. Each Shabbat morning at the conclusion of services, we would shake hands. The handshake, at first, was meek with the boy's head either down or aside, not looking at me. The regimen started: "Hold my hand firmly; squeeze it and as you do, look me straight in the face and say 'Shabbat Shalom.'" This was the procedure Shabbat after Shabbat for ten years.

Fast forward...It was Asher's bar mitzvah. He acquitted himself beautifully. I was sitting in the raised seat area in the back of the sanctuary for the occasion. The service was over. Asher was on the central *bimah* having chanted the Adon Olam; Ignoring everyone else, he bounded through the aisle leading to where I was seated, climbed the steps, stretched out his hand, pressed mine firmly, looked me straight in the face, and wished me a hearty Shabbat Shalom, to which I responded, *yasher koach,* "well done," you used your talents for good purpose; you did beautifully on your bar mitzvah—and you have mastered the proper way to shake hands.

One of the proud achievements of my synagogue life!

Rabbi Yochanan in the midrash (Exodus Rabbah 20:10) says that someone who has performed a positive act should be lauded: אָמְרוּ לְפוֹעֲלָא טָבָא יְיַשֶׁר בֹּחַךְ — *"Say to a good worker: may your strength be straight", i.e., "well done." How so? Rabbi Yochanan asked, and responded, that such was called for because the Israelites successfully resisted the evil designs of the Pharoah and Haman. What did Rabbi Yochanan mean?*

The Israelites had used their strength appropriately, for a just and legitimate cause, the midrash is saying. Their strength was "straight" or "right," as it were. Thus in the ordinary case of a person having received an aliya, for example, at the synagogue Torah reading service, we shake the recipient's hand and say to him יְיַשֶׁר כֹּח, "You have used your strength for good purpose," and this Hebrew greeting has morphed into the equivalent of "well done."

Strength is morally neutral. It can be used for good, if it is "aimed straight" at legitimate purpose, or it can be bent and twisted for negative ends. Thus יְיַשֶׁר כֹּח, yasher koach is both an acknowledgement of strength in another person, as well as a recognition that it was used in a positive, constructive ("straight") way.

A SINGLE WOMAN AT THE DOOR

A program we initiated at the University of Judaism was designed for singles ages thirty-five and up to gather and meet and perhaps forge lasting relationships. It is ever a sensitive enterprise, though, of course, needed and necessary for reasons that need no elaboration.

On one such occasion I encountered a relatively young woman standing near the door to the hall where the din of talking singles could be heard. I asked the woman why she was standing outside. With visible apprehension in her demeanor, she replied that she didn't know. Well, go in, I urged. I'm hesitant; I don't want to get hurt yet again, she said. What do you mean? I asked. She replied, it's hard for me to take the rejection. Go in, I insisted. Be persistent and patient, I asserted; your *beshert* (the one destined for you) is somewhere on the planet; you just have to locate him. He might even be inside this hall. She finally went in.

My colleague Max Vorspan and I, two men relatively advanced in age compared to the women in that hall, decided to walk through the room that night to experience firsthand the dynamics of the gathering. As we ambled through the place, the women looked us over in a way that made us both feel like the most desirable men on earth.

The reader will, no doubt, remember the famous *midrash* about the Hebrew *matrona*, the matriarch in heaven who positioned the women on one side of a line and men on the other. She proceeded to match this woman to that man. Later, they came back to her with bruises on their faces because of conflict and incompatibility. Indeed, successful matchmaking is no easy task, neither in heaven nor on earth.

———————————————

Today we did not fail
Yesterday we did not succeed
Tomorrow we need the courage to try again.
> —Saying in nurse's office in Thousand Oaks, Calif.

STROLLING ALONG THE THIRD STREET MALL IN SANTA MONICA, CALIFORNIA

Interesting, offbeat locales often rivet my attention. Such has been the case during my frequent visits to the Third Street mall in Santa Monica, California. It is a place which attracts all manner of humanity—and frequently its "underbelly." Here are some of my experiences.

• A line from a song blared out of a nearby record store: "Even though you hate me, don't leave me alone…." Another: "You're nobody 'til somebody loves you. You're nobody 'til somebody cares." (My editor tells me these are the lyrics to a Dean Martin song.)

• A bedraggled young man accosts a young woman and pleads: "Take me home" She replies: "I don't do that kind of thing." "Is it because I'm ugly?" he asks. "No…" "Is it because I'm poor?" No response. The young man casually walks away and proceeds to another young woman nearby: "Take me home…."

• A vagrant, disheveled woman suddenly grabs my shoulder and demands, "I don't have the money to pay my rent, give me some" (no "please"). Me: "Why should I give you my hard-earned money?" "Listen mister," she responds, "don't ask questions, either give me ten dollars or I move on." I gave her only five dollars because of her "attitude." She took it with nary a word and moved on to her next customer.

• A man is sitting quietly and alone about to partake of a beef sandwich he had before him. A tottering man stares at the sandwich, and stares, whereupon the sandwich man takes his meal and hands it to his onlooker who grabs it and walks away without a word. I asked the sandwich man why he gave his meal away so willingly, to which he responded, "He needs it more than I do."

• Another man is relaxing outside a café smoking a cigarette. A vagrant, with an unlit cigarette he had just gotten "free of charge" from someone else, approaches the smoker, leans toward him with his cigarette to which the smoker places his lit cigarette to the unlit one. The vagrant walked away without a word.

• I'm standing in line at a Rite Aid store about to purchase some favorite ginger ale sodas. An unkempt fellow in foul-smelling clothes approaches me and asks me to buy a bottle of vodka for him since store employees refuse to sell him any vodka. The fellow give me his Rite Aid credit card and I oblige. I then ask him where he lives. He responds, "I have a good, safe place under the freeway."

While recording the above incidents at random, I began to reminisce.

My father's brother, Falek, left his poor home in Poland when a young man. My father, Louis, also left this home and came to America and prospered. Not Falek. He became a vagrant, wandering around the world, homeless, unmarried, lonely and Jewishly vacant. On one occasion my father, a printer by trade, persuaded Falek to live with his family in Englewood, New Jersey, where Dad would teach him the printing trade so he could make a living, marry, have children and, at long last, settle down. Falek stayed a few months and suddenly disappeared. My mother told me this story and added that Falek's family never set eyes on him again.

—JS

Note

The name Falek *is a variant of the German which means "falcon." It was a common Jewish name in Eastern Europe. The falcon is a bird with thin, tapered wings which enables it to fly at high speed and change direction rapidly. They have exceptional skills required to be effective providers of their basic needs.*

—Wikipedia, The Free Encyclopedia

MENDEL MORRIS:
ON NASCENT AND REALIZED PIETY

It was during high school years at the Mesivta Chaim Berlin in Brooklyn, New York. I was sixteen years old as was Mendel Morris. Mendel was a teenager whose ways revealed a persona way beyond his years. He was caring and modest and prayed with a focus which clearly stamped him as a person of genuine piety. There was an intangible something about his calm demeanor that lent authority to the way he interacted with his peers. Untypical as it was among teens, I, as well as Mendel's classmates, respected Mendel and accepted his ever-offered gentle advice and ministrations.

I had the feeling then that Mendel Morris in later life would be a special religious leader.

Fast forward fifty years. I'm in Los Angeles; I receive a call from a Rabbi Yosef Ashinsky; he's in town from New York seeking to purchase old *sforim* (traditional rabbinic books) from rabbis who were reputed to have them in their library; he would then resell them. This was how he made his living. I invited him to my home so that he would scan my library and see what I might be willing to part with.

In the course of conversation, I told him that as a teen I attended Mesivta Chaim Berlin (he already knew this via his honed intelligence-gathering apparatus). Whereupon he asked, "Do you remember my father-in-law, Mendel Morris?"

Startled, I replied, "Yes, of course," and proceeded to describe my recollection of him. "Where does he live and what does he do?" I asked.

He replied, "He lives in Monsey, New York, is a *mashgiakh rukhani*, a spiritual guide and mentor at a Yeshiva there. He is widely known as a person of saintly character and has influenced countless young men to pursue and deepen their ways as *frum* (pious) Jews and caring *mentschen*."

A person's early youthful characteristics often portend the future nature of that person. Jonathan Sacks has articulated this phenomenon in a more "cosmic" way:

> *In the earliest stages of an embryo, when a fetus is till no more than a small bundle of cells, already it contains the genome, the long string of DNA, from which the child and eventually the adult will emerge. The gene structure that will shape the person it becomes is there from the beginning.*

—Koren Rosh Hashanah Mahzor, p. xii

PAUL DANIELS AND JEWISH "RADAR"

During my Pittsburgh rabbinate I used to stay in touch with our synagogue's young people who went off to college. Naturally, a perennial concern was whether or not these young folk were keeping in contact with fellow Jews on campus and whether they were keeping their Jewish identities intact in the context of the open, liberal and free-wheeling life of college; this is especially important since they were disconnected from their homes and the synagogue in which they were reared.

Paul Daniels had been one of our leaders in USY during his teens. At a college homecoming weekend, I asked Paul the usual questions. He replied that he did keep in contact with his fellow Jewish students, both directly and indirectly. I understood the direct contact, but what did he mean by indirect contact; how did he know who was Jewish and who was not?

Paul's reply: "There is that thing I call *Jewish radar*." He explained that there is some invisible, intangible something in other Jews that enables you to sense that they are your brethren. Paul could not clearly explain what he meant, and to this day I can't fully get my arms around the notion either. Yet I'm persuaded that *Jewish radar* is very real and still quite operative in the lives of Jews, not only in America, but wherever they live.

———————————

In this human being there is something that makes him a Jewish human being, something imponderably small yet immeasurably great, his most inaccessible secret yet which breaks form from every gesture and from every word and most of all from the most casual nod....This "something" is simply lived. It is what one is...an indefinable essence.

—Franz Rosenzweig

MARTY SMILOWITZ: BOYHOOD FRIEND

When I was in my early teens, I had a good friend. His name was Marty Smilowitz. We lived in the Brownsville section of Brooklyn, New York, a teeming area crowded with struggling immigrants whose children were striving to learn and grow into poverty-less adulthood in what was the land of opportunity. Marty and I belonged to a club of boys that met weekly at the Hebrew Education Society (HES), the Jewish Community Center, on Sutter Avenue.

I knew that Marty's family lived in difficult financial straits, in a cramped apartment—small, dark and unkempt. His mother struggled to keep the household together; his father went from job to job eking out a living. Suddenly, his father came upon an opportunity: he would manage a small restaurant and bar on Tenth Avenue in Manhattan.

With restrained pride, Marty took me to the Manhattan restaurant/bar to see the new place his father managed. It was a *flop house*—vagrants, homeless, alcoholics, drug addicts were its regular customers. It was a scene etched in my memory throughout the years.

Marty left home and joined the Marines. When he came home, he told me of the vigorous training, how it toughened him for the business of life. We subsequently went our quite different ways. But I never forgot him, or his father's new "opportunity" or Marty's pride in his dad.

A father is a man who expects his son to be as good a man as he himself meant to be.

SHELLEY: FROM "SHAYTEL" (WIG)
TO PRANCING IN THE MALL

Shelley was reared in a non-Orthodox home in Kansas City, Missouri. She became strictly observant religiously at the firm prompting of her husband who brooked no departure from the required religious lifestyle he himself adopted as a *baal teshuva*, a newly-observant, conviction-full young adult.

Shelley once told me how uncomfortable and uneasy she felt about her new lifestyle. She had a restless spirit, unrealized aspirations as a young woman now a mature adult. Yet she married her strictly religious husband and, among the many other new observances, donned a *shaytel*, a head covering worn regularly. With a quiet, sad sigh she confided that she knew well that this head covering was masking her natural hair. "Why would a religious lifestyle cover up such a God-given gift," she murmured.

Fast forward to some five years later: I'm strolling along the Third Street mall in Santa Monica. Suddenly I see a young, slim, attractive young woman. She's dressed in tight shorts, in a thin and revealing blouse, her hair flowing in all directions, prancing happily through the mall followed by a young man with a wagging ponytail. The young woman was Shelley.

I had a friend in college who was naturally left-handed. His father, a firm religious traditionalist, insisted that his son function as right-handed, especially when it came to donning the tefillin. The tefillin strap had to be placed on his left arm because that's the way a right-handed Jew is to function, the father insisted.

My friend told me that this experience had a negative psychological effect on him throughout his young life. The reason? His religious practice forced him to function in life contrary to his born nature as left-handed.

– Chapter Sixteen –

FRIENDS

A friendless man is like a right hand without the left.

—*Mivchar Happeninim,* Solomon Ibn Gabirol

GILBERT ROSENTHAL: NATURAL RAPPORT

Gil was a classmate at the Jewish Theological Seminary's Rabbinical School from which we both graduated in 1957. We were friends during college days at Yeshiva University. YU was an Orthodox institution and both Gil and I wanted to "escape" to the Conservative seminary. For me, leaving YU was not easy because my Orthodox family ties were strong and YU authorities looked askance at its students leaving for the "heterodox" seminary.

Rumor spread that I intended to go to the Conservative seminary, whereupon Rabbi Sar, the YU dean, summoned me to his office to probe if such was, indeed, my intention. I said to the good dean, "Me, a Shechter, going to the Conservative seminary; how can you think such a thing?" Nonetheless, I left Rabbi Sar's office worried, for if I were found out, I could be in trouble as was another student, Morton Narrow, who had been stripped of the honors he had earned when he was "found out."

Even though many others at the time, such as Harold Schulweis Chaim Potok and Yosef Yerushalmi, had made the move from YU to the seminary "unscathed," I remained apprehensive. My friend Gil Rosenthal was not, even though, as an honor student and on YU's debating team, he had something to lose. And so I asked Gil that when he bravely went to the seminary offices to get the rabbinical school application and other forms, he get them for me as well. (I did not want to be seen at the place and be "found out.") Gil did and we both eventually entered the august halls of the Jewish Theological Seminary.

A bond was forged between Gil and me. We dormed together at the seminary for two years. Gil was very meticulous in his personal ways, was an excellent student who valued friendship. He occupied a major pulpit in Cedarhurst, New York for many years, published several books about Jewish life, received a doctorate at Columbia University under the tutelage of the renowned historian Salo Baron, and served for a number of years as executive vice-president of the New York Board of Rabbis. Gil and I retained an inner connection throughout the years. Among other things I gained from our friendship was a consciousness of personal bearing and the importance of carrying oneself with dignity.

The test of friendship is its fidelity when every charm of fortune early on has faded away, and the bare undraped character alone remains. If regard still holds steadfast, and the joy of companionship, even at a distance, survives the passage of time, the friendship sustains even old age.

— Author unknown

MERVIN GRAY: A BOND WITH RABBIS

Mervin was the treasurer of the New England Region of the United Synagogue of America when I served as its director from 1961 to 1966. He and his wife, Rosalind, were traditional Conservative Jews and active in their synagogue, Temple Emeth in a suburb of Boston. Mervin was a past president of his congregation, a generous supporter of numerous Jewish communal causes. The Jewish way of life was their way of life.

Abiding friendship and attachment to rabbis were hallmarks of their ways. For over forty years since my leaving Boston, Mervin and Rosalind's contact with us was never-failing. They traveled to our son's Bar Mitzvah in Pittsburgh; they made their way to New Haven to join us for our son Judah's graduation from Yale; we celebrated their daughter Gila's wedding in a special way in San Diego with me serving as their rabbi; we attended the Bar Mitzvah of their grandson in that city; it was a rare occasion when Mervin and Rosalind did not call us prior to the High Holy Days to exchange well wishes for the New Year. This all at first a thousand miles and, later, three thousand miles removed from Boston.

A Scene at a Train Station

Ordinary scenes do not necessarily merit recording. For me, however, one such has remained fixed in my memory, a memento of the nature of caring friendship.

Leah and I were about to leave San Diego by train back to Los Angeles. Mervin and Rosalind had brought us to the station and waited until we boarded the train. When the train was delayed and after another long wait, they finally waved and left the station platform for their daughter's home. The train still stood still. Suddenly, I saw Mervin rushing back to the train platform, bound into the car we were seated in, asked us if we were okay and comfortable, left the train and waited and waited until it finally slowly moved on its way. And there Mervin stood, waving goodbye until the train was out of sight.

Loyalty to Rabbis

Mervin's connection with and loyalty to rabbis was visceral. Rabbi Zev Nelson, the long-time leader of Temple Emeth, was Mervin's spiritual guide throughout the years. He loved Rabbi Nelson for his compassion, revered him for his deep learning, respected him for his passionate dedication to Day School education, and unfailingly responded to Rabbi Nelson's importunities for support of his manifold causes.

Rabbi Sidney Steinman occupied a pulpit in Boston before moving to a prominent pulpit in Indianapolis. Through work together on communal matters, they grew close. In the preface to his book *Custom and Survival* about Rabbi Jacob ben Moses Halevi Molin of Mainz, Germany, known as the Maharil, Rabbi Steinman wrote this: "Heartfelt thanks are extended to Rosalind and Mervin D. Gray, whose loyalty and friendship for the author have been a source of great blessing and inspiration."

There was Rabbi Abraham Halbfinger, supervisor of the kashrut system in Boston on behalf of the City's Board of Rabbis. Mervin was his treasurer and loyalist and provided the vital layman support for that cause.

And there was Robert Miller, a retired Reform rabbi in Boston, who by coincidence was a boyhood friend of mine in our Brooklyn Yeshiva. Every Shabbat morning they got together and attended a different synagogue service in the Boston area. Mervin had a special affinity for this rabbi, felt comfortable in his presence and enjoyed experiencing Shabbat synagogue life with him.

———————————————

Appreciative men esteem and value nothing so much in this world as a real friend. Such a one, as it were, is another self, to whom we impart our inner thoughts, who partakes of our joy, and comforts us in our affliction; add to this, that his company is a lasting pleasure to us.

—Author unknown

LOUIS SHUB: UNCONDITIONAL FRIENDSHIP

Louis was the librarian at the University of Judaism in Los Angeles for some four decades. His wife, Ruth, had passed away, after which Louis remarried. He had no children. He was a man of great intellectual curiosity, an expert analyst and archivist of Israel and Middle Eastern affairs and devoted keeper of the library's many treasures.

A slight man, soft-spoken, warm and embracing in manner, he was a friend and confidante of many of his colleagues at the university. I was among them.

So, for example, whenever I would come into his office just to chat and report about the latest, he would drop whatever he was occupied with, offer a seat and listen — and emphasize, encourage, compliment, and softly criticize. He invariably made me feel good about the encounter. He spoke about himself but glancingly; he let those who came to him speak most of the time for, you see, he was the quintessential conversationalist, that is to say listener.

Someone once depicted a good conversationalist this way: Two people were talking. One spoke 90% of the time; the other but ten percent. Said the former to the latter, "You are a good conversationalist." Louis Shub was, indeed, the greatest conversationalist I've ever encountered in my life.

Toward the end, when, alas, Louis was seriously infirm, I came to visit him at his nineteenth-floor apartment on Wilshire Boulevard, which provided a panoramic view of the city. He was in a wheelchair attended by his caring wife and a Filipino aide. He greeted me with his signature warmth. His face was wan, but his eyes glowed. As usual, he asked me about my activities and welfare and spoke little about his condition.

When I was about to leave, he took my hand, kissed it and said goodbye. He implied that this was to be our final encounter. Soon after, he passed away. At his funeral, I kissed his casket as it passed by the assemblage and said goodbye to a cherished friend.

A true friend unbosoms freely, advises justly, assists readily, takes all patiently, listens intently, defends, and continues a friend unchangeable.

—William Penn

ELI SCHOCHET: BOUND IN SPIRIT

Eli, a graduate of the seminary, a pulpit rabbi in Los Angeles and warm pastor of his flock for decades, is a scholar of rabbinics. He published a set of volumes about renowned Talmudists, including the seminary's own Saul Lieberman, as well as a volume about the rabbinic views concerning the treatment of animals and another about Hasidism. I always valued Eli as a person of substance and authenticity; I attended some of his "book signing" events and installed him as a regular teacher in the Continuing Education program of the University of Judaism. In fact, I consistently gave him priority when choosing instructors for our learning ventures because of his personal qualities as well as his Jewish scholarly depth.

Yet more: We forged a personal friendship. Thus, when his son was to be a Bar Mitzvah, Eli asked me to serve as the officiating rabbi at his own congregation for the occasion. He and his wife, Penina, wanted to sit in the synagogue pews as the parents of a Bar Mitzvah usually did. I agreed. My talk at the service dealt with the Bible's Elijah and his pervasive presence in Jewish thought and life. I had inadvertently left the written text of the talk on the pulpit lectern. Some two decades later, I received an envelope in the mail with the text of that talk along with a note from Eli: "Remember?"

To let friendship die away by negligence and silence is certainly not wise. It is voluntarily to throw away one of the greatest comforts of this weary pilgrimage.

—Samuel Johnson

ALLAN BLAINE: A WINSOME PERSONA

Allan was a seminary classmate and pulpit rabbi for many years in Far Rockaway, New York, a skilled speaker with a sparkling personality marked by acid-tinged humor. He was a good friend throughout the years.

Note the following correspondence following receipt of my book the Land of Israel: Its Theological Dimensions.

July 30, 2010

Dear Jack,

Bravo! It's good to see you in print especially on the subject of Israel.

You may not recall, but over fifty years ago we sat at an evening meeting with Dr. Moshe Davis when you very boldly asked him what value Israel is to us at the present time and why should we support it. It may not be in those words, but very similar.

Prof. Davis after being "revived" gave you a dressing down and a very fine presentation on the value of Israel. And, lo and behold, this beautiful "Land of Israel" book appears under the imprimatur of Rabbi Jack Shechter. Will wonders never cease? Mazel tov—you make the class of 1957 very proud!

I will soon begin to read it and I thank you very much for sending me this complimentary copy. From Suzanne and myself our very best wishes to Leah and to your wonderful family.

Fondly,

Allan

August 7, 2010

Dear Allan,

Thanks so very much for your warm note about the Israel book.

Your reminder about the encounter with Moshe Davis really fascinated me... For, you see, I've remained throughout the years somewhat ambivalent about the focus on Israel often at the expense of focused attention on synagogue and Jewish life in America... This ambivalence probably accounts for all the time and attention I've spent on studying about the Land. The encounter with Davis fifty years ago reflects this preoccupation.

Whatever! Your reaction to the book's arrival means much to me—as has your friendship throughout the years. Please say hello to Suzanne and tell her I think she's a wise woman teaming up with her Allan.

I hope you enjoy the book. Another is in the mill: Journey of a Rabbi. We're off to Israel this Sunday for two months—a big deal for us.

Thanks again.

Your friend,

Jack

LEAH: LIFELONG FRIEND
A POEM

The reader of this vignette will be able to peruse a documentary of a record of the life and times—early and later—of Leah in the form of a formidable "scrapbook" titled *Leah Shechter: A Persona Worth Knowing*.

The record consists of a host of her materials, among them: articles and essays about Jewish thought and practice; family and professional correspondence; plays for youngsters; Hebrew verse; letters describing teaching ways; materials about scholarly pursuits…and much more.

A specialty of hers was rhymed poems. Here is one of them…

On Jack and Leah's Fiftieth Anniversary

It was now 50 years to date

The pressure was on to find a mate

Inexperienced, young and meek,

My knowledge of the world rather weak

I met a young man at a wedding one night

Who was charming, intriguing, outgoing and bright.

The attraction was there, but it needed time

To create a warmer, more comfortable clime

Jack regaled me with stories and melodies no less

And shared Divrei Torah designed to impress

We had much in common in every way

And never ran out of things to say.

Persistently, slowly, we walked through love's gate

And I, who was prone to hesitate

Had no doubt in my mind that I found the right one

There was no one comparable under the sun

So on May 19 in the year 'fifty-seven

A bride and groom, witnessed by Heaven

Stood under the Chuppa as lovers and friends

With a fervent prayer that our bond never ends.

It was thrilling, yet scary, that moment in life

When we were pronounced husband and wife

I remember the moment…so much like a dream

When we both became the Shechter team.

Partners for life to share in a mission

To live and to teach the Jewish tradition

Partners to split the sky into two

And let the face of God shine through.

And because of that moment a new home began

With two people caught up in destiny's plan

Because of that moment new births came to be

And all who are part of our family tree

Children and grandkids can truly say

"I owe my existence to that moment in May!"

It's been said that couples have their own theme song

That both people sing as life goes along

Our song was about growing and fulfilling potential

And prodding each others' 'cause that was essential.

We had peaks to climb…we went forth and slid back

But helped each other to get back on track

We had children to raise…three young souls

And we tried to help them to envision their goals

Our story and theirs won't always agree,

But we did our best so that Mentschen they'd be.

And today looking back at family and career

At those times that each of us was in high gear

We realize now how blessed we have been

In a marriage whose formula was really "win-win"

Of course we had challenges that put us to test

That forced us to examine what's base and what's best

Of course there were hardships, since we're both always
  right

But somehow we managed to squelch heat with light.

Now fifty years later—oh how the time flies

We look into the mirror and it tells no lies

We've shrunk a bit and there are wrinkles on the face

And we go about our business in a somewhat slower pace.

But there's something that's forever, that lies beneath the skin

Time can't ever really reach what blossoms from within

Devotion is forever and companionship its role

Age is not so clever as to wrinkle up a soul.

So long as God will bless us, Beloved Friends we'll stay

Living each tomorrow with the best of yesterday…

Uv-khayn yehi ratzon

A lifelong friend, indeed.

ACKNOWLEDGEMENTS

Thanks to God for fashioning—and keeping intact into my advanced years—the memory for details which enabled me to fashion the content of this book.

Thanks to Leah, my wife, who loyally shared with me in the experiences depicted in many of these vignettes—and contributed much to their content and spirit.

Thanks to Jamie Pagett, my faithful and highly skilled editor and producer of this volume. Without her considerable acumen and unstinted determination this tome would never have seen the light of day

ABOUT THE AUTHOR

For two decades, Jack Shechter served as Associate Professor of Biblical Studies and Dean of Continuing Education—renamed *The Whizen Center for Continuing Education*—at the University of Judaism (now the American Jewish University). Prior to his tenure at the University of Judaism, he served as Executive Director of the New England Region of the United Synagogue of America, followed by a decade as the Rabbi of Congregation B'nai Israel in Pittsburgh. He was ordained at the Jewish Theological Seminary and received the Ph.D. in Biblical Studies from the University of Pittsburgh, and is the author of *The Land of Israel: Its Theological Dimensions* (2010) and *Journey of a Rabbi* (2014), *The Idea of Monotheism: The Evolution of a Foundational Concept* (2018), *In Search of the Religiosity in Religion: Sacred Thought, Sacred Action Revisited* (2020) and *Monotheism: Unfolded in Historic Time* (2021).